How to Do *Everything* with Your

Palm™ Handheld

Fourth Edition

About the Authors

Dave Johnson is the editor of *Mobility* magazine and Senior Editor of *Handheld Computing*. He also writes a weekly e-mail newsletter on digital photography for *PC World* magazine. He's the author of nearly three dozen books, including *How to Do Everything with Your Digital Camera*, *How to Do Everything with MP3 and Digital Music* (written with Rick Broida), and *How to Use Digital Video*. His short story for early readers, *The Wild Cookie*, has been transformed into an interactive storybook on CD-ROM. Dave is also an award-winning photographer, conducts PDA training, and is a PADI-certified scuba instructor.

Rick Broida has written about computers and technology for nearly 15 years. A regular contributor to Cnet and *Computer Shopper*, he specializes in mobile technology. In 1997, recognizing the Palm's unparalleled popularity and the need for a printed resource covering the platform, Rick founded *Handheld Computing* (formerly *Tap Magazine*). He currently serves as editor of that magazine, which now covers all handheld platforms and devices. Rick has conducted Palm training seminars across the Midwest and authors the Tech Savvy column for Michigan's *Observer & Eccentric* newspapers. He lives in Michigan with his wife and two children.

About the Technical Editor

Denny Atkin has been writing about technology since 1987, and about handheld computers since the Newton's release in 1993. After working with such pioneering technology magazines as *Compute!* and *Omni*, he's now Editorial Director of *Handheld Computing* magazine. Atkin lives with his wife and son in Vermont, a state where PDAs are nearly as popular as maple syrup.

How to Do *Everything* with Your

Palm™ Handheld
Fourth Edition

Dave Johnson
Rick Broida

McGraw-Hill/Osborne

New York   Chicago   San Francisco
Lisbon   London   Madrid   Mexico City
Milan   New Delhi   San Juan
Seoul   Singapore   Sydney   Toronto

The McGraw·Hill Companies

McGraw-Hill/Osborne
2100 Powell Street, 10th Floor
Emeryville, California 94608
U.S.A.

To arrange bulk purchase discounts for sales promotions, premiums, or fund-raisers, please contact **McGraw-Hill**/Osborne at the above address. For information on translations or book distributors outside the U.S.A., please see the International Contact Information page immediately following the index of this book.

How to Do Everything with Your Palm™ Handheld, Fourth Edition

34567890 FGR FGR 019876543

ISBN 0-07-223082-7

Publisher	Brandon A. Nordin
Vice President &	
Associate Publisher	Scott Rogers
Acquisitions Editor	Katie Conley
Project Editors	Jennifer Malnick, Elizabeth Seymour
Acquisitions Coordinator	Tana Allen
Technical Editor	Denny Atkin
Copy Editor	Darren Meiss
Proofreader	Stefany Otis
Indexer	Jack Lewis
Composition	Carie Abrew, Tara A. Davis, Tabi Cagan
Illustrators	Lyssa Wald, Kathleen Fay Edwards, Melinda Moore Lytle
Series Design	Mickey Galicia
Cover Series Design	Dodie Shoemaker
Cover Illustration	Pattie Lee

This book was composed with Corel VENTURA™ Publisher.

Dedication

For everyone else who occasionally wonders, "is sticky ever blue?"
—Dave

For Suzi Grekin, whose simple act of kindness set me on this path.
I am eternally grateful.
—Rick

Contents at a Glance

Contents

Acknowledgments

It's hard to believe we've now authored four editions of this book. Our endless thanks to everyone at Osborne for making it possible. In particular, we'd like to thank Jane Brownlow, Katie Conley, Tana Allen, Elizabeth Seymour, Darren Meiss, and Jennifer Malnick for being great editors and fun people to work with. Extra gratitude goes to tech editor Denny Atkin, who continues to correct the wildly inaccurate things we write.

Introduction

Believe it or not, your Palm has significantly more processing power than the computers that took the Apollo astronauts to the moon. Is that reference too ancient? Then consider this: today's sophisticated Palm handhelds have almost as much power as complete desktop computers did just a few years ago. Throw in the digital music player, digital camera, and voice recorder that's built into some models, and you've got an amazingly futuristic little gadget in your hand.

Even though we use our Palm Powered handhelds on a daily basis, we can't help but marvel at how far we've come in just a few years. The first PDAs were too large to fit in your pocket, had unattractive, greenish, monochrome screens, and came with just a few megabytes of memory. The Apple Newton MessagePad, for instance, was barely smaller than many of today's subnotebook computers. Even the first PDAs from Palm were somewhat disappointing. Sure, they were smaller and easier to use—but they lacked all the cool multimedia gadgetry that made them genuinely *fun*.

In the last year or so, the Fun Gap has been bridged—with a vengeance. The Tungsten T is a sleek, beautiful handheld that plays hours of digital music and lets you wirelessly connect gadgets like GPS receivers and mobile phones. The Zire 71 has a built-in digital camera. The Tungsten C lets you connect to the Internet via any Wi-Fi hotspot. And they all play great, colorful, addictive games. What's not to like?

The Palm is such a great little device our book sometimes runs the risk of reading like promotional brochure. We have written thousands of pages about the Windows platform, and half of it always seems to be apologetic. "If you don't see the File menu, you need to reboot and send $94 in cash to Microsoft. . . ." Books about computers are often more about getting it to work in the first place or explaining why it doesn't work right than about telling you what you can actually accomplish.

The Palm family of PDAs is different. It's forgiving, user-friendly, and virtually non-crashable. And because it suffers from so few technical glitches, this book is mostly about doing things with your Palm—accomplishing stuff and making your life more fun and more efficient. In that sense, this is the most enjoyable writing experience we've ever had.

But what do we mean by Palm? We mean any device that runs the Palm operating system. That includes not only Palm-branded models, but also those from companies like Handspring, Kyocera, and Sony. No matter what kind of Palm device you have, *How to Do Everything with Your Palm Handheld* can help.

This book starts at the beginning. If you haven't yet chosen a Palm, Part One discusses the various models and which ones best suit your needs. From there, you get a guided tour of your Palm and the desktop software. We teach you things you never knew about getting around in your Palm's apps, as well as how to share data with your PC, Mac, and other Palm devices. Having trouble with Graffiti? Be sure to check out Chapter 4, which features tons of Graffiti hints, tips, and shortcuts.

Part Two of the book, called "Get Things Done," focuses on accomplishing the most important kinds of tasks you need to do every day with your Palm. We show you the Palm's core applications and then tell you stuff you'd never think of—like how to get the most out of your Palm when you go on a business trip.

Part Three goes "Beyond the Box," and that's where things get really interesting. Read those chapters and you learn how to connect to the Internet, how to use your PDA on a long trip, and how to use your Palm as a complete replacement for a laptop. You will see how to manage your finances, track your stocks, and balance your checkbook. We also delve into the arts, with chapters on painting pictures and making music. You might not think there's a lot to say about playing games, but a whole world of entertainment awaits you—and we show you how to tap into it (pun intended). In fact, you might throw away your Game Boy after reading Chapter 13. And, yes, we said people rarely have trouble with their Palms, but it does happen occasionally. We have that covered as well.

We wrote this book so you could sit down and read it through like a novel. But if you're looking for specific information, we made it easy to find. Plus, you can find special elements to help you get the most out of the book:

- ■ **How to...** These special boxes explain, in a nutshell, how to accomplish key tasks. Read them to discover key points covered in each chapter.

- ■ **Notes** These provide extra information that's often very important to gain understanding of a particular topic.

- ■ **Tips** These tell you how to do something smarter or faster.

- ■ **Sidebars** Here we address related—and, sometimes, unrelated— topics. Sidebars can be pretty interesting, if only to see us bicker like an old married couple.

Within the text, you also find words in special formatting. New terms are in italics, while specific phrases you see on the Palm screen or need to type yourself appear in boldface.

Can't get enough of Dave and Rick? See the back page of *Handheld Computing Magazine*, where we continue our lively Head2Head column. You can also send questions and comments to us at *dave@bydavejohnson.com* and *rick@broida.com*. Thanks, and enjoy reading the book!

Part I Get Started

Chapter 1

Welcome to Palm

It all started with a block of wood. In 1994, Jeff Hawkins, founder of a little-known company called Palm Computing, envisioned a pocket-sized computer that would organize calendars and contacts, and maybe let travelers retrieve their e-mail from the road. This idea of a "personal digital assistant," or PDA, was by no means new, but previous attempts—like Apple's highly publicized Newton MessagePad—had failed to catch on with consumers.

Hawkins knew he'd have a tough time selling the concept, so he decided to convince himself before trying to convince investors. His device would be roughly the size of a deck of cards—much smaller and lighter than the Newton—and would therefore fit in a shirt pocket. But would it be practical even at that size? Would it be comfortable to carry around? Hawkins decided to find out. Before a single piece of plastic was molded, before a single circuit board was designed, the Palm Computing Pilot (the original name of the device we're here to extol) existed solely as a block of wood.

Hawkins cut a piece of balsa wood to the size he'd envisioned for his handheld device, put it in his shirt pocket, and left it there—for several months. He even took it out from time to time and pretended to take notes, just to see if the size and shape felt right. Though he quickly came to realize that such a form factor made perfect sense, doors slammed whenever he showed the "product" to potential investors. "The handheld market is dead" was the mantra at the time.

Fortunately, modem maker U.S. Robotics didn't think so, and liked the idea of the Pilot so much that it bought Palm Computing outright. In March, 1996, the company unveiled the Pilot 1000, and the rest is history.

Flash forward several years. The Pilot—which would eventually be renamed PalmPilot and then just Palm—had become the fastest-growing computer platform in history, reaching the million-sold mark faster than the IBM PC or Apple Macintosh. In the interim, U.S. Robotics had been assimilated into networking giant 3Com, and Palm Computing along with it. The Palm line had grown to include a variety of models, and companies such as IBM, Sony, and Symbol Technologies had adopted the Palm Operating System for their own handheld devices.

Hawkins himself departed Palm Computing in 1998—not to take up golf, not to find a new career, but to reinvent the wheel he'd already invented. In September, 1999, his new company, Handspring, introduced the Visor—a licensed Palm clone that in many ways surpassed the devices that preceded it.

Today, the *Palm platform* (an umbrella term used to describe not only the actual hardware, but the operating system that drives it) is dominant in the burgeoning handheld market. Even Microsoft's Pocket PC operating system, a slimmed-down version of Windows that runs on competing handheld devices, has failed to topple the Palm juggernaut.

NOTE

In this book, we discuss handhelds made by Palm, Handspring, Sony, and many other companies. However, we mostly refer to them as "Palms" or "Palm devices." That's just our way of referring to all handhelds that utilize the Palm Operating System—including those from Handspring, Kyocera Wireless, Sony, and so forth. Thus, regardless of whether you own a Palm Zire 71, Visor Prism, Sony CLIÉ NX70V, or whatever, the information in this book applies to you!

What's the Difference Between "Palm" and "a Palm"?

It's easy to get confused between "Palm," "PalmSource," "Palm OS," and other terms we use frequently in this book. Therefore, here's a lexicon to help you understand the basic terminology:

- **Handheld PC**   A portable, pocket-sized computer such as the Palm Tungsten T, Handspring Visor, and Sony CLIÉ.

- **Operating system**   The core software that makes a handheld PC function.

- **Palm, Inc.**   Formerly Palm Computing, the company that makes handheld PCs that run the Palm Operating System (OS).

- **Palm OS**   The operating system used in Palm, Handspring, HandEra, Sony, and many other handheld PCs.

- **Palm Powered**   Denotes a handheld PC that runs the Palm OS. "Palm Powered" is a registered trademark of Palm, Inc.

- **PalmSource**   The division of Palm, Inc., responsible for developing the Palm OS.

- **PDA**   Short for *personal digital assistant,* a generic term used to describe any handheld PC.

- **Pocket PC**   Microsoft's Windows-like operating system for handheld PCs. Found in devices from Casio, Compaq, Hewlett-Packard, and other vendors.

Understanding Palm Handhelds

Why all the fuss? What makes a Palm OS device so special? Why has it succeeded where so many others have failed? To answer these questions, we'll first need to look at what a Palm device actually is. Put simply, it's a pocket-sized electronic organizer that enables you to manage addresses, appointments, expenses, tasks, and memos. If you've ever used a Franklin Planner or similar kind of paper-bound organizer, you get the idea.

However, because a Palm is electronic, there's no paper or ink involved. Instead, you write directly on the device's screen, using a small plastic stylus that takes the place of a pen. A key advantage here, of course, is that you're able to store all of your important personal and business information on a device that's much smaller and lighter than a paper planner.

What's more, you can easily share that information with your Windows-based or Macintosh computer. Palm devices are not self-contained: they can *synchronize* with a desktop computer and keep information current on both sides. This is an important advantage, because it effectively turns your Palm device into an extension of the computer you use every day. Changes and additions made to your desktop data are reflected in the Palm, and vice versa (see Figure 1-1).

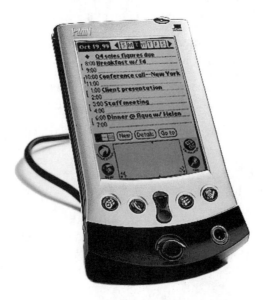

FIGURE 1-1   A Palm device connects to a PC via a HotSync cradle (or cable, in the case of certain models), which allows data to be synchronized on both devices.

Saying that a Palm is an extension of your PC is only a half-truth: in reality, it has evolved into a computer in its own right. That's because it is capable of running software written by parties other than Palm, and those parties (known as software developers) now number in the tens of thousands. There are literally thousands of programs and databases that extend your Palm's capabilities, from spreadsheet managers and expense trackers to electronic-book readers and Web browsers. Got five minutes to kill? You can play a quick game of *Bejeweled*. Need to check your e-mail while traveling? Just plug in your cell phone for wireless connectivity.

NOTE   *Although the first several chapters of this book are devoted to the Palm's core capabilities—the things it can do right out of the box—the majority of it focuses on these "extended" capabilities—the things that have elevated the Palm from a basic electronic organizer to a full-fledged handheld PC.*

Above all else, simplicity is a major key to the Palm platform's success. The devices are amazingly easy to use, requiring no more than a few taps of the stylus to access your data and a little memorization to master the handwriting-recognition software. Most users, even those who have little or no computer experience (like Dave), find themselves tapping and writing productively within 20 minutes of opening the box.

The Guts of the Machine

Whether you're still shopping for a Palm OS device or you've been fiddling with one for a month, it's good to have an understanding of all the different models—those made by Palm and other companies. Originally, only Palm Computing manufactured Palm devices, but it wasn't long before other companies licensed the operating system for similar or slightly modified devices of their own.

What's an Operating System?

Windows is an operating system. Mac OS X is an operating system. The core software that drives any computer is an operating system. Hence, when we refer to the Palm OS, we're talking about the software that's built right into the device—the brains behind the brawn. The Palm OS itself not only controls the Palm's fundamental operations, such as what happens when you press a button or tap the screen, but also supplies the built-in applications (the address book, memo pad, date book, and so on—all of which we'll discuss in detail in later chapters).

The Palm OS is the key ingredient that links the various Palm devices, whether they're manufactured by Palm, Handspring, Sony, or one of the other companies licensed to use the Palm OS.

These licensees have been granted permission by Palm to use the Palm OS in hardware of their own design. It's kind of like the way you can get PCs from a hundred different companies, yet they all run Windows.

You'll see that a Palm Tungsten T looks quite a bit different from, say, a Sony CLIÉ (see Figure 1-2), but on the inside they're fundamentally the same. They both use the Palm Operating System, and therefore operate in similar fashion and are capable of running all the same software.

When we refer to a "Palm OS device," then, we're talking about *any* of the various handheld devices that run the Palm Operating System.

Different Versions of the Palm Operating System (Important!)

If you've spent more than a few years using a computer, you've probably transitioned from one operating system to another. For instance, maybe you

FIGURE 1-2   Palm OS devices don't all look the same, and in fact can look quite different, but they all use the same core operating system.

switched from Windows 95 to Windows XP, or from an earlier version of Mac OS to OS X. Whatever the case, you probably know that operating systems inevitably evolve, and that changes are a part of that evolution. So it is with the Palm OS.

At the time we're writing this book, most Palm OS devices run OS 4. Indeed, of the eight models currently available for sale from Palm, five employ that version of the OS. However, some of those models will be discontinued by the time you read this. What's more, most of the hot new models—the Tungsten C, Zire 71, CLIÉ NZ90, and so on—are based on OS 5, which first became available in the fall of 2002. As a result, we've decided to focus this book on OS 5. It's not only rapidly capturing the present, it's also sure to occupy the future (at least until OS 6 comes along). Does that mean we're ignoring earlier versions of the Palm OS? Absolutely not! Although OS 5 does offer substantial improvements over its predecessors, it's fundamentally quite similar. In fact, using a model like the Zire 71 (which runs OS 5.2) is almost identical to using one like the Palm Vx (OS 3.5). Rest assured we're not leaving anybody out. Occasionally we'll pop in with notes or tips that alert you to things that may be a bit different in pre–OS 5 devices.

Here's an example of just such a note. Once again and for the record, whether you own the latest and greatest Palm-powered handheld or one that's four years old, this book has you covered! Okay, end of sales pitch.

Can You Upgrade Your Palm's OS?

Alas, the operating systems in most Palm OS handhelds can't be upgraded. Palm did offer upgrades for some models in the past, but it's less practical—and feasible—with current technology. Fewer models have the necessary Flash RAM required to install a new OS. And a new OS might incorporate software that's not compatible with the device hardware. Case in point: no Palm handhelds can be upgraded from OS 4 to OS 5. We won't bore you with the technical details as to why—suffice it to say, if you find yourself yearning for the latest and greatest version of the Palm OS, it's probably time to start thinking about a new handheld.

Hardware: What's Different Between Palm, Handspring, Sony, Etc?

Let's recap. You now know that many different companies make handheld PCs based on the Palm Operating System. Okay, so what are those companies, and what are the differences between their models? The latter question is easy to answer: just as Dell, Gateway, and Hewlett-Packard PCs all run Windows but have slightly different features, Palm, Handspring, and Sony PDAs all run the Palm OS—but have slightly different features. So let's look at the different makes and models, because even though the underlying software may be the same, the hardware often varies dramatically.

In Table 1-1 we list many of the latest and most popular Palm OS handhelds and their "claims to fame"—what sets them apart from the competition. Don't worry if you're confused about things like memory and screen resolution; we address those and other features later in this chapter.

NOTE *You say you bought a Palm at a Franklin Covey store? Franklin Covey, a retail operation best known for its Franklin Planner products, offers Palm-built handhelds in different packaging and with slightly modified software bundles. From a hardware and OS standpoint, Franklin Covey models are identical to their Palm counterparts—but come with Franklin's own desktop software in place of Palm Desktop (see Chapter 3). Even so, if you own one of Franklin Covey's models, most of the material in this book is still applicable (and downright useful).*

Model	Memory	Screen	Expansion Slot	OS Version	Price*	Claim to Fame
Palm i705	8MB	160×160 grayscale	Secure Digital	4.1	$199	Wireless e-mail and Web access
Palm m515	16MB	160×160 color	Secure Digital	4.1	$299	Slim, light, sexy
Palm Tungsten C	64MB	320×320 color	Secure Digital	5.2	$499	Built-in WiFi networking
Palm Tungsten T	16MB	320×320 color	Secure Digital	5.0	$399	Compact; built-in Bluetooth networking
Palm Tungsten W	16MB	320×320 color	Secure Digital	4.1	$549	Wireless e-mail and Web access; doubles as a phone
Palm Zire	2MB	160×160 grayscale	None	4.1	$99	Cheap, cheap, cheap
Palm Zire 71	16MB	320×320 color	Secure Digital	5.2	$299	A multimedia dynamo—and a digital camera

TABLE 1-1   Palm OS Handhelds at a Glance

Model	Memory	Screen	Expansion Slot	OS Version	Price*	Claim to Fame
Handspring Treo 270/300	16MB	160×160 color	None	3.5	$399/ $299	Smartphone
Kyocera 7135	16MB	160×160 color	Secure Digital	4.1	$499	Smartphone; plays MP3s
Samsung i330	16MB	160×240 color	None	3.5	$499	Smartphone
Sony CLIÉ NX70V	16MB	320×480 color	Memory Stick	5.0	$499	Large screen, built-in camera
Sony CLIÉ NZ90	16MB	320×480 color	Memory Stick	5.0	$799	Large screen, built-in 2-megapixel camera
Sony CLIÉ SJ22	16MB	320×320 color	Memory Stick	4.1	$199	High-resolution screen, low price
Sony CLIÉ TG50	16MB	320×320 color	Memory Stick	5.0	$399	Built-in keyboard, Bluetooth

*As of June, 2003.

TABLE 1-1	Palm OS Handhelds at a Glance *(continued)*

The Palm Family of Handhelds

What's in a name? Shakespeare would have had to rethink the question if faced with a company like Palm. Over the years we've seen product monikers ranging from Pilot to PalmPilot, Palm III to Palm Vx, Palm m100 to i705, and on and on. Fortunately, there's some name consolidation afoot, as Palm is moving away from the confusing "m" series in favor of two distinct product families: the business-oriented Tungsten and the consumer-friendly Zire.

Other Palm OS Handheld Makers

Although Handspring and Sony are probably the best-known Palm OS licensees, over a dozen other companies can also claim that distinction. For your edification, we spotlight a few of them:

■   **Fossil**   A company best known for handbags, Fossil offers a wristwatch with the entire Palm OS packed inside. (There's even a tiny stylus hidden in the wristband.) Thus, you can carry all your contacts, appointments, and everything else right on your wrist.

- **Garmin**　Many companies make GPS (Global Positioning System, a group of satellites used to pinpoint your position) add-ons for Palm OS handhelds. Garmin is the first to integrate the technology right into a PDA. The iQue 3600, which at press time was not yet in production, offers not only built-in GPS tracking (and real-time positioning, mapping, and driving directions along with it), but also a wealth of other advanced PDA features.

- **HandEra**　If there's a cult favorite among Palm users, it's the HandEra 330. This model was ahead of its time with a high-resolution screen, "virtual" handwriting recognition, dual expansion slots, and more. However, shortly before press time, the company announced plans to discontinue the product. HandEra, we hardly knew ye.

- **TapWave**　At press time, this new company—founded by some well-known people in the handheld and PC entertainment industries—had just announced a Palm OS handheld designed to make Nintendo's Game Boy look like a child's toy. (Okay, a really little child's toy.) Details were sketchy, but this looked to be the first PDA built specifically with games in mind.

A Word about Sony Models

Sony's first stab at a Palm OS handheld—the CLIÉ PEG-S300—was as dull as its name. But the company rebounded big time with a series of models packed with innovative and exciting features. Among the highlights: high-resolution color screens, dual expansion slots, MP3 playback, a "jog dial" for one-handed operation, and enhanced audio. If you're thinking of upgrading to one of Sony's models or you already own one, we'd like to humbly suggest a little book called *How to Do Everything with Your Sony CLIÉ*. Although much of the information in this book applies to the CLIÉ series, that book goes the extra mile with sections devoted specifically to CLIÉ features.

Our Favorite Models

Rick: Well, obviously I'm partial to Charlize Theron, who's an actress now but did start out as a model, and…oh, sorry, wrong sidebar. My current PDA is the Sony CLIÉ NX70V, which packs a remarkable amount of handheld computing power. It's great for listening to music, reading e-books, watching movies, and snapping the occasional impromptu digital photo. Of course, I'm a little bummed I paid $600 for it, when Palm's just-announced Zire 71 offers most of the same features for half the money. And in a smaller case, too. But as with all things electronic, there's always something better (and usually cheaper) just around the corner. For now, I'm extremely happy with my CLIÉ. Ten minutes from now…who knows?

Dave: I really like Sony's NX70V as well, but I have found that I simply can't live with the meager 11MB of memory the device comes with—I can't even fit most of the programs I commonly use in memory, let alone all of them. But Sony's loss is Palm's gain, because that glitch forced me to carry the Tungsten T instead, and I've fallen in love. It's compact and has built-in Bluetooth, a feature I use absolutely all the time (see Chapter 10 for some of the cool things you can do with it). No, it doesn't have the big screen that Sony puts in its N-series CLIÉ models, but that's my only real complaint with this superb PDA.

What's Important in a Handheld PC?

In the old days, it was pretty easy to differentiate between Palm OS handhelds. For one thing, there weren't that many different models. Plus, they were all pretty similar, save for a few unique features here and there. It's a different story nowadays, what with handheld makers touting things like processor speed, screen resolution, memory capacity, multimedia features, and even wireless connectivity. Let's take a look at a few of these items and how important they are—or are not—in handheld computing:

- **Speed**   Where handhelds are concerned, speed is a relative issue. Regardless of what processor is inside the device or what version of the Palm OS it uses, it takes but a second to load, say, the calendar program. So why do newer models tout faster processors? Because more advanced features, such as watching movies and playing music, do require more horsepower. If you're not interested in those kinds of features, don't worry about processor speed. A "lowly" $99 Zire works just as well as a power-packing $499 Tungsten C when it comes to scheduling appointments and viewing memos.

- **Memory**   The amount of RAM, or memory, in a Palm device is directly related to how much software and data it can store. More is always better, especially when you start loading up on games, electronic books, corporate databases, third-party software, and the like. However, because most modern handhelds are expandable—meaning you can insert memory cards that provide lots more storage space—the amount of internal RAM is less of a factor than it used to be. Sure, your Palm may have only 8MB—but slap a 128MB card in there and the sky's the limit!

- **Screen**   Although we got along fine for a long while with low-resolution (160×160 pixel) grayscale screens, we definitely prefer the high-resolution (320×320 pixel) color screens common in newer handhelds. That's not only because the higher resolution means sharper text and graphics, but also because the color screens are brighter and easier on the eyes. Plus, games and movies look significantly better in color.

- **Multimedia**   Speaking of games, movies, and whatnot, certain Palm devices fare better than others when it comes to mobile entertainment. Models like the Palm Zire 71 and Sony CLIÉ NX70V excel at it, because they come with software for listening to MP3 tunes, watching video clips, and so on. They even have built-in digital cameras. The newer the handheld, the more likely it is to support these kinds of features.

How Much RAM Do You Really Need?

Rick and Dave argue constantly about this. Dave complains that he never has enough space to hold all his applications—even though he could plug in a memory card and have all the space he'd ever need. Rick keeps the vital stuff in internal memory, but stores less-important extras such as games, MP3 files, movies, and so forth on a memory card. Problem solved.

Anyway, to answer our own question, the amount of RAM you need depends on the kind of user you are. Most late-model Palm OS handhelds come with 16MB of internal RAM—enough to hold quite a bit of software.

> **NOTE** *Just because a model advertises 16MB of RAM doesn't mean all of it is available to you. For instance, the Sony CLIÉ NX70V comes with 16MB, but 5MB of that are reserved for built-in software. For all intents and purposes, then, it actually has just 11MB. The Palm Zire 71, similarly, has just 14MB free.*

Rick maintains that even power users can solve memory-crunch problems via expansion cards and a good memory-managing utility (see Chapter 12). Dave, on the other hand, would like to state here and for the record that if Palm, Sony, or anybody else would please make a handheld with 100 terraquads of internal storage, he'd gladly buy it.

■ **Communications**   Don't want to carry both a phone and a PDA? In that case, you may want a Palm device that's also a phone—a.k.a. a smartphone. Handspring, Kyocera Wireless, and Samsung are among the vendors that offer phones built around the Palm OS. (The Palm Tungsten W is more like a traditional PDA that happens to offer phone features, if you prefer that approach.) Although these hybrids are great in that they combine two vital devices into one, they often make sacrifices in terms of screen size and/or resolution, expansion capabilities, and multimedia savvy.

Where to Find the Best Prices

Everyone likes to save a buck, and with a little smart shopping you can do exactly that. Even if you're just looking for items like memory cards and, oh, extra copies of this book to give as gifts, it pays to do some research. This section offers a few ideas regarding where and how to shop, and where to find the best deals.

NOTE *Some models are not as widely available as others. The Kyocera and Samsung smartphones, for instance, must be purchased from the cellular companies that offer service for them.*

■ If you're comfortable shopping online, you can find some of the best deals on the Web. We recommend starting with a site called PriceGrabber (www.pricegrabber.com), which provides up-to-date price comparisons for most Palm devices and many accessories, drawn from a large number of Web merchants. It even gives you shipping costs, so you know your out-the-door total before heading to the merchant's site.

■ Another worthwhile online destination: Web auctions. eBay (www.ebay.com) is a treasure trove of new, used, and refurbished Palm devices. Just remember to use common sense: sometimes people get caught in a bidding frenzy and wind up paying as much for a used model as they would for a new one. That said, there are often excellent deals to be had on last year's models.

■ Speaking of last year's models, visit Overstock.com (www.overstock.com) to find great prices on discontinued and refurbished handhelds. While you're at it, check out ReturnBuy (buy.returnbuy.com), another good source for closeouts. This site also gives you the option of purchasing an extended warranty, something to consider given that refurbished models usually come with a very short warranty—or none at all.

■ Check the Palm, Handspring, and Sony Web sites for package deals. They often offer bundles (like a handheld with a case and keyboard) you won't find anywhere else, and at discounted prices. They sometimes sell refurbished inventory as well, and those deals can be hard to pass up.

TIP *Auctions can also be a great way to sell your old Palm device if you're moving up to a newer one. You can also try a service like SellYourPalm.net (www.sellyourpalm.net), which will buy your old handheld outright.*

How to ... **Decide Which Model to Buy**

Sorry, we can't help you with this one. So many great handhelds, so few hands. Virtually every model available today—whether it's from Palm, Sony, Handspring, or any other Palm OS licensee—has its merits. The key thing to remember is that right out of the box, every one offers the same great core capabilities: contact and calendar management, easy-to-learn handwriting recognition, seamless synchronization with your PC, and access to a wealth of third-party software. With that knowledge in mind, you can focus on other aspects you might find important: price, expansion capabilities, screen size and quality, wireless options, and so on. In the end, you may just have to flip a coin. That's what we do.

Where to Find It

Web Site	Address
Palm, Inc.	www.palm.com
Fossil	www.fossil.com
Garmin	www.garmin.com
HandEra	www.handera.com
Handspring	www.handspring.com
Kyocera Wireless	www.kyocera-wireless.com
Samsung	www.samsung.com
Sony	www.sonystyle.com/micros/clie/
TapWave	www.tapwave.com

Chapter 2

Get to Know Your Palm Device

How to...

- Identify the buttons on your handheld
- Identify the infrared transmitter
- Work with the screen and Graffiti area
- Charge (or install) the batteries
- Turn on a Palm device for the first time
- Use the Graffiti tutorial
- Reset a Palm device
- Configure a Palm device's preferences
- Reset the screen digitizer
- Work with the operating system
- Check how much memory is left
- Create and use shortcuts
- Work with Palm Desktop

Okay, enough history—it's time to dive in and start having fun. At the beginning of any lasting and meaningful relationship, you want to get to know the other person as well as possible—find out what makes him tick, what his boundaries are, and where he keeps his batteries. With that in mind, we tailored this chapter as a kind of meet-and-greet, to help you overcome that bit of initial awkwardness.

Taking a Guided Tour of the Hardware

By now, your Palm device is no doubt out of the box and getting the once-over. You're seeing buttons, a screen, some little pictures, and a bunch of other stuff. What is all this? What does it do?

NOTE *Although fundamentally quite similar, the various Palm OS handhelds exhibit many minor physical differences. The Palm Tungsten T, for instance, uses a sliding mechanism to cover and uncover the handwriting recognition area—a feature no other model has. We pop in as needed to alert you to such distinctions.*

The Screen

As Palm devices have evolved over the years, their screens have changed. Early models had low-resolution (160×160 pixels) monochrome and grayscale screens, but most modern models have high-resolution (320×320 pixels or higher) color screens (see Figure 2-1). What's the big deal about resolution? More pixels means a sharper display, which is great for everything from viewing photos to reading books to playing games. Plus, the move to color has made for much brighter screens that are generally easier on the eyes.

NOTE *Garmin's iQue 3600 and certain Sony CLIÉ models have raised the bar for PDA screens by increasing both size and resolution. Instead of square, 320×320-pixel screens, these models have rectangular, 320×480-pixel screens. That translates to about 50 percent more viewing area. Of course, it also makes the devices physically larger, so your pocket pays the price.*

When you use a desktop computer, you use a mouse to navigate and a keyboard to enter data. With a Palm device, you use a plastic-tipped stylus for both navigation and data entry. That's because the screen is, technically speaking, a *touchscreen,* meaning you interact with it by tapping it and writing on it. If you want to access, say, the Expense program, you tap the Expense icon that appears on the screen. If you want to record the price of the dinner you just ate, you write the numbers on the screen.

NOTE *Many novice users think they have to double-tap the application icons, just like double-clicking with a mouse. Not true! A single tap is all you ever need when working with a Palm device.*

FIGURE 2-1   It's easy to see the appeal of high-resolution screens (right) when compared with their low-resolution predecessors.

The Difference Between Tapping and Writing

Tapping the screen is the equivalent of clicking a mouse. You tap icons to launch programs, tap to access menus and select options in them, and tap to place your cursor in specific places. Writing on the screen is, of course, like putting a pen to paper. However, most writing you do on a Palm takes place in a specific area of the screen, which we discuss in the next section. But when you're working in, say, the Note Pad or a paint program, you can scribble anywhere on the screen, just as though it were a blank sheet of paper.

TIP   *Don't press too hard with the stylus. The screen is fairly sensitive, and light pressure is all it takes to register a tap or stylus stroke. If you press too hard, you could wind up with a scratched screen—the bane of every Palm user.*

The Graffiti Area

As you've no doubt noticed, the bottom portion of the screen looks a bit different. That big rectangular box flanked by two pairs of icons is called the *Graffiti area,* referring to the handwriting-recognition software that's part of every Palm device. Graffiti makes it possible to enter information using the stylus, but you can do so only within the confines of the Graffiti area (shown in Figure 2-2).

NOTE   *We tell you more about Graffiti—how to use it and alternatives to it—in Chapters 4 and 12, respectively.*

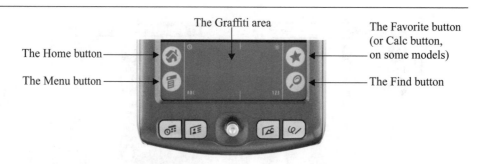

The Graffiti area

The Favorite button
(or Calc button,
on some models)

The Home button

The Menu button

The Find button

FIGURE 2-2   The Graffiti area is where you write data into your handheld and access various options such as menus and "home base."

Whoa! My Palm Doesn't Have a Graffiti Area! What's Up?

Sure enough, the Palm Tungsten W, Handspring Treo, and Sony CLIÉ TG50 are among a handful of models that don't have Graffiti areas—they have tiny built-in keyboards instead.

Because using a keyboard is fairly self-explanatory, and because you probably made a conscious choice to get one when deciding which handheld to buy, we're not going to cover keyboard operation in any great detail. That said, you may still want to read the following sections, as some of the information still applies. That's because some keyboard-equipped models also allow you to write with Graffiti—you just write directly on the screen instead of in a dedicated Graffiti area. Be sure to visit Chapter 4 for information on using Graffiti—even if your handheld has a keyboard.

What about those icons on either side of the Graffiti area? They serve some important functions. Here's an overview:

The Home Button Represented by a picture of a house and located in the upper-left corner of the Graffiti area, the *Home button* is the one you'll tap more often than any other. From whatever program you're currently running, the Home button (see Figure 2-2) takes you back to the main launcher screen—"home base," as it were (hence, the house picture).

> TIP *When you're using any program, tapping the Home button returns you to the launcher screen. While you're viewing that screen, however, tapping the Home button repeatedly cycles through the application categories, which we discuss in the section "Why Use Categories?" later in this chapter.*

The Menu Button Tapping the icon in the lower-left corner of the Graffiti area— a.k.a. the *Menu button* (see Figure 2-2)—gives you access to the drop-down menus that are part of the Palm Operating System. These menus vary somewhat from program to program, insofar as the options they provide, but they're fairly consistent within the core Palm OS applications.

> TIP *The Menu button works like a toggle switch. If you accidentally tap it or simply want to make the drop-down menus go away, simply tap it again. Also, there's another way to access menus: by tapping the top-left corner of the screen. This works both in the Home screen and in most programs. Try it!*

The Favorite (Sometimes Calc) Button Located in the top-right corner of the Graffiti area, the star-shaped *Favorite button* (see Figure 2-2) is used to launch any program you choose: Calculator, HotSync, Memo Pad, a program you've added to your handheld, or whatever. This isn't a permanent choice, either—you can change the setting whenever you want (we discuss how in the "Buttons" section later in this chapter).

The Favorite button is a relatively new addition to Palm OS handhelds—for a long time that spot was reserved for the *Calculator button*. If your handheld has what looks like a little calculator instead of a star, well, you probably don't need us to explain any further.

> **NOTE** *Some Palm OS handhelds have neither a Favorite nor a Calculator button. Kyocera's smartphones, for instance, have a "phone" button instead, used to access the dial pad. On models such as these, you can access Calculator simply by tapping its icon in the Home screen.*

The Find Button   Finally, we get to the little magnifying glass in the lower-right corner. Because a Palm can store such vast amounts of information, and because sifting through all that information to find what you're looking for can be tedious, there's a handy little search feature called the *Find button* (see Figure 2-2). We talk more about it in Chapter 9.

> **NOTE** *Keyboard-based Palms (such as the Tungsten W and Handspring Treo) have Home and Menu buttons, but you'll find them on keys instead of in the nonexistent Graffiti area. You'll sometimes need to access some of these common features by pressing a key modifier—on the Tungsten W, for instance, you get the Find tool by pressing the blue ALT key and the Caps/Find button together. It's worth your while to spend a few minutes familiarizing yourself with the many functions of the keyboard.*

The Buttons

Every Palm device has a group of "hard buttons"—buttons you press with your finger as opposed to tapping with your stylus. Most of these are application buttons, used to instantly launch the core applications (Date Book, Memo Pad, and so forth). There's also a Power button, scroll buttons, and, on some models, voice recording and other buttons. Let's take a closer look.

The Power Button

The *Power button* is fairly self-explanatory, but it serves another function on certain models. When you hold down the button for a couple seconds, one of two screen-related things may happen. First, you might see an onscreen slider tool used to adjust screen brightness. Second, the screen's backlight may turn on (or off, if it was on already). This varies from handheld to handheld, so experiment!

The Four Program Buttons

Say you want to look up a number in your address book. You could turn on your Palm device, tap the Home button to get to the main screen, and then find and tap the Address button. There's a much faster way, though: simply press the Address button, which is represented by a picture of a phone handset. That serves the dual function of turning on the Palm device *and* loading the Address Book program.

The same holds true for the three other buttons (see Figure 2-3), which launch Date Book, To Do List, and Note Pad (or Memo Pad, in some models). You can use them at any time, whether the Palm is on or off, to quickly switch between the four core programs. Some PDAs assign other functions to the rightmost buttons. The Tungsten C and the Tungsten W, for instance, have e-mail and Web browser buttons. Of course, you can always reassign any of these buttons to whatever programs you most frequently use.

The Zire (the original one, not the Zire 71) has just two application buttons: Date Book and Address. The Zire 71, on the other hand, has a Photo button in place of the To Do List. The i705, meanwhile, displaces both the To Do List and Note Pad buttons in favor of Web and e-mail buttons.

The Scroll Buttons/Navigator

Most Palm handhelds have a pair of buttons sandwiched between the application buttons. These *Scroll buttons* are used to cycle through multiple screens of data. If you're looking at, say, a memo that's too long to fit on the screen in its entirety, you'd use the *Scroll Down button* to move down to the next section—not unlike turning pages in a book. The *Scroll Up button* simply moves you back a page.

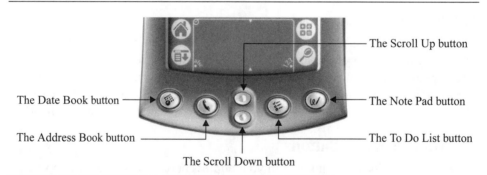

The Scroll Up button

The Date Book button

The Note Pad button

The Address Book button

The To Do List button

The Scroll Down button

FIGURE 2-3   Your handheld's hard buttons provide one-touch access to four of the most commonly used programs.

How to ... **Reprogram Your Handheld's Buttons**

Want the Date Book button to load your e-book viewer instead? Or the Calc button to load a sophisticated third-party number-cruncher instead of the built-in calculator? You can reprogram a Palm device's four hardware buttons and Calc button to run any installed program. Just tap the Prefs icon, and then select Buttons from the drop-down list in the top-right corner of the Preferences screen (or choose Personal | Buttons if you have one of the newest Palms). Now, assign your desired applications to the various buttons.

NOTE *In many programs, onscreen arrows serve the same function. Instead of having to press the Scroll buttons, you can simply tap the arrows with your stylus. This is largely a matter of personal preference: try both and decide which method you like better!*

Models such as the Tungsten T, Tungsten W, and Zire 71 take a slightly different approach, offering a five-way *Navigator* in place of scroll buttons. The Navigator affords one-handed operation of the device—it enables you to scroll through menus, select icons and options, and more without the need for a stylus. It also comes in handy with certain games.

The Navigator

What do we mean when we say the Navigator is a five-way control? Whereas scroll buttons are for up and down only, the Navigator also offers left/right scrolling. Plus, you can push the button in the center (or push the Navigator itself, in the case of the Zire 71) to activate whatever menu or icon is highlighted onscreen. Left, right, up, down, push—that's five different controls.

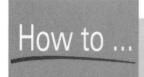 **Use the Navigator for One-Handed Operation**

The Navigator, a replacement for the traditional scroll buttons, is found on Palm models such as the Tungsten C, Tungsten T, Tungsten W, and Zire 71. It's useful not only for scrolling up and down, but also for operating your device with just one hand (no stylus required). For instance, you can launch any application from the Home screen. Just press the center Navigator button once, noting that the top-left program icon is now highlighted. Press the Navigator down or to the right—now the adjacent icon is highlighted. Keep going until you find the program you want to launch, then press the Navigator button again. Want to access the Home screen category menu? Holding down the Navigator button for two seconds will cause the menu to appear, at which point you can scroll to the category you want and select it with the button.

The Navigator works within various programs as well. While viewing the Address Book, for instance, you can press the Navigator button, scroll to the desired contact, and press it again to view the listing. The best way to learn the full extent of the Navigator's capabilities is to experiment.

 *Calling all Tungsten T owners: looking for a faster way to return to the Home screen? Instead of having to slide open the bottom section and tap the Home icon, you can simply press and hold the Navigator button for two seconds. Presto—back Home you go!*

The Back of the Palm

Flip your Palm device over. Yes, it's pretty boring back there, but there's one important feature you should know about: the Reset button. Every Palm device has a little hole on the back that's used to reset the device. Hey, every computer crashes occasionally, and the Palm OS isn't entirely glitch-free. (We talk more about resetting in the troubleshooting section in Chapter 16.)

 If you have a Zire 71, the reset button is located near the camera lens—you have to slide open the camera to access it.

The Expansion Slot

Early Palm handhelds weren't easily expandable (if at all), but virtually all of today's models have slots for adding more memory and add-on hardware (such as GPS receivers and wireless network cards). We talk more about such options in later chapters, so for now let's just identify the expansion slot. It's small, rectangular, and usually found along the top edge of the handheld (though some models have it on the side).

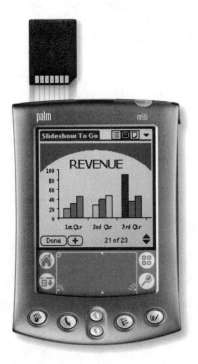

NOTE   *Handheld expansion doesn't begin and end with the expansion slot. Almost all recent Palm-branded models, for instance, have Palm's Universal Connector (UC) on the bottom. This is used not only for HotSync cradles and cables, but also for various accessories (such as travel chargers). The idea behind the Universal Connector is a great one: even if you upgrade handhelds down the road, all your accessories will still be compatible. Ironically, however, there aren't that many products that take advantage of the UC. C'est la vie.*

The Infrared Port

At the top of every Palm device (except the very oldest models), there's a small, black plastic window. This is the *infrared port,* also known as the *infrared transceiver* or *IR port.* It's used to wirelessly beam data from one Palm device to another, and has a range of about five feet. You learn more about beaming in Chapter 4.

 *By holding down the Address Book button for two seconds, you can automatically beam your "business card" to another handheld user. In Chapter 6, you learn how to designate an Address Book record as your card.*

The Stylus

Last, but definitely not least, we come to the *stylus.* Every Palm device has a small plastic or metal pen tucked away inside, usually accessible from the side or rear. As you discover in Chapter 15, dozens of third-party styluses are available—some are bigger, some are heavier, and some hide a ballpoint pen inside.

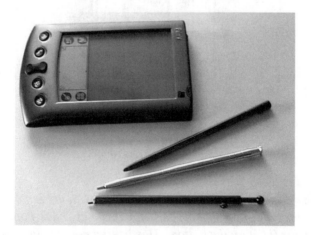

What all Palm styluses have in common is a plastic tip. Under no circumstances should you ever use any kind of ink pen or metal tip on a Palm device's screen. That's a sure way to create a scratch, and a scratched screen is a damaged screen.

TIP   *There's one exception. In a pinch, or if you just don't feel like extracting the stylus, you can use your fingernail for light taps on the screen.*

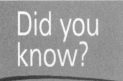

Some Cell Phones Can Beam, Too

Some cell phones have IR ports of their own. If yours does, you may be able to beam names and phone numbers from your Palm OS handheld. That would certainly be quicker and easier than entering all that information directly on your phone. We know that some Nokia phones support this option, though you have to venture into the menus to get it working. Check the owner's manual for your phone to see if it supports phone-list beaming.

Using Your Palm Device for the First Time

Now that you're familiar with the Palm hardware, you're ready to start using it. This means charging the batteries (or installing them, if the device uses alkalines), working your way through the startup screens, and checking out the Graffiti tutorial.

Charging the Batteries

Obviously there's nothing terribly complicated about this, but it's important that you charge the batteries properly, following the directions outlined in the instruction manual. Put simply, you must charge the batteries fully before using your handheld. We know you're eager to start using it, but make sure you let it charge fully before going on to the next steps. This takes about four hours. After that, you can just "top off" the battery by dropping the handheld into the HotSync cradle.

The Welcome Screens

Once the batteries are charged (or inserted, if you have an older model that uses alkalines) and you power on your Palm device, you see a "welcome" screen that asks you to remove the stylus and tap anywhere to continue. You're about to undertake a one-time setup procedure that takes all of about 60 seconds. The two key tasks accomplished here are the calibration of the screen digitizer and the setting of the date and time.

What Is Digitizer Calibration?

Put simply, *digitizer calibration* is the process of teaching a Palm to accurately recognize taps on the screen. As you know, the screen responds to input from the

Our Favorite "Secret" Uses for Palm Handhelds

Rick: Most people buy PDAs to manage their appointments and contacts. Of course, the little marvels are capable of so much more. Some of my favorite lesser-known uses for my handheld are as follows: reading e-books (mostly contemporary fiction purchased from Palm Digital Media); storing important personal data such as Web site passwords and software registration numbers (I use DataViz's Passwords Plus); and doing crossword puzzles (courtesy of Stand Alone's Crossword Puzzles for Palm OS). I've also become something of a wine lover, so I rely on LandWare's excellent Wine Enthusiast Guide to help me choose the best bottles and remember those I've enjoyed.

Dave: I get out of the house more than Rick does—he has one of those bizarre phobias that keeps him sequestered away in the basement almost 16 hours each day—so I personally appreciate AvantGo (which you can read about in Chapter 10). This is surely the single best application ever written for the Palm; I use it to read the news each day when I go out to lunch. And while I'm out, I use my Tungsten T's wireless capabilities to check e-mail (Chapter 10). It's so much more than an organizer!

stylus; this calibration process simply ensures the precision of those responses. In a way, it's like fine-tuning a TV set.

Over time, you might discover your screen taps seem a little off. For example, you have to tap a bit to the left of an arrow for the screen to register the tap. At this point, it's time to recalibrate the digitizer, which you can do in the Prefs menu. We tell you how in the section "Setting Palm Device Preferences."

Setting the Date and Time

The last stage of the welcome process is setting the date and time (and choosing your country, if you live outside the United States). To set the time, you simply tap the box next to the words "Set Time," and then tap the up/down arrow keys to select the current time (don't forget to specify A.M. or P.M.). Tapping the box next to Set Date reveals a calendar. Again, a few strategic taps is all it takes to select today's date. (Be sure to choose the year first, then the month, and then the day.) When you've done so, tap the Today button.

The Location Setting The newest Palm OS handhelds have an additional setting alongside date and time: Location. This is designed to simplify travel between time zones—it saves you from having to manually readjust the clock. Instead, just choose your location from the pop-up list that appears, and the clock changes accordingly. By the way, if your "home city" doesn't appear in the list, just choose one that's in your time zone. Here's how:

1. Tap the arrow next to Location, then tap Edit List.

2. Tap Add.

3. Scroll through the list to find your city or one that's in your time zone, tap it to highlight it, then tap OK.

4. In the next screen, you can replace the name of the city with the name of your city, if you want. You can also choose a specific time zone and enable Daylight Savings (which is already enabled by default).

NOTE *If you find yourself in a different time zone and need to change your Palm's clock, you needn't repeat the whole "welcome" process to do so. The date and time settings are located in the Prefs menu, which we discuss in the upcoming section "Setting Palm Device Preferences."*

The Graffiti Tutorial

On the last screen of the welcome wagon, you're given this option: To learn about entering text on your handheld now, tap Next. Doing so takes you to a brief but helpful tutorial on using *Graffiti,* the Palm's handwriting-recognition software. If you'd rather jump right into using your Palm and learn Graffiti later, tap Done instead of Next. You can revisit the Graffiti tutorial at any time by finding and tapping the Graffiti icon in the main Home screen.

Why Use the Tutorial?

Mastering Graffiti is arguably the most difficult aspect of using a Palm device, because it requires you to learn and use a special character set. Thus, you should definitely spend some time with the tutorial. That said, most users can gain a working knowledge of Graffiti in about 20 minutes. And, after a few days' practice, you should be writing quickly, accurately, and effortlessly. We show you the ins and outs of Graffiti in Chapter 4.

You may have discovered a Graffiti cheat-sheet sticker among the materials that came with your handheld. However, the Palm OS has a built-in cheat sheet of its own. Just draw a line from anywhere in the Graffiti area all the way to the top of the screen. Presto—a diagram of all the Graffiti characters!

An Important Note about Graffiti

As we're writing this book, PalmSource (keeper and developer of the Palm OS) is undergoing something of a sea change with regard to Graffiti. Specifically, there's a new version of the handwriting-recognition engine—Graffiti 2— and before long it'll be standard on all Palm OS handhelds. At the moment, however, most models still have the original Graffiti. What's the difference? Put simply, Graffiti 2 is based on a more traditional character set, so there's less for you to learn. We give you the full scoop on this in Chapter 4, but wanted to give you a heads-up now in case things look or act a little different on your handheld than they appear here.

Getting to Know the Operating System

We aren't exaggerating when we say working with Palm devices is roughly eight gazillion times easier than working with traditional computers. Although they're plenty powerful, Palm devices are a lot less complicated. There's no confusing menu system to wade through, no accidentally forgetting to save your document. Here we've highlighted some of the fundamental—but still important—differences between a Palm and a PC:

- When you turn on a PC, you have to wait a few minutes for it to boot up. When you turn on a Palm device, it's ready to roll instantaneously. Same goes for shutting it off: just press the Power button and the screen goes dark. There's no lengthy shutdown procedure.

- On a PC, when you're done working with a program (say, your word processor), you must save your data before exiting that program. On a Palm, this isn't necessary. Data is retained at all times, even if you, say, switch to your to-do list while in the middle of writing a memo. When you return to Memo Pad, you find your document exactly as you left it. This holds true even if you turn off the Palm!

- In that same vein, you don't "exit" a Palm program so much as switch to another one. This is a hard concept for seasoned computer users to grasp, as we've all been taught to shut down our software when we're done with it. There's no exit procedure on a Palm device, and you'll never find that word in a drop-down menu. When you finish working in one program, simply tap the Home button to return to home base or press one of the program buttons.

NOTE *We strongly encourage experimentation. Whereas wandering too far off the beaten track in Windows can lead to disaster, it's virtually impossible to get "lost" using a Palm. So tap here, explore there, and just have fun checking things out. Because there's no risk of losing data or running too many programs at once (impossible in the Palm OS), you should have no fear of fouling anything up. Play!*

The Icons

Icons are, of course, little pictures used to represent things. In the case of the Palm OS, they're used largely to represent the installed programs. Thus, on the Home screen, you see icons labeled Address, Calc, Date Book, and so on—and all you do is tap one to access that particular program.

NOTE *Say, didn't you just learn that you're supposed to press a button below the screen to load Date Book? In the Palm OS, there are often multiple ways to accomplish the same task. In this case, you can load certain programs either by tapping their onscreen icons or using their hardware-button equivalents.*

The Menus

As with most computers, *drop-down menus* are used to access program-specific options and settings. In most Palm programs, tapping the Menu button (or the program's title bar at the top of the screen) makes a small menu bar appear at the top of the screen. You navigate this bar using the stylus as you would a mouse, tapping each menu item to make its list of options drop down, and then tapping the option you want to access.

NOTE *These menus are not to be confused with those in the upper-right corner of the screen, which are usually used to select categories, Prefs options, and so on. We discuss those particular menus in the upcoming sections "Why Use Categories?" and "Setting Palm Device Preferences."*

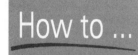

Find Out How Much Memory Your Handheld Has Left

2

As you start to add records and install new software on your Palm, you may wonder how to check the amount of internal memory that's available. From the Home screen, tap Menu | App | Info. The screen that appears shows the total amount of memory on your device and how much of it is free. Notice, too, some of the other options that appear when you tap Menu | App. There's Delete (used to delete third-party programs), Beam (used to beam third-party programs), and Copy (if you have a model with a memory expansion slot, which we discuss in Chapter 12).

The Home Screen

On a Palm device, the Home screen displays the icons for all the installed programs. (It also shows you the time and a battery gauge, as the following illustrates.)

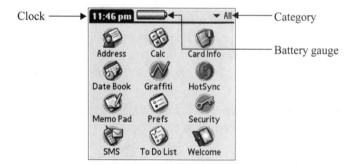

In the upper-right corner of the screen, you'll also notice a small arrow next to the word "All." What this means is that the Home screen is currently showing you all the installed programs. If you tap the arrow, you see a list of categories (see Figure 2-4) into which you can group your programs.

Why Use Categories?

The use of categories is entirely optional. They're intended solely to help you keep your applications organized. As you install more software, you wind up with more icons. Right out of the box, a Palm device has only about a dozen of them— a manageable number. But, suppose you install a few games and utilities, an

In the Home screen, categories can be used to organize your programs.

e-book reader, and some other programs. Now things are getting a little cluttered, icon-wise.

Categories offer you a way to minimize the clutter. As you saw in the drop-down list, the Palm comes with a number of categories already created. You can use them if you want, or you can create your own.

TIP *Instead of using categories, install a third-party launcher instead. These programs offer easier and more practical ways to organize your icons, such as with tabs or smaller icons. Rick is partial to LauncherX (www.launcherx.com); Dave prefers Silver Screen (www.pocketsensei.com).*

How to Create and Modify Categories   Look again at the drop-down list in the upper-right corner of the Home screen (see Figure 2-4). Notice the last option: Edit Categories. Tapping this option takes you to a screen where you can add, rename, and delete categories. To rename or delete one, first select it by tapping it with the stylus (the category becomes highlighted). Then, tap the appropriate button.

To create a new category, tap the New button, and then write in the desired name. That's all there is to it!

How to Assign Programs to Categories   Once you tailor the categories to your liking, you must next assign your programs to them. This isn't difficult, but it could take you a few tedious minutes to complete. Here's how:

1. In the Home screen, tap the Menu button, and then select Category.

2. Identify any one program you want to assign (you may have to scroll down the list, which you can do by using the onscreen arrows, the scroll bar, or the Scroll buttons), and then tap the little arrow next to it.

3. The list of categories appears. Pick one by tapping it.

4. Repeat the procedure for the other programs you want to assign.

5. Tap Done to return to the Home screen.

Now, when you tap the category arrow in the corner and select one, you see that all your reassigned icons have been placed in the respective screens.

> **TIP** *One way to change the displayed category is to tap the aforementioned arrow, but there's a quicker way. If you tap the Home button repeatedly, the Palm cycles through the categories that have programs assigned to them. Again, the Palm offers you two ways to accomplish the same goal.*

Setting Palm Device Preferences

What would a computer be without a control panel where you can tweak the settings and customize the machine? The Palm OS has one, called *Prefs*. Find the Prefs icon in the Home screen, tap it, and meet us at the next paragraph.

Divided into several different sections, Prefs is the place to reset your Palm's digitizer, change the date and time, tweak any necessary modem settings, and more. Before we delve into each individual Pref, however, we need to show you what different Prefs screens look like (see Figure 2-5). Just to keep everyone good and confused, Palm now uses three different "front ends" for the Prefs screen.

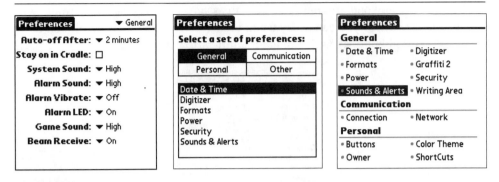

FIGURE 2-5 From left to right, the Prefs screen for Palm OS 4 and earlier, the Palm Tungsten T, and the Palm Zire 71.

Most of the options contained therein are the same from device to device, but what you'll see when you first tap the Prefs icon may vary a bit.

NOTE *Some Palm OS handhelds may have Prefs options that others don't. For instance, the Tungsten T includes one called Bluetooth, owing to its built-in Bluetooth radio. For the most part, we've covered the Palm OS 4 selection of Prefs in this section. OS 5 models such as the Tungsten T and Zire 71 may have slightly different options. Fortunately, they're pretty self-explanatory. Consult your manual if you need further help.*

Buttons

As we explained earlier, the hard buttons below the screen are used to quick-launch the main Palm OS programs. However, you can reassign these buttons to launch other programs instead. If you rarely use, say, Note Pad, but you use Memo Pad all the time, you may want to reassign the Note Pad button accordingly.

After selecting Buttons from the drop-down menu in the Prefs screen, you see an icon that corresponds to each button. You can also customize the Favorite (or Calc, if appropriate) button. All you do to change the function of any given button is tap the little arrow next to it, and then select the desired application. The buttons can launch any installed application—you're not limited to just the core Palm apps.

Notice, too, the three options at the bottom of the Buttons screen. *Default* restores the button assignments to their original settings. *Pen* (a button that's labeled *More* on some models) lets you choose what happens when you drag the tip of your stylus from the Graffiti area to the top of the screen. (This action can be made to load the built-in Graffiti help screens, invoke the onscreen keyboard, turn on backlighting, or one of several other options.) Finally, *HotSync* enables you to reprogram the HotSync button on your docking cradle or optional modem—something we don't recommend doing.

Connection

The *Connection* screen lets you set up whatever modem or cell phone you might be using with your Palm device or choose to HotSync via the unit's IR port or Bluetooth radio (instead of using the cradle). You probably won't need to fiddle with the modem settings too much. See Chapter 10 for more information on working with Bluetooth.

Date & Time

Flying into another time zone? Hit this screen to change your handheld's internal clock (an important thing to remember so you don't miss your alarms!). You can also change the date if necessary, and set the Palm to automatically adjust for Daylight Savings.

Digitizer

Noticing a little "drift" in your stylus taps? You tap someplace, but it doesn't quite register, or it registers in the wrong place? It may be time to reset your screen's digitizer. You should do so the moment you notice a problem; the worse the drift gets, the harder it may be to get to this screen. All you do is select Digitizer from the menu and follow the instructions.

NOTE *Digitizer drift does occur over time, but if it becomes a frequent occurrence, it could point to a hardware problem. If your Palm device is still under warranty, contact customer service to see if a replacement is warranted. In the meantime, there are software utilities designed to compensate for digitizer drift. See Chapter 16 for more information.*

Formats

Few users need to spend much time in the Formats screen, where you can change the way dates, times, and numbers are displayed. You can also specify whether you want the calendar week to start on Sunday (the default) or Monday.

General

Probably the most frequently visited of the Prefs screens, *General* contains the following settings:

- **Auto-off After** To help preserve battery life, your handheld will turn itself off after a designated period of inactivity. Here you can set the interval, from 30 seconds to 3 minutes. The lower you set it, the better your battery life will be.

- **Stay on in Cradle** When this box is checked, your handheld will remain on while it's in the HotSync cradle. This can be handy if you spend a lot of time at your desk and frequently need to consult your handheld for addresses, schedules, and so forth.

- **System Sound** Adjust the volume for various system sounds (such as beeps, HotSync tones, and so forth). If you want your handheld to be silent, set this to Off.

- **Alarm Sound**   Adjust the volume for alarms.

- **Alarm Vibrate**   This option appears only in models that have a vibrating-alarm feature. Set it to On if you want your handheld to vibrate when an alarm goes off. (And for totally silent alarms, set Alarm Sound to Off.)

- **Alarm LED**   On some models, the Power button doubles as an LED, which can be set to flash when an alarm goes off.

- **Game Sound**   Adjust the volume for games.

- **Beam Receive**   If this is off, you won't be able to receive programs and data beamed from other handhelds. However, keeping it off until you need it can help conserve power, but just *remember* that it's off, so you don't pull your hair out trying to determine why you can't receive a beam.

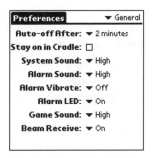

In Palm handhelds with OS 3.5 and earlier (and in some non-Palm models), the General screen is also where you set the date and time.

Network

The slightly misnamed *Network* screen is where you enter the relevant information about your Internet service provider (ISP), if you're using a modem or cell phone to dial into it. A handful of major ISPs are already listed in the Service menu, but you still need to provide your account username and password, plus the phone number for the ISP. The *Details...* button takes you to a screen with some advanced Internet settings; the *Connect* button tells the modem to go ahead and dial in.

Owner

In the tragic event that you lose your Palm device, you'd probably be very grateful to have it returned. The *Owner* screen is where you can put your name and contact information (address, phone number, e-mail address—whatever you're comfortable with). Then, if you use the Palm Operating System's security features (which we detail in Chapter 9) to "lock" the device every time you turn it off, the information on the Owner screen is displayed when the unit is turned on again. Then, if someone happens to find your handheld, they know how to return it to you, but won't have access to all your data. Smart!

TIP *Here's an even better way to retrieve a lost Palm: slap on a StuffBak or Boomerangit sticker (some Palm-branded models come with the latter). Whoever finds your handheld simply needs to call a toll-free number or visit a Web site to arrange its return. Get more information on these great services at www.boomerangit.com and www.stuffbak.com.*

ShortCuts

Next, we come to *ShortCuts,* a tool designed to expedite the entry of often-used words and phrases. Let's say you're a Starfleet engineer and you use your Palm to keep track of your repair duties. The phrase "holodeck emitters" comes up quite a bit—but do you really have to write it out every time? What if you could just write "h-e" instead and have the words magically appear? That's the beauty of shortcuts.

As you see when you reach the ShortCuts screen, a handful of the little time-savers have already been created. There's one each for your daily meals, one for "meeting," and even a couple of date and time stamps (used to quickly insert the date and time, natch). Let's walk through the process of creating and using a new shortcut:

1. Tap the New button.

2. In the ShortCut Name field, write the abbreviation you want to use for this particular shortcut. As an example, let's use "bm" for "Buy milk."

3. Tap the first line in the ShortCut Text field to move your cursor there. Now, enter the text you want to appear when you invoke the shortcut (in this case, "Buy milk").

4. Tap OK. Now, let's invoke the new shortcut. Press the To Do button to launch the To Do List, and then tap New to create a new task.

5. To invoke this or any other shortcut (in any application, be it Date Book, Memo Pad or whatever), you must first write the shortcut stroke in the Graffiti area. This lets Graffiti know you're about to enter the abbreviation for a shortcut. The stroke looks like a cursive, lowercase letter *l* (see our Graffiti guide in Chapter 4). After you make the stroke, you see it appear next to your cursor. Now enter the letter *b,* and then the letter *m.* Presto! The words "Buy milk" magically appear.

Introducing Palm Desktop

So far, we've talked mostly about the Palm itself: the hardware, the operating system, the basic setup procedures and considerations. One area is left to cover before you venture into real-world Palm use: the Palm Desktop.

What Is Palm Desktop?

Wondrous as a Palm device is in its own right, what makes it even more special is its capability to synchronize with your computer. This means that all the data entered into your Palm is copied to your PC, and vice versa. The software that fields all this data on the computer side is Palm Desktop. (If you use Microsoft Outlook or another contact manager, you needn't use Palm Desktop at all. More on that in the next section.)

Viewed in a vacuum, *Palm Desktop* resembles traditional personal information manager (PIM) or contact-management software. It effectively replicates all the core functionality of the Palm OS, providing you with a phone list, appointment calendar, to-do list, and memo pad. If you've never used such software before, you'll no doubt find Palm Desktop an invaluable addition, because it helps keep you organized at home or in the office (whereas a Palm device keeps you organized while traveling).

A Word about Synchronization

What happens when you synchronize your Palm device with your PC? In a nutshell, three things:

- ■ Any new entries made on your Palm device are added to Palm Desktop.

- ■ Any new entries made in Palm Desktop are added to your Palm device.

2

- Any existing records modified in one place (the Palm, for example) are modified in the other (the desktop, same example), the newest changes taking precedence.

Therefore, synchronizing regularly ensures that your information is kept current, both in your Palm device and in Palm Desktop.

Already entrenched in Microsoft Office? All Palm devices come with software—usually Chapura's PocketMirror, but some have a special version of Puma Technologies' IntelliSync—that allows direct synchronization with Office (bypassing Palm Desktop). If you have a different contact manager (such as Lotus Organizer), you may need to upgrade to a different sync program, such as Puma's IntelliSync.

The Differences Between the Windows and Macintosh Versions

Although functionally similar, the Windows and Macintosh versions of Palm Desktop are different programs. Palm Desktop for Windows was built from scratch, whereas the Macintosh version is a modified version of Claris Organizer, a popular contact manager.

At this writing, the Palm Desktop for Macintosh still lacks modules for viewing things such as photos (from the Zire 71) and Note Pad notes, but rest assured such items are indeed synchronized with the system and stored on the hard drive.

NOTE   *Older Palm models have serial—rather than USB—HotSync cradles, which means that you may need to buy a PalmConnect Kit. This provides the hardware you need to make the connection to your Mac.*

Where to Find It

Web Site	Address	What's There
Palm, Inc.	www.palm.com/macintosh	Mac-specific Palm information
Chapura	www.chapura.com	Outlook synchronization utility PocketMirror
Puma Technologies	www.pumatech.com	Contact manager synchronization utility IntelliSync

Chapter 3

Get Set Up with Your PC

How to...

- Install the HotSync cradle
- Configure the HotSync cradle
- Troubleshoot PC connection problems
- Install the Palm Desktop software
- Set up the HotSync Manager
- Perform your first HotSync
- HotSync with a HotSync cable
- Interpret the HotSync log
- Keep your data synchronized just the way you like
- Perform HotSyncs wirelessly via IR or Bluetooth

If you ask us, we'll tell you the coolest thing about the Palm is that it was perhaps the first handheld PC to understand it isn't all about the little computer in your hand; it's just as much about the computer back on your desk. In other words, the Palm creators made sure that the Palm fully integrated itself into your main computer system—the Windows or Mac desktop, depending on your preference—and all your data. No longer did using a handheld PC mean maintaining two different sets of contacts and appointments. No more did it mean laboriously transcribing tons of important data by hand. The Palm synchronizes with your desktop so elegantly, it's as if they were born to work together.

To be honest, the Palm wasn't the first handheld device that enabled you to share data with a desktop PC. Dave should know. He was an early handheld adopter and still has his old Apple Newton MessagePad. But synchronizing data with older handheld devices was a chore. Often, the necessary software wasn't included in the box with the handheld itself, and it worked less than optimally anyway. With the Palm, you press a button and all the important stuff you use every day is quickly shared. It couldn't be a whole lot easier.

Now that you've had a chance to explore your Palm device in Chapter 2, it's time to learn about how the device works with your PC. The Palm comes with a slew of tools designed for the desktop, including a synchronization application

Did you know?

HotSync Origins

HotSync, a term coined by Palm Computing, refers to the act of synchronizing the data stored on your handheld and desktop computers. These days, all PDA companies use a special term that means more or less the same thing—Microsoft's Pocket PCs, for instance, "ActiveSync" instead.

for making sure the Palm has the same data as the desktop. Let's get started using your PC with the Palm.

Unpacking Your Palm

If you're like us, the first thing you might have thought on seeing the Palm box is that it's way too big to hold only a tiny handheld PC. And you'd be right—there's a lot more in the box than just the Palm itself. The most important component, of course, is the HotSync cradle (the few models that don't come with a cradle come with a synchronization cable instead). The cradle is the interface that links the Palm to your desktop computer and all its data.

Installing the HotSync Cradle

Your HotSync cradle looks a little different depending on which handheld brand and model you're using, but its appearance doesn't matter; it performs the same function: transferring information between the PC and Palm. (Most cradles also charge the batteries at the same time.) Sony's unique CLIÉ cradle is shown alongside the standard Palm cradle that now works with all new models, such as the Palm m515, Tungsten T, and Zire 71, in Figure 3-1.

With rare exception, all of today's Palm models use HotSync cradles and cables that connect to your PC via a USB port. Older PDAs used a serial port. What's the difference? USB is easier to use and less prone to installation trouble.

If you have a USB cradle or cable, plug it into an empty USB port on the computer or a USB hub (but, in most cases, you need to install the Palm Desktop software first—check the instructions that came with your PDA). When you connect the cable, you don't even have to turn the computer off first. If you have a serial

FIGURE 3-1   HotSync cradles vary in appearance, but they all do essentially the same thing: let you synchronize the data on your Palm with your desktop computer.

port cradle (just about the only PDAs still using such a connection are the HandEra 330 and Kyocera 6035 SmartPhone), however, turn the computer off, then insert the serial connector from your cradle into a free serial port on the back of your PC. Remember the following information about connecting your HotSync cradle:

- Any compatible port will do. It doesn't matter which serial port you connect your serial cable to, just as it doesn't matter which USB port you connect your USB cable to.

- There are two different kinds of serial ports on the PC, and your computer may actually have one of each. Modern serial ports have nine pins. Older serial ports are wider, with a whopping 25 pins. Why? You don't want to know. Just remember this: if your nine-pin port is occupied, use a 25 pin-to-9 pin adapter, available at almost any computer store (older Palm models came with just such an adapter).

- If you are making a serial connection, play it safe and turn off the PC before plugging it in. You can leave your PC on to plug in a USB cradle.

NOTE *If you're out of sync with newer computers, all this talk about ports may be a bit confusing. What's USB, for instance, and how is it different from a serial port? In a nutshell, USB stands for the Universal Serial Bus, and it's many times faster than the serial port. In addition, it's a Plug-and-Play port that enables you to connect dozens of devices to your PC without worrying about the kind of ugly configuration issues that have hounded the serial port since the 1980s. USB has gotten so popular that some new computers don't even come with serial ports anymore.*

Powering a Rechargeable Palm

Odds are excellent that your Palm has integrated rechargeable batteries. Most PDAs that have debuted in the last few years come with HotSync cradles that can recharge your Palm whenever it's sitting idly at your desk. When you plug the cradle into the PC, make sure you connect the cradle's AC adapter, too; if the cradle isn't plugged into the wall, it can't charge your PDA. You can tell that your Palm is being recharged because a light on the cradle or the PDA itself will light up, or you'll hear a beep. If you don't see or hear an indicator when the Palm is in the cradle, check to see if the AC adapter has come loose from the wall or if the small connector where it plugs into the HotSync cradle is unplugged.

TIP *You needn't plug the AC adapter into the HotSync cradle just to transfer data between the PC and Palm. If you don't use the AC adapter, though, the batteries in the Palm won't recharge and, eventually, its batteries will die and cost you your data.*

Troubleshooting an Errant USB Port

If your HotSync cradle has a USB connector—and it probably does—don't worry. USB is usually pretty reliable, and any potential problems that crop up generally boil down to just a few simple things. For starters, you might not have anywhere to plug in your cradle, especially if you already have a few other USB devices. If that's the case, you need to run over to a local computer store and buy a USB hub. A hub plugs into an existing USB port on your PC and gives you several extra USB connectors for additional devices—it's like an extension cord that gives you a bunch of extra outlets.

If you plugged in your HotSync cradle and it doesn't seem to work, there are likely causes:

■ Your USB port doesn't have enough power to run the cradle. If your USB port has several devices connected to it, such as through a hub, it may not be able to handle the power requirements of the connected devices. Make sure you're using a "powered" hub (it will come with its own AC adapter) and that it's plugged into the wall. If that checks out, you might need to swap some devices around between your PC's various USB ports to move some high-power devices to the other port. This might take a little experimentation. This problem is pretty rare, though.

■ A related problem: your USB port might have run out of bandwidth. This can happen if you have some high-performance USB devices connected to the same port, all transferring data at the same time. Again, the solution is to move some things around between the USB ports. A few years back, Dave found he simply couldn't run all the USB devices he wanted to on his PC because they demand more total bandwidth than his PC's USB ports could deliver. If you have lots of USB devices and really need more bandwidth, you can simply buy a PCI card that gives you more USB ports.

■ One other possibility: something we like to call Windows Funkiness. Reboot your PC and it may work just fine. Heck, if you're having trouble, try rebooting the PC right away, because that may very well solve your problem.

■ Finally, you may run into trouble getting two or more Palm devices installed and properly HotSyncing on the same PC. It will work—you just need to install the software in a certain way. Specifically, you need to install the oldest Palm first, HotSync it, then install the next newer one and HotSync it, and so on. See Chapter 16 for details.

NOTE *Many new PCs have USB 2.0 ports, which are much more robust and have far greater bandwidth than older USB 1.1 ports. Nonetheless, USB 2.0 ports work like older USB 1.1 ports unless USB 2.0–compatible devices are plugged in. Right now, all Palm models are plain-old USB 1.1 devices, so there's no particular advantage to having USB 2.0 as far as your PDA goes.*

Know Your PC's Serial Ports

Still using serial? Your Palm's installation program will want to know which serial port your HotSync cradle is using. And, 99 percent of the time, the software can figure out what serial port is in use just fine all by itself. If the software encounters trouble, though, you might need to do a little detective work and figure it out yourself. This isn't as hard as it sounds. Use this table as a quick reference to decrypting your serial port:

There's only one serial port on my PC.	It's COM1.
My cradle is plugged into the small 9-pin port.	It's COM1.
My cradle is plugged into the big 25-pin port.	It's COM2.
I added a new serial port with an expansion card or a serial USB adapter and plugged the cradle into that.	It's a little hard to say from here. Experiment!

Installing the Desktop Software

Before you can synchronize your Palm and your desktop PC, you first need to install the Palm Desktop software suite on your computer. The Palm Desktop software is sort of like a personal information manager (PIM). It duplicates all the core applications from your Palm and serves as the headquarters from which you can use synchronized information from your Palm. Although you need to install the Palm Desktop, you don't need to use it. If you already use Microsoft Outlook or another PIM, you can synchronize your Palm to that program instead and avoid the Palm Desktop entirely.

The CD-ROM that accompanies your Palm includes everything you need to connect the handheld to your desktop, including your choice of synchronization to Palm Desktop or Outlook. Installation is very straightforward. Follow the installation instructions that appear after you insert the CD-ROM.

 *For most Palm models, it's very important that you install your software before you install the cradle and press the HotSync button. If in doubt, check the install guide that came with your PDA before installing anything.*

Installing Palm Desktop

The Palm Desktop CD-ROM includes an installer that places most (but, depending on which version of the software you have, not all) of the key components on your hard disk. Most of the main installation is completely automated, but you have to make a few decisions:

■ **Outlook or Palm Desktop?**   If you have a copy of Microsoft Outlook installed on your PC, the installer detects it and gives you the option of synchronizing your data to it if you so desire. What data are we talking about? Stuff like contacts from the address book and appointments from the calendar, as well as notes and tasks. If you're a regular and happy Outlook user, you should certainly choose to synchronize your Palm with Outlook. Palm Desktop, on the other hand, is a serviceable PIM, though it's not as comprehensive as Outlook. If you're not already married to Outlook, Palm Desktop just might make you happy.

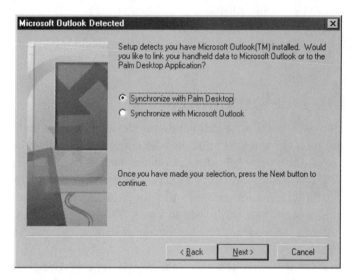

- **Assign a unique username** The User Name is actually the name of your Palm. You can use your own name or give your Palm a unique descriptor—anything from *Dave's Palm* to *Palm 33A* to just plain *Mike* is acceptable. Is the name important? Yup. If you have more than one Palm, each one absolutely must have a different name. If you give two or more Palms the same name, you can end up destroying all the synchronized data on the desktop PC and all the PDAs during a HotSync.

TIP

If you're upgrading to a new PDA, you probably want to use the same name as your old unit—that way registered software that depends upon the device name will still work on the new Palm. But if you do that, be sure to reset the old Palm and give it a different name. Or set fire to it so you can't accidentally resync it to your PC with the old name.

- **Select a COM port**   If you have a serial HotSync cradle, the installer can locate the cradle and figure out what COM port it belongs to. In some rare cases, a unique hardware configuration might make it impossible for the software to find the cradle, or you might not have connected the cradle yet for some reason. In that case, you need to choose a COM port from a list of options. If you have a USB cradle, you needn't worry about this step at all.

- **Configure mail**   The installer offers you a list of e-mail programs with which to synchronize your Palm. Just choose the one you want to use (if you want to synchronize e-mail at all—see Chapter 10 for more information). Unless you have a wireless model, the Palm's mail program will only allow you to read and write messages; sending and receiving happens when you HotSync to the desktop.

- **Set up wireless services**   If you have a wireless model such as the Palm i705, you may need to activate your wireless service, download Web applications, or perform other setup steps. Just follow the instructions in the user guide.

> TIP   *Bonus software probably won't be installed automatically. We suggest you browse the CD's main menu for cool programs such as Documents To Go, AvantGo, and games that are bundled with most Palm Powered handhelds.*

Performing Your First HotSync

Depending upon what kind of PDA you have, press the button on the HotSync cradle or cable (see Figure 3-2).

After you press the HotSync button, here's what should happen:

1. Your Palm turns itself on (if it wasn't on already).

2. You hear tones on both the computer and Palm indicating that the HotSync has begun.

3. A message box appears on the Windows desktop, which informs you of the HotSync status.

4. You hear another set of tones when the HotSync is complete.

5. The Palm displays a message indicating that the HotSync is complete.

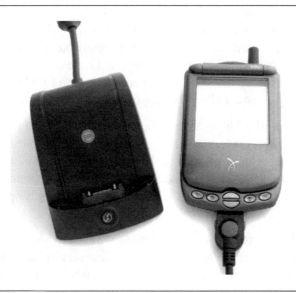

FIGURE 3-2   Most Palms have a cradle with a single HotSync button; a few models rely on a cable with the HotSync button instead.

The Best Films of All Time

Taking that TV break before the HotSync got us just a tad distracted. Truth be told, we took the opportunity to go watch some movies. And, that led to the inevitable arguments . . . what are the best movies of all time?

Dave: There's no way a rational person could disagree . . . *Aliens* is the best movie of all time. Space Marines fighting xenomorphs with 23rd-century machine guns! Woo hoo! What could possibly be cooler than that? And it has some of the best movie lines ever. This, mind you, is the film in which Bill Paxton made the words, "Game over, man," a part of my daily lexicon. After *Aliens,* my list gets a bit more introspective. *The Matrix, The Sixth Sense, Almost Famous,* and *O Brother, Where Art Thou* have to be four of the most amazing films ever made. Now let's see what lame movies Rick thinks are cool. My prediction: His favorite films include *Tron, Dirty Dancing,* and *Weekend at Bernie's 2.*

Rick: I've had just about enough of your *Weekend at Bernie's 2* bashing, mister. Don't make me tell everyone about your strange fondness for Will Smith. Anyway, in no particular order, my Top Five Movies are as follows: *Life is Beautiful, City Lights, The Shawshank Redemption, Chicken Run,* and *Star Trek II: The Wrath of Khan.* Yes, I know only one of those movies has things blowing up, which means you won't care for the other four. The age of *Ah*-nold has passed, leatherneck. Grow up already.

Exploring the HotSync Manager

The HotSync Manager software does exactly what it sounds like—it manages the connection between your Palm and your computer, enabling you to HotSync. It contains all the options and configurations needed to keep the two devices talking to each other. To HotSync, you needn't mess with anything on the Palm at all. You just need to tweak the HotSync Manager.

To get to the HotSync Manager's options in Windows, you need to see the HotSync menu. Click the HotSync Manager icon in the System Tray, and a context menu appears.

TIP   *You can click the HotSync Manager icon with either the right or left mouse button; the result is the same.*

The top of the menu lists ways available to HotSync—you'll see all or some of these options:

- Local USB
- Local Serial
- Modem
- Network
- Infrared

For now, the only one that must be checked is the Local option (Serial or USB). This means you can perform a HotSync using the serial or USB port.

Configuring HotSync Setup

Click the Setup option on the HotSync menu. You should now see the Setup dialog box. This is the place where you get to configure how the HotSync Manager behaves. Four tabs are on the Setup dialog box.

General   The General tab lets you specify how often the HotSync Manager listens to the USB or serial port for a HotSync request. It has three options, as you can see in Figure 3-3.

- **Always available**   This is the default setting. As soon as you press the HotSync button on the cradle, you synchronize your data. It's fast and convenient, and is probably the way most people use their Palms. But you needn't give in to peer pressure, because this has a downside: if you're using the serial port, HotSync Manager locks it up so you can't share the port with another serial device, such as a modem.

- **Available only when the Palm Desktop is running**   If you often share your serial port with another device, this might be a better solution. The HotSync Manager won't lock the port unless Palm Desktop is actually running. But, what if you don't use Palm Desktop? Then keep reading, because option number three is the one for you.

- **Manual**   Just like it sounds, the HotSync Manager doesn't run at all unless you choose it from the Start menu (Start | Programs | Palm Desktop | HotSync Manager). This is the least convenient of all the options, but you

3

might want to choose it if you HotSync only on rare occasion, if your serial port is frequently used by another device, or if you don't really use the Palm Desktop (meaning the second option doesn't work for you).

TIP
If you try to use another serial device such as a modem, but Windows reports that the serial port is in use, click the HotSync Manager icon and choose Exit. Then try your serial device again.

NOTE
On the Macintosh, your options are much more streamlined, so you can ignore all of this. The HotSync Software Setup dialog box (which opens when you open the HotSync Manager) lets you choose whether HotSync is available when the computer starts and lets you edit connection settings; that's about it.

Local   The Local Serial tab is where you specify the serial port and speed for your HotSync. Most of the time, the installation process correctly determines your serial port and it's all taken care of. If you move the HotSync cable to another serial port, though, this is where you tell the HotSync Manager what the proper COM port actually is. The correct COM port is almost always COM1 or COM2, and you can either experiment or use the table (see the section "Know Your PC's Serial Ports," earlier in this chapter) to determine your port name.

You can almost always leave the speed set to As Fast As Possible. If you need to troubleshoot connection problems, though, this is where you can specify a slower speed.

FIGURE 3-3   The General tab determines when the HotSync Manager runs and how easy it is to perform a HotSync.

What's a Conduit?

Conduit is the term Palm uses to describe the software that connects data on your Palm with similar data on your computer. The Calendar conduit, for instance, makes sure the Palm's Date Book and the computer's Outlook Calendar stay completely in sync. Every application on your Palm that has a corresponding program on the PC is connected with its own conduit, and the Custom menu option is where you turn to adjust these conduits.

Modem and Network   Both of these tabs are used to specify settings for more advanced HotSync techniques. After you've seen all the tabs in the Setup dialog box, click OK to save changes or click Cancel to leave the dialog box without changing anything.

Customizing the HotSync Operation

From the HotSync Manager menu, choose Custom.

TIP   *On the Mac, choose HotSync | Conduit Settings.*

This is arguably the most important dialog box in the HotSync software because it enables you to specify with great detail exactly what data will get transferred. Before we look at this dialog box, however, we should define a few essential terms the Palm uses to perform data synchronizations. If you make the wrong choice, you can destroy data you need. Here are the ways you can configure the HotSync program to manage your data:

Synchronize the files	Suppose you added new files to both the PC and the Palm since the last HotSync. The new data from the Palm is copied to the PC, and the new data from the PC is copied to the Palm. Both devices will have a copy of everything. *This is the best setting to use most of the time and is, in fact, the default for most conduits.*
Desktop overwrites handheld	This option supposes that the desktop data is correct at the expense of anything that might be on the handheld. If you add new files to both the PC and the handheld, for instance, and then perform this kind of sync, the new files on the Palm will be lost. The desktop data overwrites whatever was on the Palm.

Handheld overwrites desktop	This is exactly the opposite of the previous case. Assuming the handheld data is more correct for some reason (we assume you have your reasons), any files that are different or new on the desktop PC are lost after the synchronization. Both systems will have the Palm data.
Do nothing	With this option selected, no changes are made to either device during this HotSync.

Remember: each conduit can be adjusted separately. This means you can set the Date Book to overwrite the PC's Address Book, while the e-mail conduit is set to Do Nothing and the Notes conduit synchronizes.

TIP *If you're ever in doubt about the state of your conduits, be sure to check the action before you press the HotSync button by right-clicking the HotSync icon and choosing Custom. If you ever accidentally configure the HotSync Manager to Handheld Overwrites Desktop, for instance, you'll lose changes you made to the Palm Desktop or Outlook when you HotSync.*

With those terms in mind, let's look at the Custom dialog box (called Conduit Settings on the Mac). As you can see in Figure 3-4, the top of the box displays the name of the Palm unit. Managing more than one Palm from each PC is possible, so you select the proper unit from the list menu before continuing. If you have only a single Palm, don't worry about this option.

This dialog box displays a list of conduits and their actions. As you can see from the list, there's a unique conduit for each kind of application on the Palm. Most Palms include these conduits:

- **Calendar**   Shares data between the Palm and desktop calendars.

- **Contacts**   Shares data between the Palm and desktop address books.

- **Tasks**   Shares data between the Palm and desktop to-do lists.

- **Notes**   Shares data between the Palm and desktop memo pads.

- **Expense**   Shares expense entries between the Palm and an application such as Excel.

- **Install**   Transfers Palm OS applications from your PC's hard disk to the Palm.

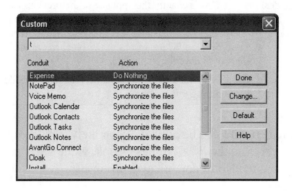

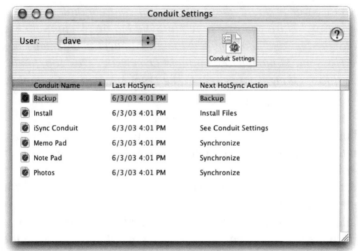

FIGURE 3-4   The Custom dialog box (called Conduit Settings on the Mac) enables you to specify how each conduit behaves when you HotSync.

- ■ **Mail**   E-mail messages are synchronized between your desktop mail application and the Palm.

- ■ **AvantGo Connect**   Used by the optional AvantGo application to transfer Web-based documents to your Palm.

- ■ **System**   Transfers other files created by Palm applications between the PC and Palm.

CAUTION   *If you install new software, you may end up with more conduits. Many programs come with their own conduits to control the flow of information between your Palm and desktop applications.*

To configure a conduit, either double-click an entry, or select it and then click the Change button. Depending on which conduit you open, you'll find that you might have all four synchronization options or, perhaps, fewer.

When you configure a conduit, whatever selection you make applies only to the very next time you HotSync unless you check the box for Set As Default.

HotSync with a Cable

You don't need a cradle to synchronize your Palm; you can also use a modem, Bluetooth, or your laptop's IR port. Here's a low-tech alternative for the road warrior: try a HotSync cable. Cables are handy because they take up less room in a suitcase than the bulky cradle, and they don't rely on finicky modems or IR ports. A HotSync cable costs about $20 and is an essential tool for the frequent traveler. You can buy peripherals such as the HotSync cable from a number of online stores, including Targus (www.targus.com), Belkin (www.belkin.com), and the Palm Web site (www.palm.com). Better still, check out the new breed of USB HotSync cables that will also charge your handheld. See Chapter 15 for details.

Reading the HotSync Log

Did your HotSync session go as planned? Did all your data get transferred properly, and did files get copied the way you expected? Usually, it's pretty obvious if everything went well, but sometimes it's nice if your computer can tell you what actually happened—especially if the HotSync dialog box reports some sort of error.

During every HotSync, the HotSync Manager makes a record of everything that happened. This log is easy to read, and it can answer that nagging question, "Why didn't the calendar update after I added an entry for the Sandra Bullock fan club?" If the HotSync Manager noticed that something went wrong during a HotSync, it'll even tell you. Figure 3-5, for instance, shows the result of a HotSync that generated an error. The log reveals what happened.

To see the log at any time, right-click the HotSync icon in the System Tray and choose View Log (if you're using Windows). On the Mac, choose HotSync | View Log from the menu. The HotSync Log window should then appear.

You can't perform a HotSync when the log is open, so be sure to close it before pressing the HotSync button.

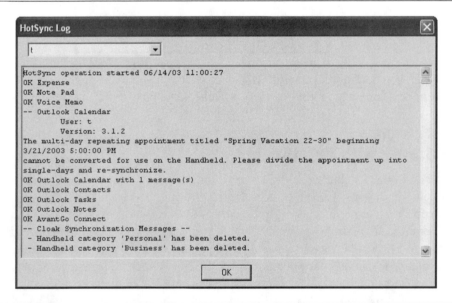

FIGURE 3-5 The HotSync log records the details of the last 10 HotSyncs, along with any errors that occurred along the way.

The log displays a list of the actions that occurred for each of your last 10 HotSync sessions. The top of the log is the most recent, and older sessions are listed as you scroll down the page. Each session is separated by a text message that indicates when it started and ended.

What kind of information does a log reveal? Each conduit reports its status, and these are the messages you're most likely to see:

- **OK**   This is good news; the conduit's action succeeded with no errors.

- **Sync configured to Do Nothing**   If something didn't happen, this may be the cause—the conduit was intentionally or mistakenly set to do nothing.

- **Truncated**   This means a file stored on the PC (such as e-mail or an address book entry) was so long that not all of it would fit on the Palm.

- **Records were modified in both Handheld and PC**   You made changes to the same file on both the PC and the Palm. Because the HotSync Manager doesn't know which change is correct, it duplicated both files on both systems. You now have a chance to update the file and delete the one you don't want.

- **Synchronization failed**   There can be any number of reasons for this, but it's probably because the COM ports were misconfigured, so the PC couldn't find the Palm.

 **HotSync**

1. Plug the cradle into your PC.

2. Set the Palm in the cradle.

3. Make sure the HotSync Manager software is running (by default, it probably is).

4. Verify that the conduits are set properly to transfer and synchronize data just the way you want (by default, they probably are).

5. Press the HotSync button on the cradle or cable.

6. Wait until you hear the "HotSync complete" tones before removing the Palm from the cradle.

 *The HotSync log is also available on the Palm itself, albeit only for the most recent HotSync session. To reach it, tap the HotSync application, and then tap the Log button.*

HotSyncing as a Way of Life

After your first HotSync, you may begin to see how convenient it is to have a duplicate of your desktop data on your Palm. But how often should you HotSync? The short answer is as frequently as you like. Some people HotSync daily, whereas others—whose data changes much less frequently—update their Palms only once a week or even less. Use this guide as a rule of thumb:

- HotSync anytime you leave the office with your PDA.

- HotSync when you return from a trip to update your PC with new info stored on the Palm.

- Many AvantGo Web channels are updated daily. A HotSync each day keeps you current with the newest content.

- HotSync to install new applications on your Palm (this is discussed in Chapter 4).

What HotSync Does to Files

After your first HotSync, you have a set of data on both your Palm and your desktop. The goal of the HotSync process is to make sure that the data stays the same on both systems. So what happens when you change data on one or both of the computers? The following table, which assumes that the conduit is set to Synchronize The Files, should help you understand the subtleties of the HotSync:

Before the HotSync	After the HotSync
You add a file to the Palm (or the PC).	That file is added to the PC (or the Palm).
You delete a file from the Palm (or PC).	The file is also deleted from the PC (or Palm).
You change a file on the Palm.	The file is changed on the PC.
You changed the same file on both the Palm and PC—they're now different.	Both versions of the file are added to both the Palm and PC. You need to modify the file and delete the one you don't want to keep.

Changing Conduits On-the-Fly

Often, you may find yourself changing all the conduits in your HotSync Manager save one or two. You might want to disable everything except the Install conduit to quickly get a new program onto your Palm, for instance, or set everything except AvantGo to Do Nothing so you can get your news onto the PDA as you're running out the door to lunch.

Whatever the reason, you'll soon find that there's no easy way to disable several conduits at once, and successively changing five conduits to Do Nothing is almost as time consuming as just doing the whole darned HotSync to begin with.

There's an easier way. Download the tremendously useful program called Ultrasoft NotSync from PalmGear.com. This program lets you quickly and easily change your conduits in just seconds. The change applies only to the very next HotSync, so it never affects your default settings.

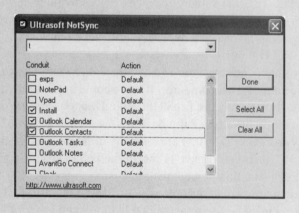

With this in mind, you might not always want to use the Synchronize The Files option for all your conduits. Why not? Any number of reasons. Here are a few situations:

■ **You might rely on your Palm to take notes that you have no interest in copying to your PC.** In other words, you want to keep one set of notes on the PC, which is relevant to what you do at your desk, and another set of notes for when you're on the road. In such a case, Do Nothing is probably the best option for your needs.

■ **You might take notes you don't need to keep after a trip is over.** In such an instance, you can use Desktop Overwrites Handheld for that conduit. After your trip is over, the handheld notes will be erased during the HotSync and replaced by the desktop notes.

TIP

Don't forget, you can configure each conduit individually, so the Address Book might be set to Synchronize The Files, while the Date Book is set to Desktop Overwrites Handheld, for instance.

Installing and HotSyncing More Than One Palm

As we've already mentioned, you can install multiple Palm devices to a single computer. Right now, in fact, Dave has a Sony CLIÉ, the Palms (a Tungsten T, a Tungsten C, and a Zire 71), and two Pocket PCs (but we won't talk about those) to one little old PC. Yes, that's neurotic since he lives by himself with 21 cats and a life-size poster of Halle Berry, but that's a topic for a whole different book. The real issue is this: there's no reason why several different Palms can't all share the same data with Microsoft Outlook.

In general, you may not have to re-install the entire Palm Desktop CD for every Palm device you connect to a computer. If two people in the same household each own Tungsten Ts, for instance, just install the Palm Desktop software once. Everything will be fine. But if you have two Palm devices that aren't the same brand—say, a Palm and a Sony—or two PDAs that are radically different ages (such as a Palm III and a Tungsten W), then you'll have to install the Palm Desktop for each. See Chapter 16 for details on this procedure.

But what if you are using Outlook as your PIM? Only the first Palm will sync with the program. The fix is easy: open Outlook and look for a folder called PocketMirror that the install process added to the program. In that folder, you'll find a note for the first Palm. Just double-click in a blank part of this folder and a new, blank note will appear. Enter the exact name of the second device and close the note. You can see Outlook configured to sync with four Palm devices in the following illustration:

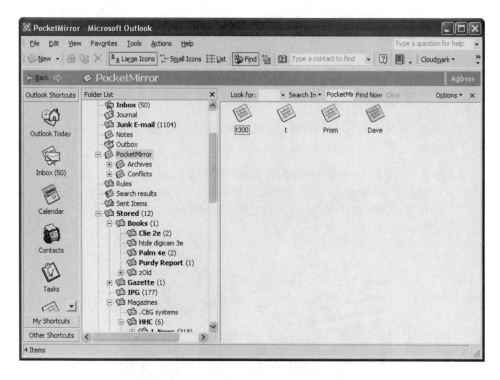

If you follow these steps, your new PDA will now sync with—and share data with—Outlook. Repeat this process for as many Palm OS devices as you attach to your PC.

Using a Notebook's IR Port to HotSync

Do you travel with both a laptop and your Palm? If you do, you can wirelessly synchronize the data between the two devices by using the IR port built into your laptop (if it has one—many newer laptops don't) and your Palm. Being able to HotSync without carting a cradle around means you can easily keep your notebook and Palm current no matter where you are.

The capability to IR HotSync doesn't exist in older versions of the Palm Operating System, so you may have to upgrade to take advantage of this capability.

Prepping the Notebook

To HotSync your Palm to a notebook, you first need to prepare your notebook. Namely, it must have the necessary infrared hardware and driver. Here's what you need to do:

1. Start by installing the Palm Desktop software if it isn't already on the system. We obviously need that later.

2. Does your notebook have an IR port? This may sound silly, but check visually for the port. It's a small, reddish plastic bubble that's usually in back of the system, but also might be located on the side.

IrDA port

3. If you have the IR port, you next need to verify that the IR driver is installed. To do this, open the Control Panel by choosing Start | Settings Control Panel. Look for an icon named Infrared. If it's there, great. The necessary software is installed.

NOTE *If you don't have the infrared driver installed, you need to download it from Microsoft's Web site. Go to www.microsoft.com/windows/downloads and click the Windows 95 link. Then find the Windows 95 IrDA 2.0 Infrared Driver and install it. This should only apply to older laptops.*

4. Next, make sure the infrared port is enabled. Double-click the Infrared icon in the Control Panel. You should see the Infrared Monitor dialog box. Click the Options tab and make sure the Enable Infrared Communication option is checked. If not, your notebook won't be able to communicate with the Palm.

3

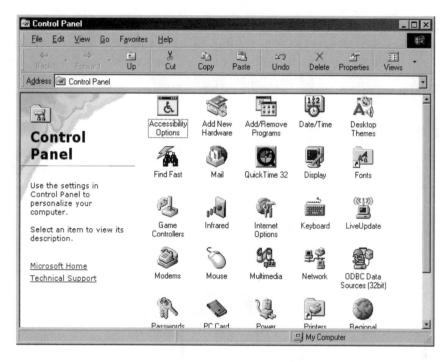

5. While you're on this tab, make a note of what COM port the infrared device is using. This should be displayed near the option you selected in step 4.

Before you go any further, be sure you perform at least one normal Local HotSync with the Palm and your notebook. That's right: you need to connect the HotSync cradle and press the button the old-fashioned way. After that, you can put the cradle back on your desktop PC and forget about it. Your first HotSync on a PC cannot be an IR HotSync, so if you arrive in Topeka with a brand-new notebook and plan to IR HotSync with it, you're in for a big surprise.

Your PC is ready to start performing IR HotSyncs.

Configure the HotSync Manager

Now that your IR port is ready, you now need to configure the HotSync Manager for IR communications. This part is easy. All you need to do is change the COM port to the same one the IR port is accessing. Do this:

1. Click the HotSync Manager icon in the System Tray and choose Setup from the menu. You should see the Setup dialog box.

2. Switch to the Local tab. Change the serial port to whatever COM port the infrared driver is using. You can find out by opening the Infrared icon in the Control Panel, as discussed in the previous section.

3. Click OK to close the Setup dialog box.

Perform the HotSync

Now it's time to perform the HotSync. Turn on your Palm and tap the HotSync icon. Make sure it's set to Local (not Modem) and choose IR To A PC/Handheld from the menu.

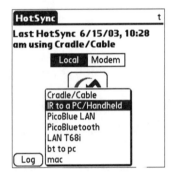

Point the Palm at the IR port on the notebook and tap the HotSync button in the middle of the Palm's screen. You should see the HotSync operation start. That's it!

HotSync with Bluetooth

The availability of Bluetooth in both Palm devices (such as the Tungsten T) and in new computers (such as some of Apple's PowerBook G4 models) opens up a whole new way of synchronizing data—wirelessly.

In principle, Bluetooth HotSyncs are pretty simple. After "pairing" your Palm and your computer, all you need to do is select the HotSync option from your PDA to wirelessly sync up to 30 feet away. Your PDA needn't be in the cradle, and everything else should work more or less the same as a traditional HotSync. For the most part, that's true. Certainly, Apple has made Bluetooth HotSyncs pretty painless. If you're trying to perform a Bluetooth HotSync on the PC, though, the exact procedure will vary depending upon which Bluetooth adapter you have

3

installed, or if you're trying to sync via a Bluetooth access point. Check the documentation that came with your Bluetooth gear or give the company's tech support a call. In general, you'll need to perform these steps for a successful Bluetooth HotSync:

1. Pair the devices. On the Macintosh, for instance, click the Bluetooth icon in the desktop title bar and choose Set Up Bluetooth Device..., then follow the wizard to associate the Palm and the computer.

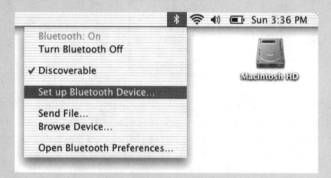

2. Tell your Palm's HotSync controls how to find the Bluetooth device you want to HotSync with. In the HotSync application on the Palm, choose Options | Connection Setup and create a new connection. Choose to connect to the PC via Bluetooth, and select the computer after your Palm searches for it (the computer needs to be "discoverable" for this to work).

3. On the HotSync application screen, select the connection you just created as the method to connect via the menu under the HotSync icon in the middle of the screen.

4. Once all those steps have been accomplished, you should be able to HotSync from now on just by tapping the HotSync icon on the Palm. The exact procedure will vary depending upon your PC and Bluetooth adapter, though.

Chapter 4

Get Information In and Out of Your Palm

How to...

- Determine whether your handheld has Graffiti 1 or Graffiti 2
- Understand the differences between Graffiti 1 and Graffiti 2
- Use Graffiti to enter data into your Palm
- Type using the onscreen Palm keyboard
- Work with built-in keyboards
- Enter data using Palm Desktop
- Use alternate gestures to write in Graffiti more effectively
- Display Graffiti help
- Beam items to another Palm
- Beam your business card to another Palm
- Install new software on your Palm
- Install software on memory cards
- Delete unwanted applications
- Work with memory cards

A handheld computer is only as good as the information you store inside it. Or, perhaps more to the point, it's only as good as the methods you have for getting information into it. After all, if storing your appointments or adding new contacts is too difficult, you won't bother doing it—and then all you have is an expensive paperweight.

Case in point: the Rex, a credit card–sized PDA that debuted a few years ago to generally favorable reviews. This little guy was so small it could actually fit into a wallet, yet it carried contacts and appointments like a champ. The problem? You couldn't add to it or make changes when away from your PC—you could only view whatever data was already loaded. For some people, this wasn't a big deal, but public reaction was underwhelming. Palm OS handhelds sell like hotcakes (the good ones, with the bananas in them) in part because they can be updated on the go, and quite easily as well.

You already know about some of the tools at your disposal for getting data in and out of your Palm device. We talked in detail about how to HotSync (some would say too much detail, but we ignore those people) in Chapter 3, and you know you can enter data directly in the device using Graffiti, an almost-ordinary method of handwriting. In this chapter, you learn everything you'll ever need to know about Graffiti. We also cover other data entry methods, including the onscreen keyboard and beaming data between Palms using the built-in IR port.

4

Three Different Ways to Enter Data

One of the first things you'll want to do with your new handheld is enter data—phone numbers, e-mail addresses, memos, to-dos, and so on—into your various applications. Hey, don't look so surprised. The core programs, such as Date Book, Address Book, Memo Pad, and To Do List, rely on you to fill them with interesting things you can later reference.

There are three primary ways to enter data into a Palm OS device:

■ Write it in using Graffiti, the built-in handwriting recognition software.

■ "Tap type" using the onscreen keyboard (or use the built-in keyboard if your device has one).

■ Enter data into Palm Desktop (or Outlook) on your PC, and then HotSync the data to your handheld. This is the preferred method for people who are just starting out with a PDA, because it's the path of least resistance. If you have an old-fashioned paper address book, for instance, and you want to copy all the names to your handheld, it's much easier to enter them into your PC than into the device itself. Similarly, if you have an electronic address book from another program or PDA, you can probably import the data into Palm Desktop or Outlook, then HotSync it all to your new PDA.

TIP *You can also connect a full-sized keyboard to your Palm and type directly into the device—no PC required. For information on PDA-compatible keyboards, see Chapter 15. Yet another way to get data into your handheld is by beaming, which we discuss later in this chapter.*

If you're on the go, you definitely need to use either Graffiti or the keyboard to enter data. If you're at your desk, though, you might find entering data into the

Palm Desktop, and then HotSyncing, easier because your desktop computer sports a full-sized keyboard.

All About Graffiti

Graffiti is a specialized handwriting recognition system that enables you to enter text into a Palm handheld virtually error-free. Before we go any further, however, we have to talk about the two versions of Graffiti that now exist. In the early months of 2003, PalmSource (the operating-system division of Palm, Inc.) announced plans to abandon the original Graffiti and adopt new handwriting-recognition software, which it dubbed Graffiti 2. We won't bore you with the details as to why (hint: lawsuits were involved—aren't they always?), but suffice it to say, our job here just got a lot harder.

That's because the vast majority of existing Palm OS handhelds have "Graffiti 1," but the latest models use Graffiti 2. PalmSource was also expected to offer an optional software patch that would endow older handhelds with the new Graffiti, though at press time that wasn't yet available. To further complicate matters, some handhelds— such as the Handspring Treo, Palm Tungsten C, and Sony CLIÉ TG50—don't even have Graffiti areas. Instead, they have little keyboards (which some people find easier for data entry than the handwriting software—either version).

NOTE   *As you'll learn a bit later in this chapter, it's still possible to use Graffiti with keyboard-equipped models.*

In the face of all these data-entry differences, what's a pair of dedicated book authors to do? Much as we'd like to throw up our hands and say, "Ahh, go read the manual," we don't quit that easily. (Actually, Dave does—he's a quitter from *way* back—but Rick dragged him kicking and screaming back to this chapter.) In the pages to come, we show you everything you need to know about entering data on your PDA. It may get a little bumpy along the way, but we think you'll come through better for the experience.

A Drive-By Introduction to Graffiti 1

Unlike other handwriting recognition systems, Graffiti 1 neither interprets your ordinary handwriting nor learns or adapts to the way you write. Instead, you need to slightly modify the way you write and make specific kinds of keystrokes that

4

How to ... Determine Which Version of Graffiti You Have

As you now know, there's the original Graffiti (let's call it Graffiti 1 just for clarity) and there's Graffiti 2. How can you tell which version is installed on your handheld? It's fairly important that you find out so you know which of the following sections to read. Fortunately, it's not hard. All handhelds equipped with Palm OS 4.1 or earlier have Graffiti 1. If your handheld has Palm OS 5 or later, it *may* have Graffiti 2. (Not sure which version of the Palm OS is on your handheld? Sheesh—do we have to teach you *everything*? Oh, right, the book title… Anyway, tap the Home button to return to the main screen, then tap Menu | App | Info. Then tap Version to see which version of the OS is installed.)

At press time, only the Palm Tungsten C and Zire 71 had Graffiti 2. By the time you read this, there will undoubtedly be more models equipped with the new software. The absolute easiest way to tell for sure is to check for a Graffiti 2 icon on the Home screen (it will be in the System category). If you've got one, you've got Graffiti 2, natch.

represent the letters, numbers, and punctuation you're trying to write. Don't worry, though, this isn't hard to do. You can learn the basics of Graffiti inside of a day— heck, you can probably master most of the characters in an hour or less.

Λ = A

$\daleth$ = T

When entering text into your Palm, you can't write directly on the part of the screen the Palm uses to display data. Instead, you write inside the small rectangle at the bottom of the display—the one that sits between the four icons. We call this the "Graffiti area." (Some models have a "virtual" Graffiti area—see the sidebar "The Virtual Graffiti Area" for more info.)

TIP   *A Palm utility, called a Hack, is available that enables you to write above the Graffiti area, right on the main screen. Some people find this way of entering text more intuitive because the characters appear directly under where they're writing. See Chapter 12 for more information on this tool.*

The rectangle is divided roughly in half: the left side is used to enter letters; the right side is used to enter numbers.

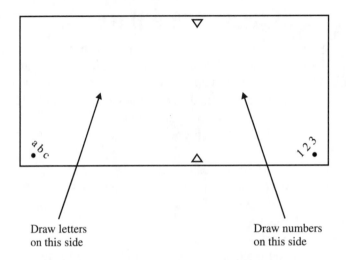

Draw letters
on this side

Draw numbers
on this side

> **TIP** *If you aren't getting the results you expect from Graffiti, make sure you're writing on the correct side of the rectangle. The right side is for numbers, the left side is for letters, and either side works for punctuation.*

Your Palm came with a Graffiti "cheat sheet," either as a laminated card or a sticker. Take a look at this guide and you will see that most characters are single-stroke shapes (called *gestures* in Graffiti-ese). The characters must be drawn in the direction indicated on the Graffiti guide: the heavy dot indicates the starting position. To write a character, mimic the Graffiti guide by drawing the shape starting with the dot and—in most cases—finish the character in a single stroke without lifting the stylus.

For more details on writing in Graffiti, see the section "Getting to Know Graffiti," later in this chapter.

A Drive-By Introduction to Graffiti 2

Graffiti 2 is a lot like its predecessor, to the extent that you should read the previous section if you haven't already. However, whereas Graffiti 1 forced you to learn a simple but somewhat unusual set of characters, Graffiti 2 allows you to write more naturally. You can't write in cursive or anything like that, but you can make a "k"

The Virtual Graffiti Area

Some Palm OS handhelds, such as the Garmin iQue 3600, HandEra 330, and Sony CLIÉ NR/NX/NZ series, employ what's called a virtual Graffiti area—a Graffiti area that's part of the software instead of part of the hardware. It looks just like a regular Graffiti area, except that it can disappear when you don't need it, thereby giving you some extra screen estate for icons, text, and so on. Think of it as "Graffiti on demand."

To open and close the Graffiti area on these PDAs, tap the arrow at the bottom of the screen. In many cases, the current application should shrink or enlarge to accommodate it. Here's an example of what a CLIÉ looks like with the Graffiti area open and closed:

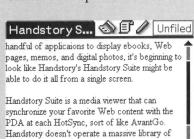

One of the coolest aspects of virtual Graffiti is that you can see your penstrokes as you make them in the Graffiti area, just as you can when writing on paper. (Of course, on a PDA the "virtual ink" disappears the moment you lift your stylus. Let's see a piece of paper do that!) Many people find that seeing their input helps them improve their Graffiti accuracy.

just like you normally would—with two strokes. Indeed, that's the primary difference between Graffiti 1 and Graffiti 2—the latter supports two-stroke characters.

NOTE *There are a few exceptions. You can't make a capital "A" with two strokes, though you can draw a lowercase cursive "a"—something you couldn't do with Graffiti 1. Thus, even though Graffiti 2 is a bit more accommodating than Graffiti 1, there's still a learning curve.*

For more details on writing in Graffiti 2, see the section "Getting to Know Graffiti," later in this chapter.

Using the Onscreen Keyboard

Even after you get comfortable writing with Graffiti, at times you'll need or want to input specific characters without using pen strokes. After all, remembering how to make some rarely used characters in the middle of taking real-time notes can be hard, and having access to a keyboard can be a real lifesaver.

TIP *When you have to enter a password, tapping it out on the keyboard is easier than writing it with Graffiti. Using the keyboard, you can be sure you're entering the right characters, error free.*

All it takes to use the onscreen keyboard is a tap. At the bottom of the Graffiti area, you see the letters *ABC* on the left and the numbers 123 on the right. Tap either spot to call up the appropriate keyboard (alpha or numeric).

NOTE *The keyboard appears only in situations where it's appropriate— specifically, when a cursor is in a data field. If no application is open into which you can insert text, you simply hear a beep when you tap the keyboard dots.*

Once the keyboard is open, note that you can switch between letters and numbers by tapping the selector at the bottom of the screen. A set of international characters is available as well.

Remember the following tips about the onscreen keyboard:

■ In handhelds that use versions of the Palm OS prior to 4.0, you can't use Graffiti at the same time you have the keyboard open. Drawing on the Graffiti area has no effect.

■ Use the SHIFT key on the keyboard in the same way you'd use a real keyboard; tap it to create an uppercase letter.

■ The CAP key is actually a CAPS LOCK key, which makes all subsequent letters uppercase until you tap it again.

■ If you're typing with the CAPS LOCK on and you want to make a single character lowercase, tap the SHIFT key.

■ The Numeric keyboard provides access to special symbols and punctuation.

Using Built-In Keyboards

There's a growing trend among handheld PCs: a real keyboard in place of handwriting recognition. Okay, maybe "real" isn't the right word—let's say "tiny" instead. Models such as the Handspring Treo, Palm Tungsten C and Tungsten W, and Sony CLIÉ TG50 don't have Graffiti areas—they have little keyboards instead (see Figure 4-1).

These keyboards are fairly self-explanatory, but allow us to offer a few tips and guidelines for using them:

■ To get an uppercase letter, you don't hold down the SHIFT key like you do with a regular keyboard. Instead, you press it once, then press the desired letter. Press it twice to effect CAPS LOCK, and a third time to return to normal.

FIGURE 4-1   The Palm Tungsten C has a keyboard instead of a Graffiti area—though this particular model also lets you input data with Graffiti. You just write directly on the screen.

■ The same applies for the "function" key—the (usually blue) key used for symbols, numbers, and so on. Just press it once—don't hold it down. Or press it twice to "lock" it, which is useful if you need to enter a lot of numbers. A third press unlocks it.

■ On some models, you can press and hold a letter key to get a capital letter.

Using Graffiti on Models with Built-In Keyboards

Just because your PDA lacks a Graffiti area doesn't mean you can't use Graffiti— or something like it. There may be times when it's quicker, easier, or just plain preferable to write instead of type. Fortunately, most keyboard-equipped models have some kind of handwriting-recognition option, either built in or accessible via third-party software.

■ **Handspring Treo**   Many Treo models don't have Graffiti as part of the Palm OS. However, you can use a third-party program such as Jot (www.cic.com) or SimpliWrite (www.simpliwrite.com) to add handwriting recognition. They effectively turn your handheld's screen into one large handwriting area, and also recognize a somewhat more natural character set than Graffiti. Bonus!

■ **Palm Tungsten C**   The Tungsten C has a Graffiti option built in. To access it, tap the Prefs icon on the Home screen, then choose Writing Area. Tap On to enable "anywhere onscreen" writing. Doing so turns the entire screen into a Graffiti area, complete with an invisible line down the middle separating the letter and number sides. Now you can input data using either the keyboard or Graffiti. One caveat: to press buttons (such as Done or OK), you have to hold your stylus down on them for a second or two.

■ **Sony CLIÉ TG50**   This CLIÉ pops up a virtual Graffiti area. Unfortunately, it obscures everything else, but at least the option is there if you want it.

Using Palm Desktop

Graffiti and the onscreen keyboard are great when you're on the go, but what about getting data into your Palm when you're comfortably sitting at your desk? Nothing is wrong with entering notes into the Palm with Graffiti, even in the office, but long notes can get tiresome. Instead, you can use the keyboard on your desktop PC to type into the Palm much more quickly and efficiently.

How? By using Palm Desktop or another program with a HotSync conduit. In other words, suppose you need to enter a long note into your Palm. Instead of writing it slowly using Graffiti, create a note in Palm Desktop or Outlook, depending on which program you use, and then HotSync.

Let's add a note to the Palm's Memo Pad using the Palm Desktop. Do this:

NOTE   *If you configured your Palm to synchronize with Microsoft Outlook or another PIM, use that program's memo or note pad for this exercise.*

1. Start Palm Desktop in Windows by choosing Start | Programs | Palm Desktop | Palm Desktop. On the Mac, you can find it in the Chooser or in the Palm folder.

2. In Windows, switch to the Memo Pad view by clicking the Memo button on the left side of the screen. On the Mac, choose View | Note List instead.

3. If you're using Windows, click New Memo and type a note. On the Mac, click the Create Note button on the toolbar at the top of the screen.

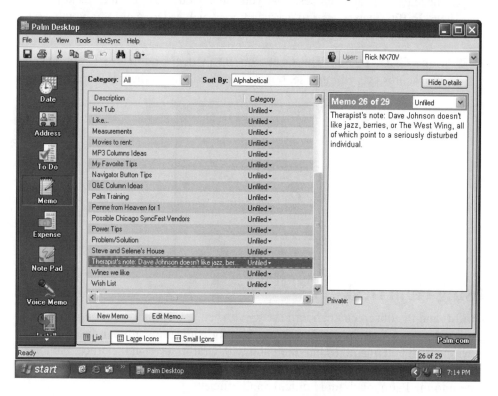

4. When you finish typing your note, close the New Note dialog box (on the Mac) or click anywhere in the Memo list (in Windows). The note is automatically saved, and the memo's subject line shows as much of the note as would fit on the line in the list.

5. When you finish entering data, place the Palm in its HotSync cradle and press the HotSync button. For details on how to HotSync, see Chapter 3.

Getting to Know Graffiti

Earlier in the chapter, we took a quick look at using Graffiti to enter data into your Palm. Graffiti deserves a lot of attention, though, because it's your principal way of interfacing with your favorite handheld PC. We're willing to bet that more than 90 percent of the time you need to add a note, contact, or to-do, you end up whipping out the Palm stylus and entering your info with good old Graffiti. Knowing Graffiti like the back of your hand is essential to using your Palm effectively.

NOTE   *In this section, we mostly refer to Graffiti in a generic sense, meaning the information applies to original Graffiti (a.k.a. Graffiti 1) and Graffiti 2. We jump in where necessary to note any important differences.*

TIP   *If you just upgraded to a newer Palm OS handheld that has Graffiti 2, but you're fluent with Graffiti 1 and miss it horribly, all is not lost. TealPoint Software's TealScript, which is discussed in detail in Chapter 12, effectively restores Graffiti 1. Now wipe those tears away.*

As we pointed out earlier in this chapter, Graffiti doesn't rely on interpreting whatever chicken-like scrawl you happen to draw into the Palm's Graffiti area. While it might be nice if the Palm could interpret unmodified handwriting, we've all seen what happened to that technology.

Specifically, Apple's Newton MessagePad—the first PDA—tried hard to understand free-form handwriting. And while it did a darned good job, first-time users faced an uphill battle getting it to understand them. Not until you had a chance to use the Newton for a few hours did it start behaving like it comprehended English. To make matters worse, Apple insisted on putting MessagePads in stores with big signs inviting people to saunter over and try them. The result? People would scratch out a sentence in sloppy handwriting and the Newton would convert the result into total gibberish, kind of like what you think Lou Reed might be muttering in a Velvet Underground song. The public never got any confidence that Apple had a workable handwriting recognition engine, and even though the Newton actually was a great little PDA, it failed largely because of public perception. (For the record, Rick thinks it failed because it was an overpriced brick.)

Palm didn't make the same mistake. Its handwriting recognition engine is designed to recognize particular gestures as specific characters, thus reducing the possibility of error. In fact, if you routinely draw the characters according to the template, you should get just about 100 percent accuracy. Graffiti doesn't have to understand 50 different ways of making the letter *T,* so it's both fast and accurate.

TIP   *There's a Graffiti cheat sheet built into the Palm. By default, you can see it by making an upstroke from the Graffiti area up to the top of the LCD screen.*

General Tips and Tricks for Graffiti

Before we get started with the nuts and bolts of writing with Graffiti, it might help to remember a few things. Despite Graffiti's simplicity, a few tips and tricks can make writing on a Palm a lot easier.

- Draw your characters as large as possible, especially if you're having trouble with Graffiti misinterpreting what you're writing. Use the entire Graffiti area (top to bottom), if necessary.

- Don't cross the line between the letter and number portion of the Graffiti area. Make sure you make your gestures on the correct side of the fence to get the characters you want.

- Don't write at a slant. Some handwriting recognition engines can account for characters being drawn at an angle to the baseline, but Graffiti can't. Vertical lines should be perpendicular to the Graffiti area baseline.

- Don't write too fast. Graffiti doesn't care about your speed; but if you write too fast, you won't have sufficient control over the shape of your gestures and you can make mistakes.

- If you have a hard time making certain gestures consistently, try the character a different way. Specifically, refer to Table 4-1 (which is specific to Graffiti 1) for a list of primary and secondary gestures for each character. Use the ones that work best for you.

Writing Letters and Numbers

The easiest way to learn Graffiti is simply to practice writing the alphabet a few times. Use the Graffiti reference card that came with your Palm, or refer to Table 4-1 for a guide on how to draw each character. The advantage of using this book, of course, is that we show you a few alternate gestures that might make certain characters easier to draw consistently. Give them a shot.

In Graffiti 1, you might notice some letters and numbers have identical gestures. The letter *L* and the number 4, for instance, are both made in the same way (see Figure 4-2). How does Graffiti tell the difference? That's an easy one—don't forget, the Graffiti area is divided into a number side and a letter side.

Letter	Gestures		Letter	Gestures
A	∧		S	S 5
B	B B 3		T	7 ⟩
C	C <		U	U ✓
D	D D △		V	V V
E	Ɛ ξ		W	W W
F	Γ Γ		X	X X
G	G G		Y	y Y
H	h M		Z	Z 2
I	∣		0	O O U
J	J J		1	∣ ∧
K	⍺		2	2 2
L	L ∠		3	3
M	m m		4	L <
N	N N		5	5 5
O	O O		6	6 6
P	P P		7	7 ⟩
Q	O O		8	8 8
R	R R		9	9 Ɛ

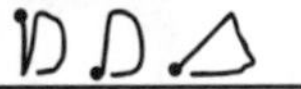

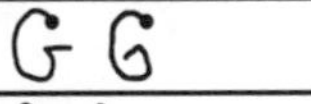

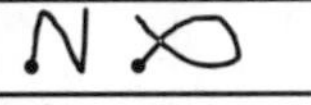

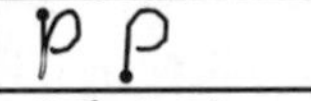

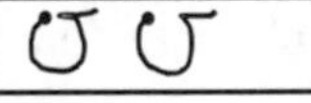

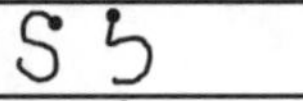

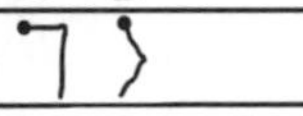

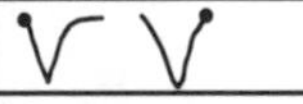

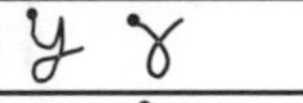

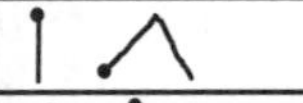

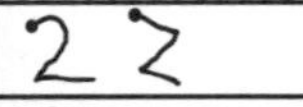

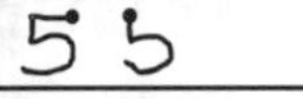

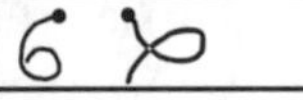

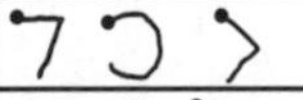

TABLE 4-1 Graffiti 1 Numbers and Letters

Graffiti 2 Numbers and Letters

Graffiti 2 is very similar to Graffiti 1, though there are a few exceptions. In the following screenshots, captured directly from Graffiti 2's built-in help screens (draw a stylus stroke from the Graffiti area to the top of the screen to view them yourself), you can see the basic strokes. What this cheat sheet doesn't illustrate is that you can also draw lowercase characters for many letters. Open a blank memo and try it for yourself. Whichever version of Graffiti you have, practice and experimentation is the hands-down best way to learn.

If you're really having trouble mastering Graffiti 1, there's a great tutorial program called PenJammer (www.penjammer.com). It's not for Windows or Macintosh—it works right on your handheld, teaching you every Graffiti character via animated helpers. Very cool, very helpful, and very inexpensive (it's just $7.95).

The Hardest Characters

Everyone seems to have trouble with some Graffiti character. Even if you can never get your Palm to recognize your letter *B,* that doesn't make you a failure— it just means you should learn an alternate stroke for that letter or put extra care into drawing it carefully and slowly. Even we have trouble with some letters.

Dave: It's unfortunate my last name is "Johnson," because I can't get Graffiti to take my letter *J* to save my life. Half the time, it's my own fault. As many times as I've made the *J,* I can't remember it starts at the top and curves down. I always try to start at the bottom and hook up—which gives me a letter *U* every time. But, even when I remember how to do it, I end up with a *V* or a new paragraph. Of course, now that I'm drawing it for this chapter, I can't seem to do it wrong—10 perfect Js out of 10. I think the letter just hates me. And I know I'm not crazy, by the way, despite what my dog keeps telling me.

Rick: If you'd ever seen Dave's chicken-scratch excuse for handwriting, you'd understand why he sometimes has trouble with Graffiti. To be fair, though, a few characters seem tougher to make than others. It's the *V* that drives me up the wall—I always forget to put the little tail on the end of the upstroke. But I know a secret: if you write the letter backward, it comes out perfect every time—and you don't need to draw the tail!

Gesture	Character	
L	L	4
↑	I	1
3	B	3

FIGURE 4-2   The letter *L* and the number 4 are made exactly the same. So is the letter *I* and the number 1.

Capitalizing Letters

You've probably noticed there's no distinction in the Graffiti gestures for lowercase and uppercase characters. That's a good thing, actually—you don't have to learn 50+ gestures because uppercase and lowercase letters are drawn the same way. Here's how to tell Graffiti you want to make an uppercase letter:

NOTE   *If you have Graffiti 2, you can ignore most of this advice. To make a capital letter, just write it across the invisible line separating the letter and number sides—that is, the middle of the Graffiti area.*

- **One capital letter**   To make the next character uppercase, first draw an uppercase gesture: a vertical line from the bottom of the Graffiti area to the top. This works only on the left side of the screen; it won't work in the number area. You see a symbol like this one, which indicates that you're now in Uppercase mode:

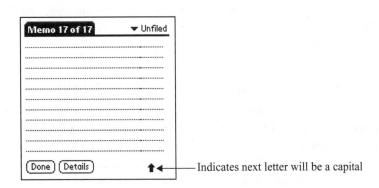

Indicates next letter will be a capital

■ **All capital letters**   To switch to All Caps (or Caps Lock) mode and write all capital letters, draw the vertical gesture twice. You see this symbol to indicate All Caps mode:

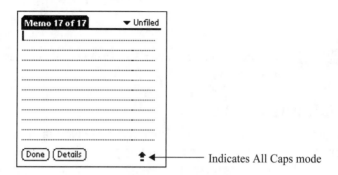

Indicates All Caps mode

■ **Lowercase letters**   If you're already in All Caps mode, you can exit and write in lowercase again by making one more vertical gesture. The All Caps symbol should disappear to show that you changed modes.

 Uppercase mode doesn't affect numbers, so it doesn't matter which mode you're in when writing numbers. This means you needn't drop out of Uppercase mode just to write numbers amid a bunch of capital letters.

 One of our all-time favorite Hacks (see Chapter 12) is called MiddleCaps. It saves you having to write the upstroke before each capital letter. Just write the letter across the imaginary line separating the letter and number sides of the Graffiti area. Absolutely indispensable, and it's a freebie! Find it at PalmGear (www.palmgear.com). Of course, Graffiti 2 has this capability built right in.

Spaces, Backspaces, and Deleting Text

Words are arguably more useful when you can put a space between them, thus enabling the casual reader to discern whereeachoneendsandthenextonebegins. In Graffiti, inserting spaces is easy. So easy, in fact, you might be able to figure it out on your own (but we'll tell you anyway). Draw a line that starts on the left and goes to the right (not all the way to the right—it's just a little dash, really), and you'll see the cursor skips ahead a space. You can use this gesture to insert spaces between words or to perform any other space-making task you might need. And, yes, you can insert multiple spaces simply by performing this gesture as many times as needed.

The backspace, not surprisingly, is exactly the opposite. Draw a gesture from right to left and the cursor backs up, deleting any text it encounters along the way.

TIP *Space and backspace gestures work fine in both the letter and number sides of the Graffiti area.*

4

Using the backspace gesture is great if you want to delete one or two characters, but what if you want to delete a whole sentence? That backspace swipe can get tiring if you have a lot of text to kill or replace all at once. Luckily, there's an easy solution: select the text you want to delete. The next thing you write replaces the selected text. Here's how to do it:

1. On the PDA, find a region of text you want to replace.

2. Tap and hold the stylus down at the start of the text you want to select, and then drag the stylus across the text and pick it up when you've selected all the text in question. This is not unlike selecting text in your favorite word processor, but the stylus takes the place of the mouse.

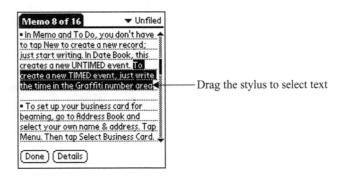

Drag the stylus to select text

3. In the Graffiti area, write some new text. The old text is immediately erased and replaced with the new text. If you simply want to delete the text, use the backspace gesture instead.

Adding Punctuation

To add punctuation to your prose, you need to (surprise, surprise) enter Graffiti's special Punctuation mode (punctuation in Graffiti 2 is a bit different—see Figure 4-3).

FIGURE 4-3   Most punctuation in Graffiti 2 approximates normal writing. You make a period just by tapping (once, not twice like in Graffiti 1), an exclamation point with a line and a dot, and so on.

All it takes is a tap in the Graffiti area. You see a dot appear, which indicates that you can now enter punctuation. Table 4-2 displays the punctuation gestures you commonly need. Note that this refers solely to Graffiti 1. There's no special punctuation mode that precedes your strokes—but there are some special strokes to learn.

The most common punctuation mark is a period; and because it's simply a dot, you can add a period to the end of a sentence by performing a quick double-tap (a single tap in Graffiti 2). Some other symbols are trickier, though, and may take some practice. The comma, parenthesis bracket, and apostrophe are so similar, for instance, it's not unusual to get one when you're trying for another.

If you have a lot of trouble with specific symbols, you can always use the onscreen keyboard along with Graffiti to write your text.

If you enter the Punctuation mode by tapping on one side of the Graffiti area, you need to complete the punctuation gesture on the same side. Tapping once on the number side and again on the letter side has no effect, for instance.

Using Shortcuts

Everyone loves shortcuts. In desktop applications such as Microsoft Office, many folks eschew the mouse for keyboard shortcuts that speed tasks such as text formatting and saving files. The Palm also has the capability to save you time and effort using shortcuts. Even better, Palm shortcuts are user definable,

Punctuation	Gestures
Period	•
Comma	╱ (draw low)
Question mark	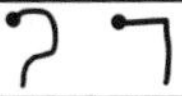 ʔ ˥
Exclamation point	 ǀ˙
Colon	∨
Semicolon	 �
Open parenthesis	(
Close parenthesis	)
Tab	⌐
Apostrophe	ǀ (draw high)
Quotes	N
Slash	╱
Backslash	╲
At symbol	∪
Asterisk	 ⅗
Number sign	 ʋ ɦ
Greater than	<
Less than	 >
Percent	 ∪∪ ⅄
Equal sign	 Z
Plus sign	 ∝
Dollar sign	S

TABLE 4-2   The Most Common Graffiti Punctuation Gestures

so you can create your own library of them, and you needn't be satisfied with whatever came in the box.

So what are *shortcuts,* exactly? If you have a word or phrase you frequently write over and over (such as "Dave throws like a girl"), you can assign an abbreviation to it and let Graffiti do the hard work of writing the phrase in its entirety. To see how easy using shortcuts is, try this, using one of the shortcuts that come built into your Palm:

1. Open the Memo Pad and tap the New button to open a new memo page.

2. Draw the shortcut gesture (shown at left). The *shortcut gesture* tells Graffiti that the next thing you write is going to be an abbreviation, which should be expanded in accordance with the shortcut library.

3. Write "br," which is the shortcut for "breakfast." As soon as you finish writing the *R,* the text should expand into the word "breakfast."

That's all there is to it. We hope you can see the value of creating shortcuts that are relevant to what you frequently write.

Storing Your Own Shortcuts

Your Palm comes with roughly half a dozen shortcuts and you can easily create new ones whenever you want. To create a shortcut, do this:

1. Display Preferences by tapping the Prefs icon.

2. Choose Shortcuts from the list of Preferences in the upper-right corner of the screen (or choose it from the list of options if that's what your model displays).

3. Tap the New button to display the Shortcut Entry window.

4. Give your shortcut a name. This is the abbreviation you write to summon the entire shortcut text. If you want to create a shortcut that reads "Dear Sir," for instance, you might want to use "ds."

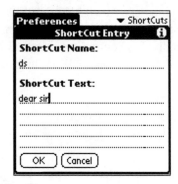

5. Enter the complete shortcut text. Remember, you're limited to a maximum length of 45 characters. If you reach that limit, you hear a beep when you try to write additional text.

6. Tap the OK button to save your shortcut.

Once you create a shortcut, you can use it anywhere in your Palm that you can write with Graffiti. And they work in Graffiti 2, too.

TIP *Don't go overboard with shortcuts right away. Shortcuts become a lot less cool if you have so many of them that you can't remember what the abbreviation is to summon the entire text. Start with two or three, and, once you know them like the back of your hand, add a few more.*

Another Kind of Shortcut: Menu Commands

If you're a big fan of hitting CTRL-S in Microsoft Word to save your work, then you should love this. The Palm has its own menu shortcuts you can access with Graffiti. To do that, though, you must be prepared by remembering two important items:

- How to draw the Graffiti command stroke

- What the shortcut character is for the menu command you want to invoke

 The command stroke is easy. To put your Palm in Command mode, draw the gesture on the left. After you draw the gesture, your Palm displays the Command

The Command Bar

So, you tried entering a command, but you're curious about the Command bar. What are all those little symbols, and what do they do?

Actually, the Command bar is a clever tool you can use to access common features of your Palm rapidly. It's context sensitive, which means the bar will look different—it'll have different icons—depending on when you make the command stroke.

Try this: make the command stroke when you're viewing the Home screen. The three icons on the right side of the Command bar represent Info, Beam, and Delete (just as if you tapped the Menu button and selected Info, Beam, or Delete from the App menu).

Now open the Date Book and select an appointment by dragging the stylus across some text. Make the command stroke again. Voila! You now have different choices, such as Cut, Copy, and Paste. You can experiment with the Command bar in various locales around your Palm to see what kinds of shortcuts you can effect.

bar. You simply need to write the proper character to invoke the menu item—say, C for Copy or F for Font.

As you can see in the following screenshot, the Command bar also displays icons that allow quick access to certain commonly used functions, such as beam, copy, and delete. These icons appear in a context-sensitive fashion, so don't be surprised if you don't always see the same ones. If you haven't selected any text, for instance, there's nothing to copy, so you won't see the copy icon.

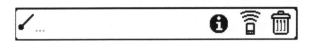

Most menu items have no corresponding icon in the Command bar, however, so you have to learn what the shortcuts are for each item. To do so, display the menu (tap the Menu button and you'll see something similar to Figure 4-4). As you can see, many menu items have associated shortcuts.

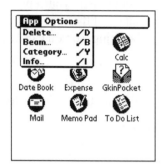

FIGURE 4-4   Many menu items have Graffiti shortcuts associated with them.

    The Command mode lasts only a few seconds, after which the bar disappears. If you don't write the shortcut character quickly enough, you'll need to perform the command stoke again.

Beaming Data Between Palms

On *Star Trek,* transporters are used to beam people and equipment from one location to another. Although we're a long way from being able to beam physical things around, the Palm OS makes it possible to beam almost any kind of data between handheld PC users.

All Palm models (except for first-generation Palm Pilots) have an infrared (IR) port. On most models, you can find it on the front edge of the case. If you haven't located your Palm device's IR port yet, find it now. It's a small, dark-red, translucent strip of plastic. Using this IR port (and add-on software, of course), you can beam information in a surprising number of ways. You can:

- Use your handheld as a TV and stereo remote control.

- Send data between your Palm and a cell phone or pager.

- Print Palm data on an IR-equipped printer.

- Beam data to other Palm users.

- Give another Palm user your "business card."

- Play two-player games "head-to-head."

These things are pretty cool, but mostly you'll probably use beaming for exchanging mundane business data. All the core applications (Address Book, Memo Pad, and so on) support beaming, so you can beam the following:

- Contact listings

- Your own "business card" from the Address Book

- Appointments and meetings

- Memos

- Tasks

In addition, you can beam entire applications to other Palm users. If you download a freeware program from the Internet and want to share it with friends or co-workers, go ahead: it's a snap to transmit the item wirelessly.

How to Beam

No matter what you're planning to beam—or receive—the process is essentially the same. Actually seeing the process demonstrated is faster than reading about it; but because neither Dave nor Rick is handy to stop by your office today, here's the process in a nutshell:

1. Orient the two Palms so their IR ports face each other, and are between three to four inches and three feet apart. If you're any closer than four inches, the PDAs may have a hard time locking onto each other. Too far away, the signal won't be strong enough to reach.

2. As the sender, you should choose the item you want to beam.

3. Choose the Beam command from the menu.

TIP

If you beam often, you might want to use the beam shortcut—a command slash gesture followed by the letter B. Or you can configure your Palm so a stroke from the bottom of the Graffiti area to the top of the screen can start a beam of any given item. To do that, tap the Prefs icon, and then select the Buttons item in the list at the top-right corner of the screen. Tap the Pen button and choose Beam Data.

4. A dialog box appears, indicating that the beam is in progress. First, you see a message that your Palm is searching for the other Palm. That message then goes away and the data is transmitted.

After the beam, your Palm goes back to business as usual—you won't get a message indicating that the beam was successful. The receiver Palm, on the other hand, gets a dialog box that asks permission to accept the beamed data. As the receiver, you need to decide what category to file the information into and tap either Yes or No, depending on whether you want to keep the item. If you tap Yes, the data is integrated into your Palm in the category you specified. (There's no category decision to make if you're receiving an application or some other non-core-app data.)

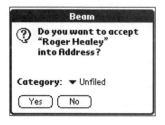

TIP   *As the receiver, a good idea is to specify a category in which to file the data you just received. If you let stuff such as Address Book entries accumulate in the Unfiled category, it can later become difficult to find what you're looking for.*

To Accept or Not to Accept

By default, your Palm is set to automatically receive beamed items. However, there are two reasons you might want to disable auto-receive for beaming:

■ Because the IR port is constantly on and searching for transmissions from other Palms, your Palm uses slightly more battery power. Is this a big deal? We don't think so. The extra power consumption is marginal.

■ With all the concerns about viruses and other malicious programs that exist for PCs today, some folks are nervous about leaving their Palm in a state that receives data all the time. Our call: viruses for the Palm aren't a threat (yet), and you have to manually accept a beamed program after reception anyway. Don't worry about it.

So, while we obviously don't think auto-receiving beamed items is a big deal, here's how to disable that feature if you want to:

1. Open the Palm's Preferences by tapping the Prefs icon.

2. Choose the General category from the list at the top right of the screen (or the Power option, on some models).

3. Change Beam Receive from On to Off.

After changing your preferences to disable beaming, other Palms can't send you data unless you re-enable beaming from Preferences.

Selecting Items for Beaming

So, now that you know the rudiments of beaming, you're no doubt eager to start. Although we're usually a pretty down-to-earth couple of guys, we have to admit a certain coolness factor is involved in beaming things in the middle of a meeting or on the show floor at a trade show. It's definitely better than writing notes by hand or trading easily scrunched business cards.

Beaming Appointments

If you work with other Palm users, you can make sure everyone is on the same schedule by beaming entries from the Date Book. To do that, select an appointment, and then choose Beam Event from the menu.

| TIP | *Speaking of keeping everyone on the same schedule, Palm DualDate 1.0 (a freeware utility available from PalmGear.com) lets you display two calendars side by side on your PDA—ideal if you want to keep track of, say, a spouse's or co-worker's schedule. It's basically an enhanced replacement for the stock Date Book application. Check it out!* |

Beaming Contacts

If you're like most people, the Address Book is the most well-exercised part of your Palm. And instead of exchanging paper-based business cards, now you can beam the information between Palms, which can later be HotSynced back to Palm Desktop (or Outlook). In recognition of just how important the Address Book is, you have not one, not two, but three options for sending data from this application:

- ■ **Beam the current entry**   To send an Address Book entry to another user, find the name you want in the address list, tap it, and choose Beam Address from the menu.

- ■ **Beam a whole bunch of entries**   You can send any number of contacts— even every name in your Palm, in fact—using Beam Category. To do that, first choose the category you want to beam by picking the category from the list at the top-right corner of the screen. Then tap Menu and choose Beam Category. To beam all the entries in your entire Address Book, you should set the category to All—but if you do that, the recipient loses the categories, and everything ends up on the destination Palm as "Unfiled."

 *Be careful before you beam or try to receive a whole category's worth of contacts—make sure it's something you really need to do. This operation could include hundreds of entries, which will take more time than either of you are willing to spend pointing your PDAs at each other.*

■ **Beam your own entry** What's more common than handing your business card to someone? You can configure your own Address Book entry as your personal business card and beam it to other handhelds. For details on configuring an entry as your business card, see Chapter 6. Once configured, however, you can send it by opening the Address Book, tapping Menu, and choosing Beam Business Card.

 *There's a faster way to beam your business card to someone: hold down the Address Book button for two seconds. This automatically tells the Palm to beam your business card.*

Beaming Memos and Tasks

Memos are handy to pass off to other Palm users. You can beam notes, action items, short documents, and even meeting minutes. Likewise, if you want to delegate a task to someone else in your office, tell that person to "visit my cubicle—and don't forget to bring your Palm." There are two ways to beam memos and To Do items:

■ **Beam a Memo or a To Do** To beam a single item, select it, tap Menu, then choose Beam Memo (for a Memo) or Beam Item (for a To Do).

■ **Beam a bunch of stuff at once**   As with Address Book, you can select a category in Memo Pad or To Do List, and then choose Beam Category from the menu. To beam all your memos or tasks at once, remember to set the category to All.

Beaming Applications

Now for the best part. You can use the Palm's beaming prowess to transfer entire applications from one Palm to another. If you meet someone who shows you his cool new Palm game or utility, for instance, you can ask him to beam the program to your handheld.

> **NOTE**   *Not all applications are free, so don't use your Palm's beaming capability for piracy. Actually, many commercial programs are "locked" to prevent beaming, and shareware applications often require an unlock code to access all the features in the registered version. You can beam trial versions around, but don't share registration codes—that's piracy.*

Not all programs can, in fact, be beamed. The core applications that come with your Palm are "locked," making them nonbeamable. Many commercial programs are also locked, and some programs have a resistance to beaming—such as Hacks (discussed in Chapter 12). In addition, if you have a program that requires supporting database files, the files won't be beamable. This means you must go home and install the program the old-fashioned way, using your PC.

Now that we've told you what you can't do, let's talk about what you can do. Beaming an application isn't much different than beaming data from one of the Palm's programs. Do this:

1. Tap the Home button on your Palm to return to applications.

2. Tap Menu, then choose Beam. You see a dialog box with a list of all the applications on your Palm, as in Figure 4-5. Some applications have little locks; these aren't beamable.

3. Select an application and tap the Beam button. If the desired program is stored on a memory card, tap the arrow next to Beam From and choose the card instead of Handheld. You'll then see a list of the programs stored on the card. This designates only where programs are beamed from—programs you receive from others are always stored in main memory (though you can easily offload them to a memory card later on).

┌─────────────────────────────┐
│   **Beam**   ⓘ   │
│ **Beam From:** ▼ Handheld │
│ **Quick Tour**   942K ▲│
│ **Address**   🔒 98K   │
│ **AudiblePlayer**   375K   │
│ **AuthenticationMgr** 🔒 9K │
│ **Brightness**   🔒 9K   │
│ **Calc**   🔒 104K   │
│ **Card Info**   🔒 18K   │
│ **CardEngine Library** 176K │
│ **Date Book**   🔒 127K ▼ │
│ (Done) (Beam)   │
└─────────────────────────────┘

FIGURE 4-5   Choose a program from the list to beam it to another Palm. If it has a lock, however, it can't be beamed.

TIP   *If you want to beam more stuff, get a program called FileZ. This freeware file manager makes it possible to beam certain kinds of apps (such as Hacks and databases) that the Palm OS can't do on its own.*

Installing New Software on Your Palm

Did you know that you can install tons of additional programs on your Palm? Thousands of free and commercial applications are out there, just waiting to be installed. They include enhancements to the core applications, utilities, games, and more. In fact, one of the best reasons for choosing a Palm OS device (instead of a Pocket PC device or some other kind of organizer) is that there's such a wealth of software.

But you might wonder: how the heck do I get all this cool stuff onto my Palm?

The answer is that Palm Desktop includes a handy Install Tool for loading Palm apps. (If you sync with Outlook, don't fret—the Install Tool works independent of your desktop contact manager. You can run it directly from within Palm Desktop, and you can also access it directly as a standalone program.)

Drag program files here to install to main memory

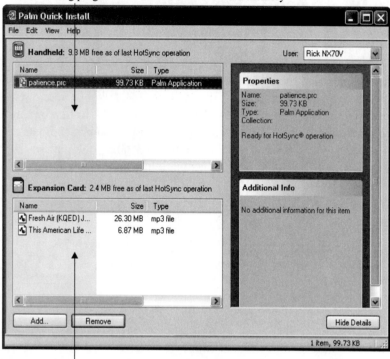

Drag program files here to install to a memory card (if you have one inserted)

FIGURE 4-6   Palm's new Quick Install tool lets you drag and drop program files directly to the handheld's internal memory or to a memory expansion card. It also shows how much storage space is available as of your last HotSync.

NOTE   *At press time, Palm had just introduced an updated installation program called Quick Install (see Figure 4-6). It works much like the original, except that it's divided into two windows (one for installing to internal memory, the other for installing to a memory card) and offers a few extra amenities. If you have a Palm Tungsten C, Zire 71, or an even newer model, the installation information on the following pages still applies—but consult your documentation for more information on the new tool.*

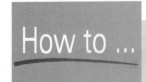

Install New Palm Applications on a Macintosh

There are two ways to install applications and data on a Mac. If you are a Palm Desktop user, the easiest way is to simply run the Install tool: from the Palm Desktop menu, choose HotSync | Install Handheld Files, and then use the dialog box to add your files. You can use the Add To List button to select files from your hard disk or simply drag and drop apps and data directly into the dialog box. Want to install an app to your Palm's memory card instead of main memory? Click the Change Destination button.

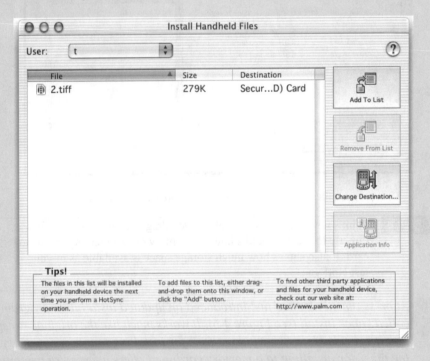

You don't have to open Palm Desktop to install files—you can use the Send To Handheld droplet instead. You can find Install To Handheld in the Palm folder on your hard disk. Once running, it places a droplet icon in the Mac's Dock at the bottom of the screen. Drag and drop apps and data files to this droplet, and the Install dialog box automatically appears, with the files in the queue ready for install.

 **Install New Palm Applications on a Windows PC**

4

1. Run the Install Tool by choosing Start | Programs | Palm Desktop | Install Tool. (If you have a Sony CLIÉ, the folder in question may be called Sony Handheld instead of Palm Desktop.)

2. Click the Add button. You see the Open dialog box for selecting Palm applications.

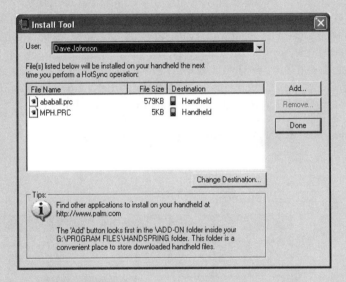

3. Locate the program you want to install (you'll have to navigate to the correct folder on your hard drive) and select it. Click the Open button.

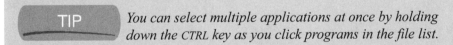

TIP   *You can select multiple applications at once by holding down the CTRL key as you click programs in the file list.*

4. With your application displayed in the Install Tool dialog box, click Done.

5. The next time you HotSync your Palm, the selected application is installed.

You can skip most of these steps by simply opening the Windows folder containing the program you want to install, then double-clicking the program's icon. That will launch the Install Tool and add the program to the queue. Click Done, HotSync, and you're finished!

Install to a Memory Card

If your have a memory card, you can install applications directly to it. That's handy, especially if you want to install a huge application or data file that simply wouldn't fit if copied to the Palm's more limited internal memory.

After you've used Install Tool to select a program for installation, click on the Change Destination button. You'll see the Change Destination dialog box. Then just click on the program that you want to install directly to the memory card, and click the arrow to move it to the right side of the screen, which represents the PDA's memory card. (Note: the Change Destination option appears only if you're using a handheld that runs Palm OS 4.0 or later.)

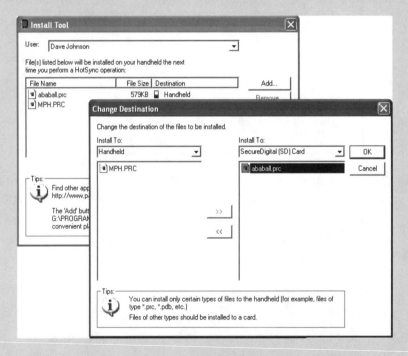

When you've configured your to-be-installed applications to your liking, click OK, close the Install Tool (by clicking Done), and HotSync.

Prepping Applications for Installation

As we've said, a ton of Palm applications are available—many free, others not. Throughout this book, we make reference to our favorite applications, and we recommend that you try them. Perhaps the single best resource for Palm applications is a Web site called PalmGear.com (see Figure 4-7).

Most of the time, downloaded applications aren't immediately ready for installation. If you download an application from the Internet, it usually arrives in the form of a SIT file (if you're a Mac user) or a ZIP file (if you use Windows). You need to expand these SIT and ZIP files to get to the actual program files before they can be installed on your Palm. We recommend these tools for managing compressed files (of course, if you already happily use another program, keep up the good work; these are just our favorites):

- ■ **Windows**   Use WinZip to uncompress ZIP files.

- ■ **Macintosh**   Use Aladdin StuffIt Expander to manage SIT files.

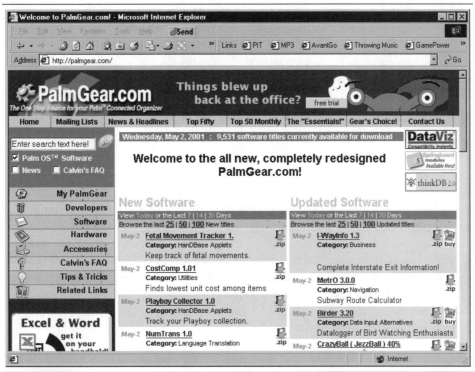

FIGURE 4-7   PalmGear.com is where Dave and Rick typically go for Palm software.

Once expanded, most Palm files have the file extension ".prc." In a ZIP or SIT with lots of little files, you can generally grab the PRC file and install that. Of course, if in doubt, read whatever documentation accompanied the application.

Deleting Applications

You won't want every application you install on your Palm forever. Some programs you won't like, others will outlive their usefulness. And sometimes you'll need to remove some software to make room for more, because the Palm has limited storage space (unless you have a memory card, that is—see "Working with Memory Cards" for more details).

Deleting programs is easy. Tap the Home button, then tap Menu | Delete. You see a list of all the applications currently stored on the handheld. At the top of the screen, you also see a bar that shows how much memory remains on your Palm.

If your handheld has an expansion slot, you can tap the arrow next to Delete From, then choose the memory card from the list. That allows you to delete applications stored on the card.

To delete an application, select it and tap the Delete button. This is similar to the Beam interface—in fact, it's so similar, you should be careful you don't accidentally delete an app you're trying to beam to a friend.

When you delete an application, you also delete all the data it generated. If you have a document reader, for instance, deleting the app also trashes any Doc files it may contain. To preserve these files, HotSync before deleting anything—that way you can later restore the files from the Backup folder on your hard disk if you need to.

4

Do You Really Need More Memory?

In the old days of handheld computing (we're talking 1999-ish), there was no such thing as adding memory to a PDA. Once you filled up your 2MB or 8MB, that was it—you had to delete programs and/or data if you wanted to make room for more. Fortunately, now you have almost limitless storage space at your disposal. But do you really need it?

Many users don't. Contacts, appointments, memos, and other such data consume very little space. Many third-party programs are the same way, nabbing just a few dozen kilobytes of the thousands you have available. If you don't plan to get into games, e-books, photos, music, movies, and other memory-hungry applications, you may never need a memory card.

Ah, but there's one other reason to consider buying one: backups. With a memory card and the right software, you can make quick and easy backups of your entire handheld. That could come in very handy when you're traveling, especially if disaster strikes and you lose some precious data. See Chapter 12 for more information on making backups—and consider keeping a memory card installed for just that purpose.

Working with Memory Cards

By now you know the 21st-century spin on the old adage: you can never be too rich, too thin, or have too much memory. Sure, it's grammatically iffy—but it is accurate. What with RAM-devouring e-books, games, AvantGo channels, productivity software, and even MP3 files, 16MB just don't go as far as they used to. Fortunately, the latest and greatest Palm Powered handhelds offer simple, inexpensive, potentially limitless memory expansion.

And not just memory expansion. It may be possible to add accessories such as GPS receivers, Bluetooth and WiFi adapters, and other products to your handheld. We talk more about such accessories in Chapter 15; for the remainder of this chapter, we teach you the ins and outs of Palm OS memory media.

It's in the Cards

It all started with Handspring's Visor, the first Palm Powered device to shatter the storage barrier. Simply pop an 8MB module into its Springboard socket and you immediately double your available memory (or quintuple it, if you have a 2MB Visor). Then came the TRGpro, which served up an industry-standard

CompactFlash (CF) slot. Finally, Palm got into the act, equipping new models with a slot for razor-thin MultiMediaCard (MMC) and Secure Digital (SD) media. In the interim, Sony kept things in the family with its proprietary Memory Stick cards for the CLIÉ series. See Figure 4-8 for a look at these different kinds of cards.

NOTE   *What's the difference between MMC and SD cards? Physically, they're almost identical: about the size of a postage stamp. MMC media tends to cost a bit less; SD media offers faster data transfer rates and higher capacities. There's really no reason to opt for MMC these days, unless you find a great closeout deal (SD is rapidly becoming the dominant of the two media).*

Yep, the good news is that virtually every Palm Powered handheld introduced in 2001 featured some flavor of expansion slot—and so has nearly every model since. The bad news is these slots are largely incompatible with one another. You can't, for instance, stick a Memory Stick into an SD slot. This isn't a major issue, but you may want to do a little planning as you shop for your next handheld PC, digital camera, and MP3 player. By making sure all your hardware supports the same media, you'll lower your operating expenses and have an easier time sharing files between devices.

As of press time, SD was emerging as the preferred choice for PDAs. Every model in Palm's current lineup has an SD slot, and the latest smartphones from

FIGURE 4-8   Pick a card, any card. Different Palm Powered handhelds use different kinds of memory media, including (from left to right) CompactFlash, Secure Digital, and Memory Stick.

Should You Buy Software on a Card?

Palm sells a variety of memory cards that come preloaded with software. Because the software resides on the card, you can run it without sacrificing any of your handheld's internal memory. But if memory conservation is your only concern, don't bother with software cards. Usually it's a better bet to buy a blank memory card, and then load it up as you see fit. Same end result, but you can get a lot more storage capacity for the money.

However, there are some good deals to be had. Some of Palm's eBook and Game cards, for instance, pack multiple titles onto a single card—titles that would cost more if purchased separately. But the key thing to remember is that virtually any software you can buy on a card, you can buy separately from sites such as PalmGear.com.

Handspring and Kyocera have one as well. Sony is the dissenter, sticking with Memory Stick for its CLIÉ series (a few models also have CompactFlash slots). As you shop for memory cards, be sure to get the right kind for your handheld.

What Price Memory?

Just what will it cost you to add, say, 128MB to your handheld? For starters, it depends on the media. We spent some time shopping at eCost.com, where we found 128MB SD cards selling for about $50 and 128MB Memory Sticks for about $25 (after a mail-in rebate). In general, you can find lower prices online than you can in retail stores, and many Web-based vendors offer free shipping, thus saving you even more.

TIP   *You needn't buy media directly from Palm or Sony just because you own, say, a Zire 71 or CLIÉ NX70V. Memory cards from companies such as Lexar Media and SanDisk tend to cost a lot less and work just as well.*

Memory 101

With the introduction of Palm OS 4.0, Palm also introduced the Virtual File System (VFS)—a way for the operating system to recognize removable memory cards, and access the programs and data stored therein. Thus, you could relocate, say, Palm Reader and all your e-books to a card, freeing a fair chunk of your handheld's internal memory.

More Memory on the Inside

If you own a Palm OS device that doesn't have an expansion slot, or you're simply not satisfied with its 2MB, 4MB, or 8MB of internal memory, take heart. It's possible to increase the internal memory—provided you're willing to part with your handheld for a few days. Just send it to STNE (www.stnecorp .com) or Tony Rudenko (www.palmpilotupgrade.com). Both can upgrade virtually any model.

It's important to note that utilizing either service will void your handheld's warranty, but both vendors offer a 90-day warranty of their own.

Getting Started with Memory Cards

You can get programs and data onto a memory card in two basic ways. First, if you have software that's already loaded in internal memory, you can use the Palm OS Copy tool to copy it to the card. (This works both ways: you can copy items from a card back to internal memory as well.) To access it, tap the Home button to return to the main screen, and then tap Menu | App | Copy. Select the program you want to copy (you have to copy them one at a time), making sure to select the desired Copy To and From destinations. Tap Copy to begin the process.

Copy	
Copy To: ▼ ▯Card	
From: ▼ Handheld	
Beam Box	14K
Graffiti	15K
ScreenShot	0K
Tweak User	10K
X-Master	52K
(Done) (Copy)	

Alas, because there's no "move" option, the original file remains on your handheld. To claim the extra storage space you were after, you must then delete the software from internal memory.

This is exactly as tedious as it sounds, which is why we strongly recommend a third-party file manager such as FilePoint (www.bachmannsoftware.com) or PocketFolder (www.PalmGear.com). These programs make it much easier to move, copy, beam, and delete files than the Palm OS. Just be sure you move the right files. If a program relies on more than one file for its operation (a good example is LandWare's Wine Enthusiast Guide 2003, which consists of the program file and several databases) and you move the wrong files or not enough of the files, you could wind up in trouble (as in the program no longer runs).

| TIP | *File managers can actually be a bit overcomplicated, especially for novice users who simply want to shuffle programs between internal and expansion memory. Instead, try an application launcher, which will not only organize all your programs, but also provide drag-and-drop simplicity for relocating them. Read on to learn more about them, then head over to Chapter 12 for the full scoop.* |

A better way to place apps into external storage is by installing them there directly. The Palm OS Install Tool lets you specify the destination for new software at the time you install it, meaning you can HotSync apps right onto a memory card. See "Installing to a Memory Card" a few pages back for instructions.

Ah, but what happens to them after that? Novice users often fall into the same trap: they install programs on their memory cards, and then can't understand why they don't see the icons in the Home screen. The answer lies in a quirk of VFS: all applications stored on a memory card are automatically segregated into a category called Card. Thus, you must look in that category to find your newly installed stuff.

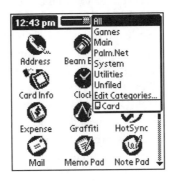

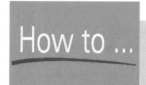

Make a Backup Using a Regular Memory Card

Psst! Have we got a great tip for you. Let us preface this by saying that if your handheld has an expansion slot, you should be making regular backups of your data. Glitches and catastrophes happen—consider yourself warned. However, you needn't buy one of those special backup cards or modules (such as the ones offered by Palm). Instead, buy a standard memory card and use a utility such as PiBackup II. It creates a backup of your entire handheld (or just specific files), storing the data in a folder on the memory card. Now you have only one card to keep track of and one less thing to buy!

This can be inconvenient, to be sure, especially for users who like to keep their icons orderly. If you wind up with, say, 30 apps on a storage card, now you've got an organization problem—you can't subcategorize the Card category. Fortunately, there's a solution in the form of third-party launchers, most of which now support external storage. One of our longtime favorites, Launcher X, lets you organize your icons however you see fit, regardless of where the actual applications are stored. MegaLauncher and Silver Screen, two more launchers we like, offer VFS support as well. (Read more about launchers in Chapter 12.)

Memory 102

Although memory cards open the door to carrying much more software than you ever could before, there are a couple hitches. Suppose you have a favorite document reader and a fairly large collection of Doc files that go with it. You decide to move the files to your memory card to free some internal storage space. But the next time you fire up the Doc reader, you discover your Doc files are gone. Why? Because the Doc reader doesn't know to look for them on the memory card. They're still stored there, but the software can't see them. This is true of many older programs (and by "older" we mean those written prior to summer 2001). The good news is that developers are rapidly updating their wares to support VFS, meaning this problem should disappear before long. (For the record, plenty of Doc readers already support VFS, including Palm Reader, TealDoc, and WordSmith.)

To overcome VFS-related issues such as this one (and have an easier time overall working with applications and data stored on memory cards), power users should check out utilities such as MSMount, PiDirect II, and PowerRun. In a nutshell, these programs trick the operating system into thinking that programs and data stored on a memory card are actually stored in main memory, so everything is accessible all the time.

If your handheld runs Palm OS 5 or later, be sure to choose a utility that supports that version of the OS. At press time, PowerRun and MemHack for OS 5 were among the few that did.

4

Part II

Get Things Done

Chapter 5

The Date Book

How to...

- Use the Day, Week, Month, and Agenda Views
- Customize the Date Book's appearance
- Add appointments to the Date Book
- Beam an appointment to someone else
- Create an appointment using the Address Book
- Create repeating events
- Add a note to an appointment
- Make an appointment private
- Edit appointments in the Date Book
- Delete events in the Date Book
- Set an alarm for an appointment
- Use the Windows Date Book
- Use the Palm with Outlook
- Use the Macintosh Date Book

Are you busy on Tuesday at 3 P.M.? If you have your Palm handy, you'd probably already know the answer to that question. In an informal survey, we found the Date Book is the single most popular core application on the Palm. Heck—some people buy the Palm just for its scheduling prowess.

The Date Book is a modern miracle. That may sound like an overstatement, but consider how useful it is. It can track all your appointments. It can show you your schedule by day, week, or month. The Date Book handles recurring appointments and can notify you about upcoming events with an alarm. It synchronizes precisely with your desktop calendar. And the Date Book fits in the palm of your hand. It's better, Rick might tell you, than *Star Trek: Voyager.* Dave, on the other hand, might be inclined to say it's better than *24.*

Viewing Your Appointments

When you switch to the Date Book, by default, it starts by showing you any appointments you have for today. Start the Date Book by pressing the Date Book

Operating System Oddities

Although Palm devices all work more or less the same way, they don't all use exactly the same operating system. Likewise, the Palm Desktop software on your PC may vary a bit depending on which model you own. We wrote most of this book with Palm OS 5 in mind, since that's what all the newest PDAs come with—models such as the Tungsten T, Tungsten C, and Zire 71. If you have an older PDA or one that runs a different version of the Palm operating system, don't worry—the differences are minor. Most of the time, in fact, you probably won't even notice a difference.

button on your Palm or tapping the Date Book icon, found in the Main category of the Palm's Application screen.

Navigating the Day View

When you start the Date Book, the first thing you see is the Day View. You can see that it shows the currently selected date in the tab at the top of the screen. Next to that are seven icons, one for each day of the week.

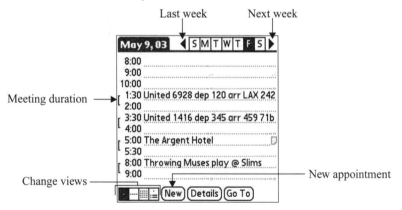

In the middle of the screen, you see the current day's calendar. You can enter new events on the blank lines. If you have any appointments already entered, note that long appointments (those lasting for more than 30 minutes) have *duration*

> **TIP** *Tap and hold the date tab to see the current time. If you let go too quickly, the Record menu will drop instead.*

brackets, which appear to the immediate left of the appointment time and show you what time an appointment is scheduled to end.

Other icons also appear near appointments. In fact, you should get used to seeing these three icons:

- **Alarms** This icon indicates you'll get notified by the Palm alarm sound that the appointment is due to start.

- **Notes** If you attach a note to your appointment (perhaps with directions to the location or agenda details, for instance) you see this icon.

- **Repeating meetings** If the meeting is configured to happen more than once, this icon appears.

If you tap any of these icons, shown in Figure 5-1, you see the Event Details dialog box, which we discuss in detail later in this chapter.

Finally, the bottom of the screen has several important controls. Icons exist to change the current view, as well as to create a new appointment, to view the Event Details dialog box, and to go to a specific day.

Changing View Options

By default, the Day View compresses your calendar by not showing blank times of the day. This way, you can have appointments that span from 6 A.M. to 11 P.M. and have them all appear onscreen without needing to scroll at all. Whenever it can, it includes blank events between existing events for better readability.

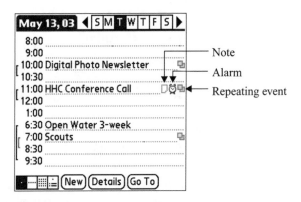

These icons tell you valuable information about your appointment. Tap on them to edit the details.

What happens if you have such a busy day that all your appointments won't fit onscreen at once, even with the Palm's compression in place? You need to tap the scroll button at the bottom of the screen. It appears only when needed.

Lots of users try using the Scroll button or Nav Pad on the Palm's case to see more appointments in the same day. Of course, that simply changes the view to the next day.

Not everyone likes the Day View compression. If you frequently add events to your schedule during the day, for instance, you might want to have blank lines available for all the hours of the day. If this sounds like you, here's how to turn off compression:

1. Choose Options | Display Options from the menu.

2. Uncheck the Compress Day View option.

3. Tap the OK button.

Now when you use the Day View, you see all the blank lines for your day. On the other hand, using this setting virtually guarantees you need to use the stylus to surf around your daily schedule.

When you configure your Day View, you also have to decide what kind of person you are. Are you

■ Neat and orderly—and opt for less clutter whenever possible?

■ Impatient—and want everything at your fingertips all the time?

■ Apathetic—and don't want to bother changing the default settings?

5

You can change the display of the Date Book to accommodate the way you want your Palm to look. If you're the neat and orderly sort, for instance, you might want the Date Book to be a blank screen, unless it actually has appointments already scheduled for that day. If this is the case, choose Options | Preferences and set the Start Time and End Time to be the same thing—like 7:00 A.M. After configuring your Palm in this way, you should find days without appointments are essentially a blank screen with a single blank line—the time you set in Preferences.

More of an impatient sort? Then choose Options | Preferences and configure your Start Time and End Time to span the full range of hours you plan to use. If you ever add events to the evening, for instance, set the End Time for 10 P.M. or later. This way, you have a blank line available immediately for writing a new entry.

If all this sounds extremely pointless to you, leave the Preferences alone. The default settings cover most of the hours you routinely need.

Getting Around the Days of the Week

As you might expect, there are several ways to switch to a different day. You can figure out most of them on your own, but we bet you can't find 'em all. Here's how you can do it—use the method that's easiest for you:

- Switch to a specific day by tapping the appropriate day icon at the top of the screen, or change weeks using the arrows (see Figure 5-2).

- To move forward or backward one day at a time, press the Scroll button or Nav Pad on your Palm. If you hold it down, you scroll quickly, like holding down a repeating key on a computer keyboard.

- If you want to find a specific day quickly, tap the Go To button and enter the date directly in the Go to Date dialog box. When you use Go To,

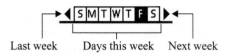

Last week   Days this week   Next week

FIGURE 5-2   Get around the Date View with these controls.

remember to choose the year and month first, because you go to the selected date as soon as you tap a date.

■ To get back to "today" from somewhere else in the calendar, tap Go To, and then tap Today on the Go to Date calendar dialog box.

Navigating the Week View

Now that you're used to the Day View, we'll let you in on a little secret: there's more where that came from. That's where the icons at the bottom of the screen come in. Tap the second one to change to the Week View.

TIP *The Date Book button also serves as a view changer. Every time you press the button, the view cycles from Day View to Week View to Month View to Agenda View and back to Day View again. It's convenient to jab with your thumb as you view your various schedule screens.*

This screen uses a grid to display your appointments. The top of the grid is labeled by day and date; the left side contains time blocks throughout the day. The gray blocks represent scheduled events. Obviously, this view isn't ideal for determining your daily schedule in detail, but it's handy for getting your week's availability at a glance. Use it to pick a free day or to find a clear afternoon.

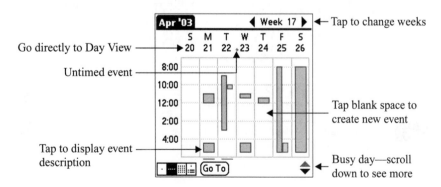

5

 *If you have an appointment you need to move to another time anywhere in the week, tap the event, hold the stylus down, and then drag it to another place on the schedule. As you move the block around, you can see the exact time to which the event is being moved. To abort this process without changing anything, move it back to its original location without lifting the stylus.*

Navigating the Month View

If you press the Date Book button again or tap the third icon at the bottom of the screen, you're transported to the Month View. It displays an entire month at a time.

Blocks of busy time are now replaced by little hash marks. You can't tap on these marks to see the appointment details because they don't actually represent individual events. Instead, the three possible marks represent events in the morning, afternoon, and evening, as shown in Figure 5-3. In addition, this view shows untimed events as plus signs and multiday events as a series of dots that span several days. If you tap any day in this view, you're automatically taken to the Day View for that day.

NOTE *Depending upon which Palm OS device you own, both of these special display features may be initially disabled. If yours are off to begin with, turn them on by choosing Options | Display Options from the Day View screen. Then, in the Month View section of the Display Options dialog box, enable Show Untimed Events and Show Daily Repeating Events.*

FIGURE 5-3   If you enable the right features in preferences, you can see untimed and multiday events in the monthly calendar.

Adding Some Holidays

One thing that the Palm's Date Book doesn't come with is a database of holidays. When's Christmas? That one is easy—but if you want to know when we celebrate President's Day, Veteran's Day, or Arbor Day, then it helps to have a calendar with holidays already nailed down for you.

Thankfully, there are a number of holiday databases online, many of them free or extremely inexpensive, and all of them easy to install on your Palm. After loading the appropriate files, your Date Book will know exactly when all the major holidays are, and display them in all the various views.

Try either one of these, or if you prefer, search online and you'll find many others as well:

- **TinyDates**   For a mere $4, you get a huge database of holidays that synchronizes with the Date Book, includes free updates in future years, and has a detailed description of the background of all the holidays.

- **MegaHolidays**   This holiday database costs $13 and comes in its own application that resides outside of the Date Book.

Both of these programs are available on www.Palmgear.com.

Managing Your Day from the Agenda View

The last of the Date Book views—the Agenda View—is a favorite for many people. Like some desktop day planners, it combines your appointments and to-do tasks into a single screen. You can see at a single glance all your responsibilities for the day without switching screens or pressing buttons. Take a look at the Agenda View:

You can see that the top of the screen shows you any appointments and untimed events that may be scheduled for the day. After a horizontal line, your Palm lists your to-dos.

You can change the current day by tapping the arrows at the top of the screen to change a day at a time. If you want to hop directly to another day, tap the date between the arrows. This displays the Go To Date dialog box, just as if you had tapped the Go To button at the bottom of the screen.

To jump to the current date, tap the Go To button and then tap the Today button at the bottom of the Go To Date dialog box.

Filtering Your To-Dos

You might not always want to see all the to-do tasks stored in your Palm. If you're at work, for instance, you might not want to see any to-dos filed in a personal category.

To fine-tune the To Do List, tap the down arrow for the category list and choose the category you want to see displayed. You can choose any category you like, including All.

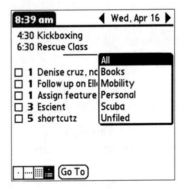

The Agenda View

The Agenda View is great for viewing your day's schedule, but it's also a cool way to make changes to your daily itinerary. Just tap on a calendar item to switch to the Day View so you can make schedule changes. Or tap a to-do item to go to the To Do List for editing.

The Best Sci-Fi

Dave: The Palm is like science fiction come alive, which begs the question, which sci-fi? Rick obsesses over some of the lamest sci-fi shows ever, such as *Star Trek: Deep Space Nine* and *The West Wing* (Martin Sheen as the president? Yeah, that's gotta be sci-fi). I am partial to shows with plausible technology, engaging plots, and a real sense of drama—that's why *Babylon 5* ranks up there among the best television ever. Meanwhile, Rick is watching a repeat of another "very special" episode about Kira. Apparently, she lost the bracelet her mom gave her this week.

Rick: Speaking of sci-fi, aliens have taken over Dave's brain. I know because for years . . . *years* . . . I have stated my disdain for *Deep Space Nine* and my total love for *Star Trek: Voyager*. But alien-Dave can't seem to compute that. And, obviously, anyone who doesn't like *The West Wing* must be controlled by some evil influence. Oh, that's right, Dave's a Republican.

NOTE *It would be great if you could automatically start your Palm in a specific mode, such as Agenda View, all the time. Alas, you can't quite do that. But, if you set your Palm to the Agenda View and then visit another application, the Agenda View automatically appears when you return to the Date Book. If you're in a hurry, remember that you can press the Date Book button several times to cycle through the Date Book's various screens to arrive at the Agenda View.*

Creating New Appointments

Now that you've mastered the fine art of viewing your schedule from every conceivable angle and perspective, you probably want to know how to add new events to the schedule. As you can probably guess, there are two ways to add appointments to your Palm: via the Palm Desktop—which we discuss later in this chapter—and right from the Palm itself. The only place you can actually enter data about a meeting is from the Day View.

Adding Timed Events

Most of the time, your schedule will be full of meetings that take place at a specific time of day, such as

```
Meet with Susan from accounting
3-5pm in Conference Room A.
```

This is what Palm refers to as a *timed event*—but most people call it an appointment. In any event, several ways exist to add an event like this to your Palm:

■ **Use the New button**   Tap the New button on the Day View. Then, within the Set Time dialog box, select a Start Time and an End Time, and then tap OK. Now, enter the meeting information on the blank line provided for you.

■ **Start writing**   Tap on a blank line that corresponds to the meeting start time and write the details of the meeting on the line.

■ **Pick a time from the Week View**   If you're looking for a free space to place a meeting, the Week View is a good place to look because it gives you the "big picture" of your schedule. When you find a spot you like, tap it, and the Day View should open to the desired start time. Then write the meeting info.

A Closer Look at the Set Time Dialog Box

To set a time in this dialog box, tap an hour (in the selector on the left) and a minute (on the right) for both the Start Time and End Time. You can change your mind as often as you like, but the time must be in increments no smaller than five minutes. You can't set a Start Time of 11:33, for instance.

You can also use Graffiti to set the time, a real convenience for folks who are faster at writing than tapping. 335 is interpreted as 3:35. To change between A.M. and P.M., write an *A* or a *P* in the letter side of the Graffiti area.

If you need to back up and start over, use the backspace gesture. When you want to move between the Start Time and the End Time box, use the Next Field gesture. Finally, when you've finished entering times, use the Return gesture to simulate tapping OK. Now, you're back at the Day View, ready to write in your meeting name.

 *A fast way to create a new event at a specific time is to simply write the start time. A Set Time dialog box appears, and you can proceed from there. For example, writing a 4 automatically launches the Set Time dialog box for 4 P.M.*

Adding Untimed Events

If we wrote about something called a timed event, you must have assumed we'd get to something called an untimed event, right? *Untimed events* are pretty much what you'd expect—they're events associated with a day, but not with a specific time. Typical untimed events include birthdays and anniversaries, reminders to pick up the dry cleaning, and deadline reminders (though you might also consider putting those kinds of things in the To Do List, described in Chapter 7). To create an untimed event, perform one of these two techniques:

■ On the Day View with no time selected (in other words, the cursor isn't waiting in a blank line for you already), just start writing. The event appears at the top of the screen as an untimed event.

■ Tap New to display the Set Time dialog box. Instead of setting a Start Time and an End Time, though, tap the No Time button and tap OK.

Make a Date

If you're setting up an appointment with someone in particular, you can have a lot of fun with your Palm. Okay, it's not better than listening to Pink Floyd with the lights out, but it's pretty cool nonetheless. Suppose you need to meet with someone who's already in your Address Book. Switch to the Day View and tap on a blank line at the time you want to start your meeting. Then choose Options | Phone Lookup. You see the Phone Number Lookup dialog box, which displays all the names in your Address Book. Find the name of the person you're meeting with and tap it. Tap Add. What do you get? The person's name and phone number positioned at the start time of the meeting.

 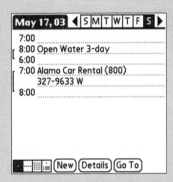

Now it gets even better. Does your associate have a Palm? If so, point your Palm at theirs. Make sure the appointment is still selected and choose Record | Beam Event. You've just given your associate a copy of your meeting.

Making Your Appointments Repeat

Some schedule events just don't go away. Weekly meetings, semiannual employee reviews, and the monthly dog grooming sessions are all examples of events you might want the Palm to automate. After all, you don't have the time or energy to write the same weekly event into your Palm 52 times to get it entered for a whole year. An easier way exists. To create a recurring event, do this:

1. Select the entry you want to turn into a recurring event and tap the Details button at the bottom of the Day View screen.

2. In the Event Details dialog box, the Repeat box is currently set to None; tap it. The Change Repeat dialog box should now appear.

3. Now you need to tap a repeat interval. Will the event repeat daily, weekly, monthly, or annually? In other words, if the event takes place only once a year—or once every five years, tap Year. If you have a meeting that takes place once a month, or every other month, tap Month. For meetings that occur every week or every five weeks, use the Week button. Finally, if you need to schedule a meeting daily, every other day, or every ten days, tap Day.

4. You now have more options, depending on which interval you choose. A common interval is Week, which would enable you to set up a weekly meeting. Tell the Change Repeat dialog box how often the meeting will occur, such as Every 1 Week or Every 3 Weeks.

5. If you chose a monthly interval, you can also choose whether the meeting will repeat by day (such as the first Monday of every month) or by date (as in the 11th of every month).

6. If the event will repeat more or less forever (or at least as long as you can imagine going to work every day), then leave the End On setting at the default, which is No End Date. If you are creating an event with a clear conclusion, tap End On to set the End Date for this repeating event.

7. Your selection is turned into a plain English description. If you agree the repeat settings are what you want, tap OK.

TIP   *If you're attending a multiday event, such as a trade show, you can display this in your Palm by creating an untimed event and setting it to repeat daily (Every 1 Day). Don't forget to set an End Date.*

Making an Appointment Private

You may not want all your appointments to be available to the public. Although we generally believe honesty is the best policy, you can flag certain appointments as private—and they'll be hidden from everyone except you. If you want to hide an appointment, do this:

1. On the Day View screen, select an appointment.

2. Tap the Details button.

3. On the Event Details dialog box, tap the Private box to add a check mark. Once you select this option, the current record is flagged for privacy. Tap the OK button, and you see this dialog box:

4. Tap OK to close the dialog box.

You might notice the event probably isn't hidden yet. To make it go away, you need to enable the Private Records feature in the Security app. For details on how to do this, see Chapter 9. Using this feature, you can hide and show private data whenever you want.

Editing Recurring Meetings

With most appointments or events, you can make a change just by tapping and entering the needed change with a little Graffiti. Changes to repeating meetings require a little more care. In general, when you change some aspect of a meeting that repeats, the Palm asks you whether you want to change only this one meeting, future meetings, or every meeting in the series.

If you need to move a specific meeting—such as the one in November—to a different time, but all the other meetings continue to be held at the traditional time, select Current. The event is actually unlinked from the series, and any changes you subsequently make to the rest of the repeating event don't affect the one you changed. On the other hand, if the meeting is moving to a new day permanently, choose All:

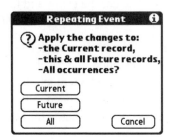

There's an exception to this rule: if you change any of the text in the name of the appointment, then the Palm makes the change to the entire series without asking. If you want to change the text of one instance of the event without changing the rest, you need to unlink it from the series. To do that, try this:

1. Change something else about the event, such as its time.

2. You're asked if you want to change the current event or all of the events. Choose Current. The event is now unlinked from the series.

3. Change the name of the unlinked event.

4. If you need to, fix whatever you changed in step 2.

Deleting Old Appointments

As time goes on, your Palm starts to accumulate a considerable number of appointments. Often, after an event has passed, you no longer need a record of it. If that's the case, you might want to delete it to save memory. Granted, each appointment takes up a miniscule amount of memory; but eventually this can add up. Even if you don't care about memory savings, meetings do sometimes get canceled—and you need a way to delete them. A few ways exist to get these events off your Palm:

■ **Erase it**   Open the Day View. Tap the stylus at the end of the line and backspace over it to delete all the characters. Or, you can highlight the text by dragging the stylus over the name of the meeting, and then use a single backspace gesture to erase it.

CAUTION   *Watch out! If you use this method to delete a repeating event, the Palm erases all the events in the series without warning.*

- **Use the Delete button**   Select the event and tap the Details button. Then tap Delete (or select the item and choose Delete from the menu).

- **Purge a bunch at once**   If you want to delete a bunch of appointments at once, a special tool was designed just for this task. Choose Record | Purge from the Day View. Then choose how much data to delete—you can choose to delete events that are more than a week old or, if you want more of a safety cushion, delete events more than a month old.

TIP   *If you purge your appointments, you have the option to "save an archive copy on PC." If you do that, the Palm automatically saves your deleted data in a file called "archive" on your PC. You can restore those appointments from the desktop later by opening the archive file within Palm Desktop by choosing File | Open from the menu. It works only if you HotSync with Palm Desktop instead of another program, such as Outlook.*

Working with Alarms

If you need a reminder about upcoming events, then you should use the Palm's built-in alarm feature. Any event you enter can be set to beep shortly before the event, giving you enough time to jump in your car, pick up the phone, or start saving for the big day. You can assign an alarm setting to your events as you create the event or at any time afterward.

NOTE   *Timed events play an audible sound. Untimed events don't play a sound, but simply display a screen advising you the event is pending.*

Picking Your Own Alarm Sound

If, like us, you're easily bored, you might be interested in changing your Palm's default alarm sound. It's easy to do—just visit a Palm software Web site such as PalmGear.com and search for alarm sounds. You'll find tons of downloads that give your Palm alternative sounds. Some give you special effects such as science fiction or animal sounds; others are complete songs. If you've ever wanted your Palm to sound like a Star Trek communicator, here's your chance. Of course, it's not all fun and games—a distinctive alarm sound can make your Palm easier to hear in a crowd.

Setting Alarms for Specific Events

To enable the alarm for a particular appointment, do this:

1. In the Day View, select an appointment.

2. Tap Details.

3. In the Event Details dialog box, tap the Alarm check box. You should see a new control appear that enables you to set the advance warning for the event.

4. Select how much advanced warning you want. You can choose no warning (enter a zero) or set a time up to 99 days ahead of time. The default is five minutes.

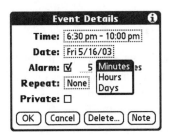

5. Tap OK.

Setting Alarms for Everything

By default, the Palm doesn't turn the alarm on for your appointments. Instead, you need to turn the alarm on for every event individually. If you find you like using the alarm, though, you can tell the Palm to turn the alarm on automatically for all your appointments. Then, it's up to you to turn the alarm off on a case-by-case basis when you don't want to be notified for any events.

To enable the default alarm setting, do this:

1. In the Day View, choose Options | Preferences.

2. Tap the check box for the Alarm Preset. Set your alarm preference; configure the alarm time, the kind of alarm sound, and how many times the alarm will sound before giving up.

> **TIP** *You can try out each of the alarm sounds by selecting them from the list. After you choose a sound, it plays so you can hear what it sounds like.*

3. Tap OK.

Importing Alarm Settings

Much of the time, you probably get appointments into your Palm via your PC—you HotSync them in from the Palm Desktop or Outlook. In that case, the rules are different. The Palm keeps whatever alarm settings were assigned on the PC and doesn't use the Preference settings on the Palm. If you want a specific alarm setting, you need to change the alarm setting on the desktop application before HotSyncing or change the alarm on the Palm after you HotSync.

> **TIP** *Some folks would like to have two separate sets of alarms for their appointments: one for the Palm and another for their desktop calendar program. If you have a PC and Microsoft Outlook, try Desktop to Go. This alternative conduit enables you to configure the Palm to use a completely independent set of alarms from Outlook.*

Controlling Your Alarm

If you use an alarm clock, you must surely know the only thing better than having an alarm is actually being able to turn it off.

Keep in mind that the Palm really isn't all that loud. If you need to hear your Palm, don't bury it in a backpack or a briefcase, where the sound will be hopelessly muffled. But what if you're in a quiet meeting room and the last thing you need is for your Palm to start chirping in front of the CEO? In that case, temporarily silence it. Open Prefs and choose the General view, where there's an option for Alarm Sound. Choose Off from the Alarm Sound list. Some Palm models even have a vibrating alarm, which is a great way to keep on top of alarms without disturbing the people around you.

5

Working with the Palm Desktop

If you use the Palm Desktop as the calendar on your desktop PC, you benefit because it looks similar to the version on your Palm. Granted, the Palm Desktop is a lot bigger than your Palm screen, and it's in color. But aside from that, the modules share a common appearance, and the overall philosophy of the program is similar.

Using the Windows Date Book

After you start the Palm Desktop, you can switch to the Date Book by clicking the Date icon on the left side of the screen or by choosing View | Date Book from the menu. To change views, click the tabs at the right edge of the screen. You should see tabs for Day, Week, Month, and Year.

Using the Day View

The Day View looks similar to the Palm display. Look at Figure 5-4 for an overview of the major elements in this display.

TIP   *The easiest way to double-book a time slot is to click the Time box. A new blank appears to the right of the existing appointment.*

You might recall that on the Palm, you can create an appointment by using the Phone Lookup feature—this grabs a name and phone number from the Address Book and places it in a time slot in the Date Book. You can do the same thing in the Palm Desktop. Under the calendar, you can see the To Do List and Address Book minilists. Choose which one you want to see by clicking Address or To Do. Then drag a name (or even a To Do) into a time slot.

Go to today   Add untimed event

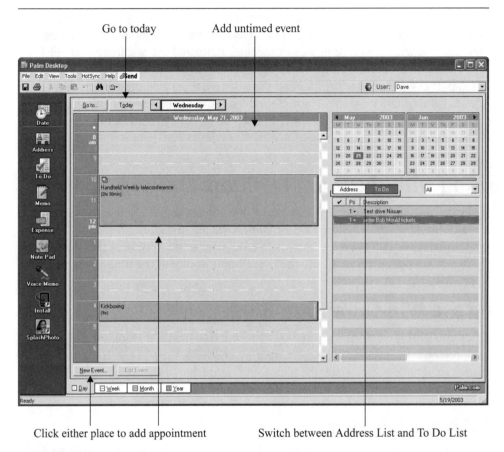

Click either place to add appointment   Switch between Address List and To Do List

FIGURE 5-4   The Day View combines appointments with either to-dos or addresses, depending upon how you configure the screen.

Editing Appointments

You can make lots of changes with the mouse. To change the duration of an event, drag the arrow-shaped duration handle up or down. To move the appointment, drag it by its event handle on the right edge. To see the Edit Event dialog box, which lets you edit the text and includes alarm and privacy controls, double-click anywhere in the event.

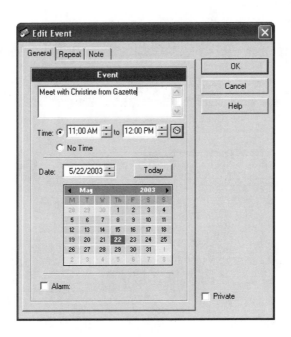

5

You can move an appointment to another day by dragging it via the event handle to the calendar and dropping it on the desired day.

Using the Long Range Views

The Week and Month Views are quite similar to their Palm counterparts. In the Week View (shown in Figure 5-5), though, the event blocks work a little differently than you might expect:

■ To move an event to a different time, drag it by the event handle.

■ To display the Edit Event dialog box and change options such as text, time, repeat settings, or the alarm, double-click the event.

■ To change the duration of the event, drag its duration handle up or down.

The Month View is a bit more helpful than the one in your Palm. The Month View actually shows you what events are scheduled, not only that you have a mysterious "something" scheduled. You can't edit the events in this view, though.

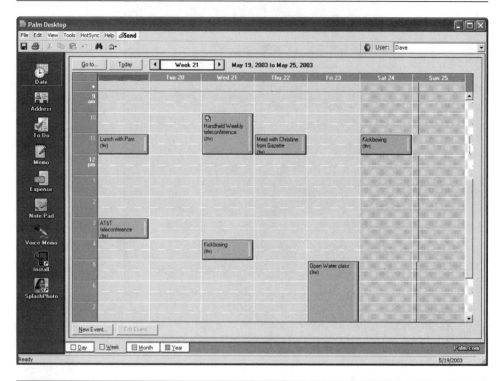

FIGURE 5-5   The Week View enables you to add and edit appointments.

Instead, you can double-click the appropriate day to get to the Day View or add a new event to a specific day by right-clicking the day and choosing New Event from the menu.

Finally, the Year View lets you see 12 months at a glance. If you look closely, you'll see that the calendar marks busy days with little tick marks. To see appointments, just hover the mouse over the appropriate day. Double-click to go directly to that Day View.

Using Alarms on the Desktop

Want to be notified about upcoming events while working at your desk? You need to use the Palm Desktop's Alarm Manager. Although Alarm Manager is linked to the Palm Desktop, it's technically not a part of it. What we mean is that it runs outside of the program and hangs out in the Windows System Tray, just like HotSync Manager.

To activate the Alarm Manager, choose Tools | Options and then click the Alarm tab. You'll see three choices in the Options dialog box:

- **Always Available**   When you choose this option, Alarm Manager loads when you start Windows, even if Palm Desktop itself isn't running. It ensures that you hear all of your alarms. Most folks, we think, want this option.

- **Available only when the Palm Desktop is running**   This is pretty self-explanatory—but we can't think of a lot of reasons why you'd use this option.

- **Disabled**   Alarms won't ring at all—which makes sense if you don't need to worry about event alarms or you actually use another PIM, such as Outlook.

Once you set up the Alarm Manager to your liking, you can configure alarms in the Palm Desktop when you create new events. At the bottom of the New Event or Edit Event window, you'll find the alarm options (which work just like they do on the Palm itself).

Using Outlook

Of course, Microsoft Outlook synchronizes with the Palm just fine, and many people use it instead of the Palm Desktop. We should point out, though, that some people categorize appointments in Outlook. The Palm doesn't let you categorize events in the Date Book, but you can add this capability by upgrading to programs such as Chapura's PocketMirror Professional or DataViz's Beyond Contacts.

Switching Between Outlook and Palm Desktop

When you first install your Palm software, you're offered the option of synchronizing with Palm Desktop or another PIM such as Microsoft Outlook. You can change your mind later, but you'll need the original Palm Desktop installation CD-ROM.

To change synchronization from Palm Desktop to Outlook—or vice versa—run the Palm Desktop installation again. There's no harm in installing the software "on top of" the copy already on your hard disk. When the installer asks you which program you want your Palm to sync with, make the appropriate choice and finish the install.

Synchronizing Multiple Palms with Outlook

Some households or offices have more than one Palm device, and each needs to sync with the same copy of Outlook. That's easy: just open Outlook and look for a folder called PocketMirror. It was installed during the initial Palm software setup. It should be a folder with a single note bearing the HotSync name of your Palm device. To sync Outlook with more devices, create a note for each PDA and type the device's HotSync name exactly as it appears on the top right of the HotSync screen on the Palm. The next time you sync the PDA, it will exchange data with Outlook.

It's worth pointing out that if you synchronize multiple PDAs with a single copy of Outlook, everyone's data will be combined on the PDAs and within Outlook into a big, friendly broth of data. No secrets here! If you sync multiple PDAs with Palm Desktop, though, Palm Desktop keeps everyone's data separated by device, so everyone doesn't end up with everyone else's data on their handhelds.

Tweaking Alarms for the Palm

By default, every Outlook appointment comes with an alarm that sounds 15 minutes before the event. If you create most of your appointments within Outlook, you might end up with alarms you don't want on the Palm after a HotSync. To change the length of the default alarm—or to disable alarms entirely—choose Tools | Options from the Outlook menu and click the Preferences tab. In the Calendar section, edit the Default Reminder option to suit your needs. If you remove the check mark, the alarm is then disabled for new appointments.

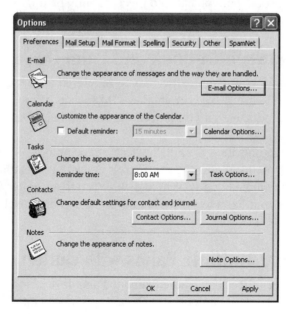

Using the Macintosh Date Book

If you have a Macintosh, your Palm Desktop looks quite a bit different than the PC version—thanks largely to the elegant OS X interface and the top-of-screen toolbar. But navigating around this program is still a snap. (We based the Mac portion of this book on OS X since it's clearly the way of the future.)

To see the Date Book, click the Date Book button on the Palm Desktop toolbar atop the screen, or chose View | Date Book | Day from the menu. Like the Palm's Date Book button, you can click this button over and over to cycle among the Day View, Week View, and Month View.

You can go directly to the current Day View by clicking the Today icon in the toolbar. Likewise, you can scoot to a specific calendar day by clicking the Go To button.

If you opt to synchronize your Palm with Apple's iCal via iSync, you lose the ability to synchronize with the Palm Desktop's Date Book. To switch back, reinstall the Palm Desktop from the CD-ROM.

Using the Day View

The Day View (in Figure 5-6) is divided into two parts: the appointments and the To Dos view. You can create new events two ways:

- Click and drag the mouse to define the start and end time of the appointment. When you release the mouse, you can type the appointment name.

- Double-click in a time slot to display the Event dialog box. You can fill out the event time, alarm, and frequency information here. Click OK to save the appointment.

If you need to add an appointment in the same time slot as an existing event, you can either double-click or click and drag in the space between the event and the hour markers, at the left edge of the window.

Adding an Untimed Event

To add an Untimed event to the current day, double-click above the time slots, but below the date. You then see the New Event dialog box already set to No Time. Fill it in and click OK.

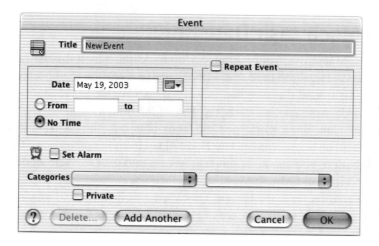

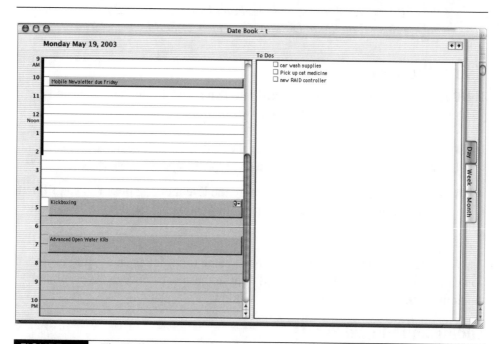

FIGURE 5-6   The Daily View stacks appointments in layers for better readability.

Using the Week and Month Views

The Week View works much the same as the Day View. Adding and editing appointments—both timed events and untimed events—is done in the same way.

> **TIP** *If you want to see more days or fewer days in the Week View, click the plus and minus buttons on the right edge of the window. Depending on your preferences, you can see as few as one day or as many as seven days onscreen at once.*

5

The Month View has the most surprises. Unlike on the Palm, this Month View is fully editable and enables you to see the contents of your appointments (they don't just appear as gray blocks). Here's what you can do with the Month View:

■ Double-click an empty space to display this dialog box:

■ Click the item you want to create in the designated day.

■ Click and drag an appointment to move it to another time.

■ Double-click an appointment to open the Appointment dialog box and edit the event details.

■ Double-click the gray date bar across the top of any day to switch to the Day View.

> **TIP** *Gray events in the Week and Month Views are untimed events.*

Better Date Books

Looking for an alternative to the Date Book that comes with your Palm? You have quite a few choices. The Palm Date Book hasn't changed much in the past decade, and it still has many of the same limitations it had back in the mid '90s. You can't categorize appointments the way you can in Microsoft Outlook, for instance, and you can't synchronize with Microsoft Exchange Public Folders. Another annoyance: you can't "link" appointments with items elsewhere in your Palm, such as the contact information for people attending your meeting. Don't worry, though, since there are numerous alternatives available.

Some of the best replacements for the Date Book include the following:

DateBk5	www.pimlico.com
Agendus	www.iambic.com
Beyond Contacts	www.dataviz.com
KeySuite	www.chapura.com

These programs offer a wealth of features and capabilities you won't find in the integrated Date Book. DateBk5 and Agendus, for instance, take advantage of larger screens, such as the big 320×480-pixel display on some Sony CLIÉs. They also let you attach colorful icons to appointments, making it easy to tell them apart at a glance in any calendar view. The other programs integrate with Outlook more coherently, utilizing categories, more data fields, and other important features.

So Many Preferences

Since this is the fist time we've played around inside the Palm Desktop, it's worth pointing out that the program has a rich set of preferences. To see them, choose Palm Desktop | Preferences from the menu. Be sure to experiment with the Décor tab, where you can choose from among a dozen or so styles for the program's appearance. The Date Book tab lets you specify many personal Date Book settings, such as the start of the work week and the default length of appointments.

Chapter 6

The Address Book

How to...

- View Address Book entries
- Customize the Address List display
- Search for an entry by name
- Search for an entry by keyword
- Create new Address Book entries
- Display a specific phone number in the Address List
- Use the custom fields
- Assign a category to an entry
- Delete Address Book entries
- Use the Windows Address Book
- Use your Palm with Outlook
- Use the Macintosh Address Book

What's the big deal? It's only an address book. Yes, but as one of the four big "core" applications—the main programs that ship with your Palm— you'll use the Address Book a lot. And the Address Book is an elegant program, designed to get the information you need quickly, perhaps more quickly than any other contact manager on the market.

We're sure you'll get a lot of mileage from the Address Book. You can store literally thousands of entries and not run out of memory. Regardless of how many names you add to the list, your Palm never slows down to a crawl—that's a claim desktop applications simply can't make. In addition, the Address Book isn't really a stand-alone application (though it can be if you want). The Address Book synchronizes with desktop applications such as the Palm Desktop and Microsoft Outlook. This means you need to create a contact list just once and then it's maintained on both your PC and your Palm.

Viewing Your Addresses

When you switch to the Address Book, the program displays all the entries in your list onscreen. As you might expect, you can start the Address Book by pressing the Address Book button on your Palm or tapping the Address icon in the Home screen.

> **NOTE**   *On some Palm smartphones, the Address Book button may actually launch the Speed Dial screen. You may have to press the button several times to get to the Address Book.*

As you can see in Figure 6-1, the Palm lists your contacts alphabetically in a view called the Address List. Unless you have a Palm device with a bigger screen (such as the Sony CLIÉ NX70V), there's room for 11 entries onscreen at one time; the rest appear above or below the screen, depending on where you are within the Address List. To get around in the Address List, just use the scroll buttons or the Navigator. Each time you scroll, the Palm moves the list by one complete page of entries.

You can also get around with categories. If your contacts are divided into more than one category, every time you press the Address Book button, you switch categories. You can cycle through the first page of names in each category by repeatedly pressing the Address Book button.

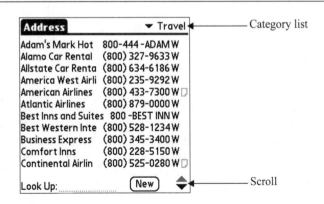

FIGURE 6-1   The Address List is a database of all your contact information.

Viewing by Company Name

For most folks, the default Address List is great. This list displays the entries by name (last, first) and a phone number. If you prefer to work with your contacts according to the company they work with, you can change the Address List.

To change the View mode of the Address List, do this:

1. Display the Address List View.

2. Choose Options | Preferences from the menu.

3. Choose Company, Last Name from the List By list.

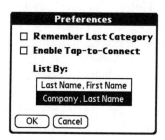

4. Tap OK to save your changes.

Notice that after making the change, you can see the company name in the list. If no company is associated with a particular entry, then you see only the individual's name, as you did before. You can switch back to the default view at any time.

Finding a Specific Name

If you're looking for a specific entry in the Address List, you can simply scroll down until you find it. If you have only a few dozen contacts, that's not so hard. But what if you're like us and your Address List is brimming with over a thousand contacts? Scrolling might take a while, especially if the guy you're looking for is named Nigel Walthers or Earnest Zanthers. That's when you use the Look Up function.

To search for a specific name, start writing the person's last name in the Look Up field at the bottom of the screen. The Address Book adjusts the display as you write; so if you enter the letter **J**, it displays all the names that begin with the letter *J*. If you write **JO**, it narrows the search and shows names that begin with those letters.

> **NOTE**   *If you're using the List By: Company, Last Name option in the Address List View, it's a little more complicated. If the entry has a company name, you need to search for that entry by company name. If the entry doesn't have a company name, though, you must find it by the last name.*

6

Once you start searching, you can keep writing letters until the Palm displays exactly the name you want, or you can write one or two letters, and then use the Scroll button to find the name you need. If you want to clear the Look Up field to write in a new name, just press one of the Scroll buttons.

> **TIP**   *If you try writing a letter, but your Palm beeps at you, this means no name in the list is spelled with the letter you're trying to add. You've probably misspelled the name.*

Conducting a Detailed Search

You may have noticed that the Look Up field searches only by last name. What happens if you want to find someone, but you can only remember that person's first name or the company where he works? The Look Up field won't do any good.

In this case, use the Find tool. Tap the Find button, enter the word you want to search for, and then tap OK. You get a list of every entry in the Palm with that word—even items from the other Palm applications—as shown in Figure 6-2. The current application is searched first, so make sure you're in the Address Book before you start using the Find tool.

Viewing a Name

Once you locate the name you were looking for, tap on it. You see the Address View, which displays the contact's name, address, and phone numbers, as shown in Figure 6-3.

FIGURE 6-2   The Find tool is a powerful way to locate an entry even if you don't remember the person's exact name.

FIGURE 6-3   The Address Book shows you all the details about the selected individual.

Dialing a Phone Number

If you have a wireless Palm (such as a Tungsten T paired with a Bluetooth phone) or smartphone, you can dial a number in the Address Book and immediately take the call. When you find the name you're looking for, tap the Quick Connect icon at the very top of the screen (it looks like a pair of envelopes and a cell phone) and then tap the phone number you want to dial. Be sure to check out Chapter 10 for details.

Creating New Entries

To create a new Address List entry on the Palm, tap the New button at the bottom of the screen. From there, start filling in the blanks. Start by writing the last name of the person you're adding. When you're ready to move on to the first name, you need to change fields. You can do this in two ways:

- Tap the next field with the stylus, and then start writing.
- Use the Next Field gesture to move to the next field.

The Future of the Address Book

Dave: There's little doubt that thanks to the Palm Address Book—the PDA's best application—all Palms will inevitably, someday, turn into wireless devices or smartphones. After all, why carry an address book in your PDA and another one in your mobile phone? If your PDA were a phone, you'd just tap the name you want to dial to place the call. I do that already with my Tungsten T—it uses Bluetooth to dial my mobile phone—and it's clearly the way of the future. Only losers like Rick could see the advantages on carrying one device yet willingly continue to carry both a Palm and a phone.

Rick: Let's see...you have to carry your Tungsten, your phone, and a Bluetooth headset (the biggest "I'm a nerd" badge since the calculator watch). There's no debating the value of the Palm Address Book, especially when it's integrated into a smartphone. Hence the appeal of models such as the Handspring Treo and Kyocera 7135. Of course, you think your needs are all people's needs, so whatever you decide is right must be the future. Here in the real world (you should visit sometime!), there's no perfect smartphone (yet), so there are still advantages to carrying both a non-wireless Palm and a regular phone.

 *The Next Field gesture takes a little practice because it's easy to get the letter U by mistake. Although the gesture template shows a curve in the first part of the stroke, you get the best results by going straight down, and then straight up again.*

Even though you see only a single line for text in each field, the Address List secretly supports multiple lines of text in each field. If you're entering the company name, for instance, you can use two or more lines to enter all the information you need about the company, department, and so on, for the individual. To write multiple lines of text in a field, use the Return gesture to create a new line. You won't see the multiple lines in the Address List, but you can see them when you select the entry and view the Address View.

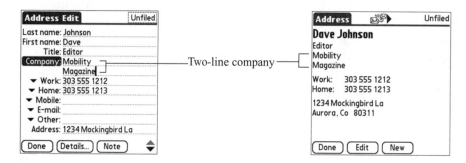

When you've finished adding information about this new person, tap the Done button.

 What if you're Canadian, French, or living in some other non-American location? The Palm defaults to address details such as city, state, and ZIP code—which may not be appropriate for your locale. The solution is to tap on the Prefs icon in the System category of the Home screen and select Formats from the menu. Then, set the Preset To: menu to whatever country you desire.

Using Multiple Phone Numbers

The Address List gives you a few options when you enter contact information. Specifically, you can set what kinds of phone numbers your Palm has for each contact. Conveniently, this needn't be the same for everyone. For one person, you might list a home phone and a pager, for instance, and another entry might have a work number and an e-mail address. The Palm keeps track of everything for you.

To control these numbers, tap on the phone number list and choose the desired label. Then, write the number or e-mail address in the field next to the label. You can specify up to five entries for each person in your Address List.

If you're on the ball, you might wonder which of those numbers shows up in the Address List View. Remember, the list shows the name and a phone number for each contact—this means you may not have to open an entry simply to dial a phone number because it's right there in the List View. The answer, though, is that the first phone number you enter into the Edit View is the one that appears in the List View—no matter where it appears in the list of phone numbers.

 *If you later decide you want a different number to appear in the List View, tap the Details button and select the number label you want from the Show in List menu.*

Don't like the font? You can choose from four font sizes by choosing Options | Font in the Address Book menu. You can even set the display and edit screens differently.

Using Extra Fields

The Address List has plenty of preconfigured fields (such as name, company, and phone numbers) for most users, but it's flexible enough also to accommodate the special needs of everyone else. You might want to track birthdays, Web pages, spouse names, or other personal information. If so, you're in luck—four custom fields are at the bottom of the Address Edit View, which you can rename as you like.

To label these four bonus fields into something more useful, do this:

1. Choose the Address Book. Any view will do.

2. Choose Options | Rename Custom Fields from the menu.

3. Select the text on the first line (which should say Custom 1) and write a name for the field. Name the other fields—or as many as you need—in the same way.

4. Tap OK when you finish.

Once you create labels for these fields, you can find them at the bottom of the list of contact info in the Address Edit View.

 *The custom fields are global. This means you can't have different custom fields for each entry or even for each category. Once named, the custom fields apply to all entries in the Address List. You needn't fill them out for every entry, though.*

Assigning Categories

Your new contact can easily get lost within a sea of names and addresses if you aren't careful. With only a few names to manage, this isn't a big deal. But what if you have 500 or 1,000 contacts in your Address List? This is when categories could come in handy.

Choosing a Category

As you might remember from Chapter 2, categories are simply a way of organizing your Palm data more logically into groups you frequently use. To assign a contact to a specific category, do this:

1. From the Address Edit screen, tap Details. The Address Entry Details dialog box should appear.

2. Tap the Category List and choose the category name you want to assign to this contact.

3. Tap OK to close the dialog box.

Of course, you needn't assign a category if you don't want to do so. By default, new contacts are placed in the Unfiled category.

Editing and Deleting Addresses

In this fast-paced world, a contact once entered in an address book isn't likely to stay that way for long. You may need to update an address, phone number, or e-mail address, or to delete the entry entirely.

To edit an entry, all you must do is find the entry in the Address List and tap it. You're taken to the Address View where you can see the existing information. Then, tap on the screen and the display changes to the Address Edit screen, which you can change to suit your needs.

If you have a contact you simply don't need anymore, you can delete it from the Palm to save memory and reduce data clutter. To delete a contact, do this:

1. Choose the entry from the Address List. You see the Address View.

2. Choose Record | Delete Address from the menu.

NOTE   *If you check the box marked Save Archive Copy on PC, then a copy of this entry is preserved in a file called "archive" on your PC, which you can load into Palm Desktop using the File | Open menu. In general, you probably needn't archive your data, but this option lets you restore deleted data in a crisis.*

Creating and Beaming Your Business Card

As mentioned in Chapter 4, one of the coolest things about taking your Palm to meetings and trade shows is the capability to beam your personal information into other peoples' Palms. This is a lot easier and more convenient than exchanging a business card. Heck, a paper business card? That's so . . . '80s! Use your Palm instead.

Before you can beam your personal information around, though, you need to create a business card. That's not hard to do. Find your own personal information in the Address List (or, if you haven't done this yet, create an entry for yourself). After you select your card and you can see your personal information on the Address View screen, choose Record | Select Business Card from the menu.

Record	Options
Delete Address	⁄D
Duplicate Address	⁄T
Beam Address	⁄B
Send Address	
Connect	⁄I
Attach Note	⁄A
Delete Note	⁄O
Select Business Card	
Beam Business Card	

From here on, you can beam your card to others either by choosing Record | Beam Business Card from the Address List menu or, more simply, by holding the Address List button down for two seconds.

TIP *Is your Address List entry selected as your business card? It's easy to tell. On the Address View, you can see an icon representing a business card at the top of the screen, to the right of the title.*

 **How to ... Create an Address Book Entry**

1. Press the Address Book button on your Palm to switch to that app.

2. Tap the New button on the bottom of the Address List View.

3. Enter all the information to create an entry for the person in question.

4. Tap the Details button and assign the entry to a category, and then tap OK.

Working with the Palm Desktop

The Palm Desktop obviously has its own counterpart to the Address Book found in the Palm. Using the Palm Desktop, you can not only create, edit, and refer to entries on your PC, but you can also put them to use in ways unavailable on the Palm itself. Next, we look at the Palm Desktop—both on the PC and the Mac.

The Windows Address Book

Using the Address Book in the Palm Desktop is a radically different experience than using the Palm. In most respects, it's better because the larger desktop screen, keyboard, and mouse enable you to enter and use the data in a more flexible way. After you start the Palm Desktop, you can switch to the Address Book by clicking the Address icon on the right side of the screen or by choosing View | Address Book (see Figure 6-4).

6

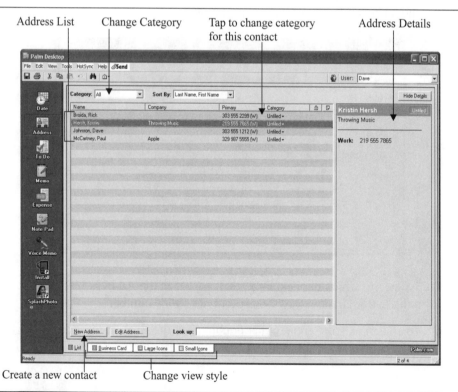

Address List   Change Category   Tap to change category for this contact   Address Details

Create a new contact   Change view style

FIGURE 6-4   The Address Book looks sparse, but has more features than the Palm itself.

The Address Book interface enables you to see both the Address List and Address View simultaneously. To see a specific record's contents, click it in the list, and the information then appears in the column on the right.

You can print a detailed address book based on your Palm contacts by choosing File | Print. The address book is nicely formatted.

Creating and Editing Entries

Some of the most dramatic differences in the Address Book appear when you create and use the Address Book. Remember these notes:

■ To create a new entry, click the New button at the bottom of the screen or double-click a blank spot in the Address List.

■ The Edit and New dialog boxes allow you to enter the same information as on the Palm. The dialog box also has a list box for specifying the category and a check box to make the entry private.

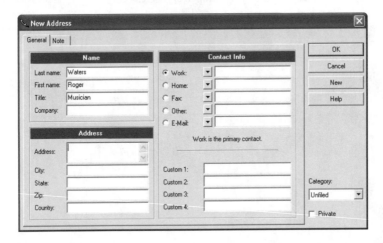

■ To specify which phone number will appear in the Address List, click the radio button to the left of the appropriate phone number.

■ To edit an existing entry, either double-click the entry in the Address List or its equivalent in the Address View on the right.

■ You can also change the custom fields on the Palm Desktop. To do that, choose Tools | Options and click the Address tab.

Importing Contacts into the Palm Desktop

If you have a history with another contact manager, you could have dozens or even hundreds of names and addresses that should be copied over to the Palm Desktop to be synchronized with the Palm. Thankfully, the Palm Desktop makes importing all those contacts possible with a minimum of fuss. All you need is a contact manager capable of saving its data in either a comma-separated values (CSV) or a tab-separated values (TSV) format. To import your data from another program, do this:

6

1. In your old contact manager, find the menu option to export your data in either CSV or TSV format. If the program gives you an option to remap your data as it's saved, don't worry. We'll map it properly as it's imported into the Palm Desktop. Save the exported data to a file on your hard disk. Make a note of where you save this file because you need to find it again in about two steps.

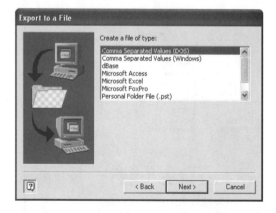

2. In the Palm Desktop, choose File | Import. The Import dialog box should appear.

3. Select the file you just created with the old contact manager. You may have to choose the proper file extension (such as CSV or TSV) from the Type of File list box to see the file you created. Choose Open.

4. Now you see a Specify Import Fields dialog box, as shown in Figure 6-5. This is the hardest part of the process and the one part that isn't terribly automated. Here's the deal: the data in a typical contact entry includes items such as name, phone numbers, and address. But those fields won't be in the same order in any two contact management programs, so you need to help the Palm Desktop put the old data in the right fields as it imports. To map the fields properly, drag each field on the left (which is the Palm Desktop) until it's lined up with the proper field on the right (which represents the old program). Line up last name with last name, for instance, and match phone numbers, e-mail addresses, and any other important fields. If you don't want to import a certain field, deselect its check box.

You can use the arrows to cycle forward through the database and make sure you assigned the fields properly.

5. When you finish lining up the fields, click the OK button.

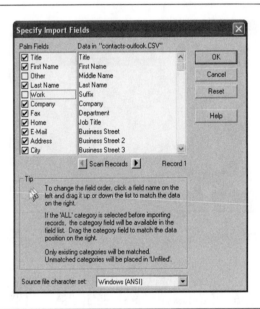

FIGURE 6-5   Carefully rearrange the fields in the Specify Import Fields dialog box so your old data is imported properly into the Palm Desktop.

If you did everything right, you should see your contacts in the Palm Desktop. Any newly imported entries are highlighted. If you messed something up, all isn't lost. Simply delete all your records, and then try to import your contacts file again.

Using Outlook

As we mentioned in Chapter 5, Outlook is a perfectly good alternative to the Palm Desktop. To see your contacts in Outlook, start by clicking the Contacts icon in the Outlook Shortcut bar. Outlook should switch to the Contacts View, and then you see a complete list of your names and addresses.

 *To find a contact quickly from any view in Outlook, type the person's name in the Find a Contact field on the Outlook toolbar and press* ENTER. *Outlook displays a list of names that matches your criteria or, if only one name appears, displays its entry.*

Working with the Palm

Outlook can hold a wealth of information, but it's important for you to understand the Palm's limitations when synchronizing to Outlook. Not all the fields in Outlook get transferred to the Palm because there simply aren't enough fields. Specifically, the limitations in the HotSync from Outlook to the Palm are the following:

- By default, only the business address is stored on the Palm. You can upgrade to other HotSync conduits that let you synchronize the personal address. Specifically, try PocketMirror Professional or Intellisync.

- Work, Home, Fax, Mobile, and E-mail are typically the only contact fields transferred to the Palm. If you create a contact with alternative fields, such as Business 2 or alternative e-mail addresses, Palm tries to include these entries, space permitting.

- None of the data from the Details tab is stored on the Palm.

This illustration should help you see how the Palm's Address Book entries correlate to Outlook:

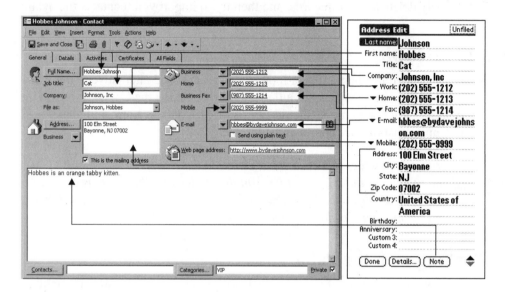

The Macintosh Address Book

Once you've mastered the Address Book aspect of the Palm Desktop (see Chapter 5) the rest—including the Address Book—is pretty straightforward as well. Click the Addresses icon in the toolbar to see a complete list of contacts synchronized with your Palm.

 If you're synchronizing with the Mac's Address Book via iSync, your Palm will sync only with iSync—not Palm Desktop. To return to Palm Desktop synchronization, you'll have to reinstall the Palm Desktop from CD-ROM.

The Address List is essentially the only view or module in the program—you needn't learn to switch between multiple views to use all the features in the Address Book:

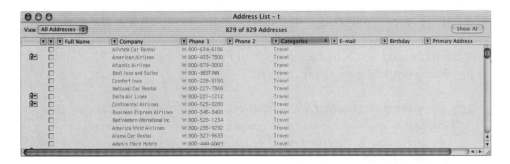

 *When you create a new contact, the first phone number in the list (not the first one you complete) is the one the Palm uses in the Address List as the main number. Also, to synchronize properly with the Palm, you should enter the e-mail address in the field in Other Information.*

Sorting and Filtering Your Contacts

You can customize the way your contacts are displayed by using the controls at the top of each column. If you want to see only some of the contacts, for instance, you can filter the display to show only certain entries. You can establish filters based on any column. To see only contacts in your own area code, for instance, choose Phone 1 and set the filter accordingly. Here's how:

1. Click the menu for the column you want to use as the filter criteria. You should see the filter and sorting menu.

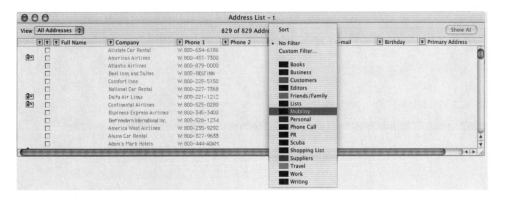

2.   If the criteria you want to sort appears in the menu, click it. If you want to sort by multiple items, click Custom Filter, which displays the Custom Filter dialog box. Choose the items to filter by—then click OK to close the dialog box and display the results.

You can create detailed filters by combining different columns. You can apply a filter to both the Phone 1 and Company columns, for instance. Anything that passes the first filter must then also pass the second filter to appear in the Contact List.

If you create a filter set you want to use often, you can tell the Address Book to memorize it. To do this, click the View menu and choose Memorize View. Give this view a name, and then you can display it in the future without going through the process of setting up one or more filters every time. To exit this memorized view and revert to the normal view, click Show All.

You can also sort your results alphabetically. To sort, decide which column you want to use as the sorting column. Then click the column menu and choose Sort.

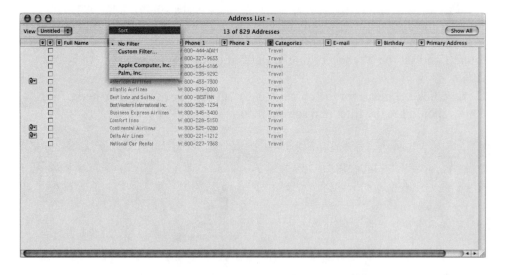

Address Book Alternatives and Enhancements

Don't think you have to stick with the Address Book just because it came with your trusty old Palm. Personally, we prefer the Palm Address Book to most of the alternatives, but here are a few you might want to look into if you feel like expanding your contact management horizons:

- **KeySuite**   This program from Chapura could well be the answer to every power user's dreams. The ordinary Address Book doesn't synchronize many of Outlook's fields, but KeySuite is a replacement that transfers absolutely everything—including all those extra fields in the other Outlook Contact tabs and all the categories as well. Visit www.chapura.com.

- **Agendus**   This Address Book replacement combines the To Do List, Date Book, and Address Book to deliver a single, integrated interface for tracking, alarming, and viewing your daily itinerary. This program has lots of die-hard fans because of its many powerful features for managing contacts. You can try it out at www.iambic.com.

- **Beyond Contacts**   Yet another aggressive Address Book alternative, Beyond Contacts comes with a slew of cool features—the most important of which is a comprehensive, integrated interface that does the work of all four Palm apps, making it work more like Microsoft Outlook. It even has an Outlook-like Today screen that summarizes your appointments. Visit www.dataviz.com for more information.

6

Where to Find It

Web Site	Address	What's There
Chapura	www.chapura.com	PocketMirror Professional and KeySuite
Pumatech	www.pumatech.com	Intellisync

Chapter 7

The To Do List, Memo Pad, and Note Pad

How to...

- View To Do List entries
- Create new To Dos
- Prioritize your To Dos
- Add notes to To Dos
- Customize the To Do List View
- Beam To Dos to others
- Use the Palm Desktop for Windows
- Use Outlook with the Palm
- Create Tasks on the Mac
- Create new memos
- Cut, copy, and paste text in a memo
- Assign categories to memos
- Customize the Memo List
- Make memos private
- Import text files into Windows memos
- Use memos in other Windows applications
- Configure attachments to HotSync properly on the Mac
- Sort and filter notes on the Mac

Three other programs constitute the core features of the Palm's personal information management: To Do List, Memo Pad, and Note Pad. For a lot of folks, these programs don't get the same constant workout as the Address Book and Date Book, and that's too bad. These programs are great for making your day smoother, more efficient, and less troublesome. Well, think of it this way: would you be more organized if you actually carried a list of things you needed to do—big and small—with you all the time? Would you stay on top of your tasks and remember important brainstorms if you simply wrote them down as they occurred to you? That's the magic of this trio of apps. In our never-ending quest to improve your life, we've dedicated this next chapter to illuminating these programs.

Viewing the To Do List

As with most of the core applications in your Palm, you can start the To Do List by pressing its button on the Palm (it's the one to the right of the scroll buttons) or by tapping its icon on the Application screen.

On some newer Palm models, though, the To Do List button has been eliminated in favor of other apps. The Tungsten W, for instance, makes the third button an e-mail launcher. If you have such a device, you have two choices:

1. Always start the To Do List from the Main category of the Apps screen.

2. Reassign one of the buttons to launch the To Do List—for details on that, see Chapter 2.

As you can see in Figure 7-1, the Palm lists your To Dos in a fairly straightforward list that you can use to see what tasks you have coming up or, in some cases, past due (you might want to take care of those pretty soon). Getting around is easy. Simply scroll down to see more To Dos, either with the onscreen scroll arrows or the scroll buttons/Nav button on the Palm's case.

Each time you scroll, the Palm moves the list by one complete page. This means that if you scroll down, the bottom entry on the page becomes the top entry after scrolling.

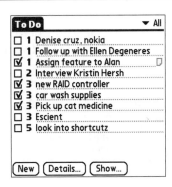

FIGURE 7-1   The To Do List displays all of your pending tasks.

The Agenda View Is Handy!

You can view your To Do items in the Date Book. The Agenda View lets you see all of today's appointments and upcoming To Dos at a glance, all on the same screen. See Chapter 5.

Another way to get around is by using the categories. If your tasks are divided into more than one category, every time you press the To Do button, you switch categories. You can cycle through the first page of tasks in each category by repeatedly pressing this button.

Creating a To Do

To add a To Do to your Palm, just start writing. The text appears automatically in a brand new To Do entry.

 *If you want to create a task with a specific priority, tap on a To Do entry that has the priority you want, and then tap New. The new To Do takes the priority of the previously selected task, saving you the trouble of choosing a priority later.*

Although most tasks can be summarized in only one line of text, there's no reasonable limit to how long you can make a To Do entry. If you need more than one line of text to describe your task, you can use the Enter gesture to get the Palm to display a new blank line in the same To Do. Remember, though, creating multiline To Dos might make it hard for you to read your tasks later, as you can see here:

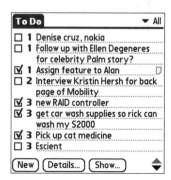

Friends Are a Chore

It's true! Having friends and coworkers can be actual work. Suppose you need to meet with Ed Grimpley from accounting sometime this week to talk about why you've gone through 18 mouse pads in the space of one week. You don't have an appointment in your calendar; you'd rather pop in sometime when it's convenient. The To Do List is your answer. Create a new To Do and choose Options | Phone Lookup from the menu. Find Ed in the Phone Number Lookup dialog box and tap Add. What you get is Ed's name and phone number in the To Do entry. It's a handy way to remind yourself to call someone without setting up a rigid appointment in the Date Book.

Instead of making long, multiline tasks, we recommend you add a note to your task instead (explained later in this chapter).

Adding Some Details

Once you finish entering the name of the task, tap elsewhere on the screen to save the entry. If you prefer, you can add additional information, such as a priority, category, and due date. You don't have to enter any of these special settings, but using them enables you to track your tasks with greater accuracy. Here's what you need to do:

1. Select the task you want to edit by tapping the name of the To Do.

2. Tap the Details button.

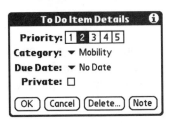

3. Tap a number to represent the priority of your task. You can select any number from one to five (the lower the number, the higher the priority).

4. Choose a category from the Category list.

To Do or Appointment?

We know what you're thinking—if you can assign due dates to items in the To Do List, why bother with appointments? Or, from the other perspective, why use To Dos if you have the Date Book? That's a good question. We use the To Do List whenever we have tasks that need doing by a certain date—but not at a certain time of day. If it requires a time slot, we put it in the Date Book. So, stuff like "buy lemons" and "finish Chapter 8" (hint, hint, Rick . . .) are To Dos. "Meet with Laura for lunch at 11:30" is a Date Book entry. There's also the matter of alarms: your Palm has an alarm for appointments, but not for To Dos.

5. Choose a due date from the Due Date list. You can choose to make a task due today, tomorrow, or in a week, or you can choose a date directly from the Calendar dialog box.

6. Tap OK to save your changes to the task.

 *Although you can make a task almost any length, most people find it's better to keep the To Do short, and add a note. To add a note to a To Do, select your To Do, tap the Details button, and then tap Note.*

Working with the List View

When you switch to the To Do List, all of your existing tasks are arranged onscreen, usually in order of importance (as determined by the priority number assigned to each To Do). As you can see in Figure 7-2, six elements are associated with each task:

- **Check box**   If you complete a task, you can indicate it's done by tapping the check box. That places a check mark in the task. Depending on how you configured the To Do Preferences, the entry either disappears or remains onscreen, but is marked as done.

- **Priority**   Not everything is the most important thing on your task list. If you want to arrange your tasks by importance or urgency, use the priority numbers, from one through five. Tap the number to get a list of all the priority choices.

To Do ▼ All

☐ 1 Denise cruz, nokia
☐ 1 Follow up with Ellen Degeneres
      for celebrity Palm story?
☑ 1 Assign feature to Alan
☐ 1 nterview Kristin Hersh for back
   2 age of Mobility
☑ 3 ew RAID controller
☑ 4 jet car wash supplies so rick can
   5 vash my S2000
☑ 3 Pick up cat medicine
☐ 3 Escient

(New) (Details...) (Show...) ◆

FIGURE 7-2 The To Do List lets you modify your tasks without tapping the Details button.

7

TIP *We recommend that you use priority numbers for your tasks—they help you sort through the clutter of your various To Dos and determine what's really important from one day to the next.*

- **To Do description** You can edit the description of the task by tapping in this field and editing the existing text.

- **Note icon** If you already created a note for the task, you can read the note or edit it by tapping the icon to the right of the To Do name field. If no note already exists, you can add one by selecting the task and choosing Record | Attach Note from the menu.

- **Due date** You might have tasks that need to be accomplished by a specific date. If this is the case, use the final column. If a dash is in that slot, this means you haven't yet assigned a due date. Tap it and choose a date. You can also change the due date in the same way.

NOTE *Watch out! The To Do List uses* month/date, *an unusual format in the U.S.*

- **Category** Change the category to which a task is assigned by tapping the Category column and choosing the desired category from the list.

NOTE *Some of these columns aren't displayed by default—to enable them, tap the Show button and choose the columns you want to appear in the To Do Preferences dialog box.*

Changing the View Options

If you're anything like us (and that could be a very, very bad thing, if you know what we mean), you may be perfectly happy with the default look of the To Do List. It's easy to modify, though. Tap the Show button and you see the To Do Preferences dialog box. Here are your options:

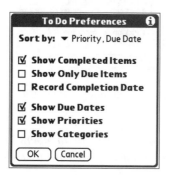

Sorting Options

The first item you encounter in the Preferences dialog box is a Sort By list. This determines the way the To Do List shows the tasks onscreen.

■ **Priority, Due Date** This groups all the priority 1 tasks first, then priority 2, and so on. Within each priority group, the earliest deadlines are listed first, and no-deadline tasks are listed last. This option works best if you need to work on tasks with the highest priority and due dates aren't particularly important to you.

■ **Due Date, Priority** This selection arranges all the tasks by due date, with the soonest due dates listed first and no due dates listed last. If several tasks have the same due date, they're listed by priority order. This is probably the best display option for most people—it lists your tasks with the ones due soonest at the top of the page and, within each due date, you can see the top priorities arranged first.

■ **Category, Priority** Arranges your tasks by category. The categories are arranged in alphabetical order. If you have more than one task in a given category, they're arranged in priority order within the category. Use this category if seeing tasks visually arranged into different categories— such as work and personal—is more important for you than arranging them by due date or category.

■ **Category, Due Date**   This selection also arranges your tasks by category, and the categories are arranged in alphabetical order. If you have more than one task in a given category, they're arranged by due date within the category. Soonest deadlines appear first, and no-due-date tasks are placed last within each category.

Using Filters to Customize the Display

The next section in the To Do Preferences dialog box controls what kind of tasks are displayed onscreen. Actually, that's not true, but we're trying to apply some logic to the way Palm chooses to group the items on this screen. Here's what each of these three items does:

■ **Show Completed Items**   As you check off tasks you complete, slowly but surely they clutter up your screen unless you do something about them. If you uncheck this option, completed items are hidden. If you need to see items you have completed, simply check Show Completed Items and they reappear.

NOTE   *If you hide completed tasks in this way, they're not deleted. They still take up memory on the Palm. Turn the page to find out how to delete old To Dos.*

■ **Show Only Due Items**   If you're concerned only about tasks due today, check this item. Any tasks with a due date after today disappear from the screen and reappear only on the day they're due.

CAUTION   *Be careful with this option because it hides To Dos from the screen that aren't due today, regardless of priority. It's easy to get caught off guard by a major deadline this way.*

■ **Record Completion Date**   This interesting little feature changes the due date of a completed item to the date it was completed. If you didn't assign a due date to a task, the completion date becomes the due date. In this way, you can track what day you completed each of your tasks.

CAUTION   *This option overwrites the due date with the completion date. You can't get the original due date back, even if you uncheck the task or turn off the Record Completion Date option.*

7

Modifying the Task Columns

As you probably already saw, you can tweak the data the To Do List shows you for each task in the list. That tweaking occurs here, in the last three options of the To Do Preferences dialog box. Your To Do List can look sparse, highly decorated, or anything in-between by changing the Show options.

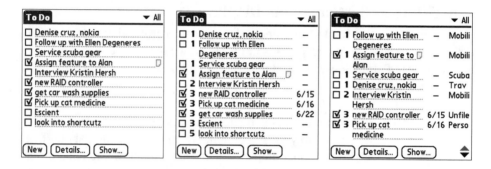

- ■ **Show Due Dates**   The due date format is day/month, which takes some getting used to. If you don't assign a due date to a task, you see a dash instead. On the To Do List, if you tap a due date you see a list for changing the date.

- ■ **Show Priorities**   This displays the priority to the left of the To Do name. The priority can be adjusted by tapping the number on the To Do List View.

- ■ **Show Categories**   The category of the task appears on the right edge of the To Do List View if you use this option. You can assign a category to an unfiled To Do (or change the category of a previously filed entry) by tapping the category name on the To Do List view.

Deleting Old To Dos

For most people, To Dos are not like diamonds—they don't last forever. After you check off a task that says "pick up a loaf of bread," how long do you need a record of having accomplished that goal? That's why your Palm provides a method of removing tasks you no longer want. The Palm offers you two ways to eliminate tasks:

- **Delete them one at a time**   If you need to delete only one To Do, tap in the To Do to select it. Now choose Record | Delete Item from the menu and the To Do is gone forever.

- **Delete a whole bunch at once**   If you use the To Do List a lot and occasionally develop a back list of dozens or hundreds of completed tasks, axing them one at a time could become a full-time job. Instead, purge them. A *purge* deletes all completed tasks. To purge your To Do List, choose Record | Purge from the menu. The Purge dialog box appears, asking if you really want to delete your completed To Dos. Tap OK.

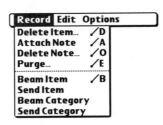

7

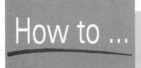 **Create Tasks on Your Handheld**

We've talked a lot about To Dos, so here's a summary of how to create tasks on your Palm:

1. Press the To Do button on the Palm.

2. Start writing—this creates a new To Do.

3. Tap the Details button.

If you want to, assign a priority, category, and due date on the Details dialog box. Tap OK to close this dialog box.

If you want to preserve a copy of your completed tasks, check Save Archive Copy on PC. If you later want to refer to deleted tasks, load the archive file (which is automatically created on the PC when you HotSync) into Palm Desktop when you need to refer to the entries. This works only if you do, in fact, synchronize with Palm Desktop instead of Outlook or another program.

Using To Dos in Palm Desktop

Who says the only place you can enter To Dos is on your Palm? Not us! The Palm Desktop—both the Windows and Mac versions—has a module dedicated to tracking your tasks. Using the Palm Desktop, you can enter To Dos and have them appear on your Palm when you're away from your desk.

The Windows To Do List

The To Do List's interface is a bit more spacious than the one in your Palm. As a result, the Palm Desktop pulls off a cool trick—it displays both the list itself and the contents of the Details dialog box onscreen simultaneously. Click a To Do and the details automatically update to show you more information about the particular task you selected.

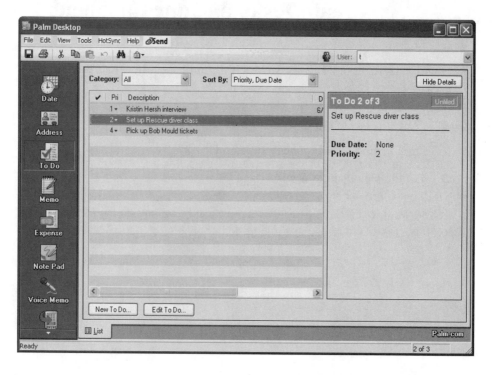

Turn To Dos into Appointments

Your Palm understands there's a tight relationship between your calendar and your To Do tasks. Switch to the Date Book in the Palm Desktop and you'll find the right side of the screen has a window for displaying either addresses or To Dos. Click the To Do box to show To Dos; click Address to return to the Phone Number Lookup mode. What good is that? Well, you can actually grab a To Do and drag and drop it into a calendar appointment. That lets you turn a task into a bona fide appointment. You can't go the other way, though, and turn an appointment into a task.

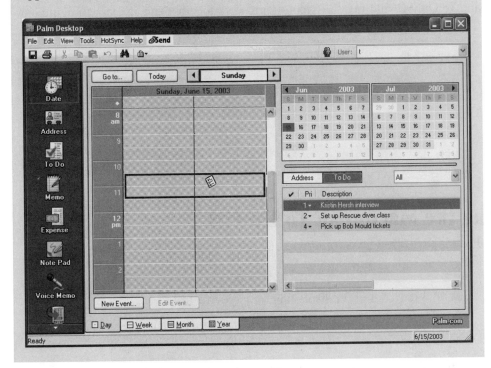

Creating and Editing To Dos

To create a new To Do, just click the New To Do button at the bottom of the screen. You'll see the New To Do dialog box, where you can enter text, assign priorities, and even set a due date for your task.

Using To Dos in Outlook

If you're an Outlook user, you probably already know that Palm's To Do items become Tasks in Outlook. In fact, that's pretty much all you need to know to use Outlook with your Palm. To see your To Dos in Outlook, click the Tasks icon in the Outlook Shortcuts bar. The tasks are also displayed in the Taskbar section of the Calendar.

Understanding Task Priorities

The Palm and Outlook use two slightly different ways of assigning priority to tasks and To Dos. Thankfully, the two systems work together and are easy to figure out. Use this guide to correlate the Palm and Outlook systems:

Palm	Outlook
1	High
2	Normal
3	Normal
4	Normal
5	Low

Using the Macintosh To Do List

The Mac's To Do List is composed of a few key elements and is shown in Figure 7-3.

- A View control for displaying only specific tasks.
- Filters for sorting and displaying the tasks, found at the top of each column.
- The task entry, which includes the name, priority, date, category, completion status, and note.

Creating and Editing Tasks

You can create a new task either by double-clicking anywhere in the Task View or by clicking the Create Task icon in the Palm Desktop toolbar. The Task dialog box

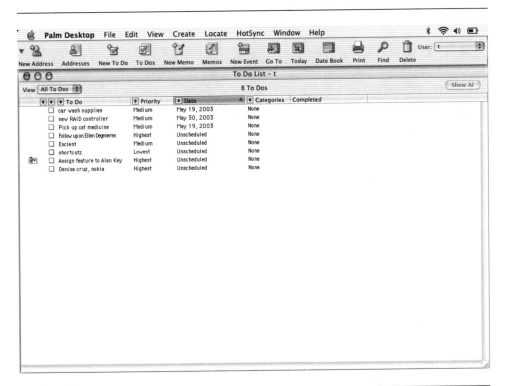

FIGURE 7-3 The Task List displays all of the pertinent information about your tasks on one screen.

has everything you need to complete your task, but it looks somewhat different than the Palm equivalent.

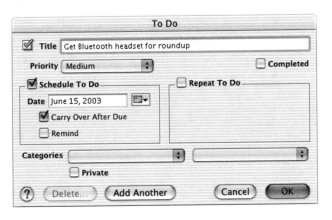

Here are a few things to watch for:

- **Priority** The Mac uses a word-based priority system (highest to lowest) instead of numbers (1 to 5). Highest corresponds to 1, and Lowest corresponds to 5.

- **Categories** Two categories are in the Mac's Palm Desktop, but only the first one is used by the Palm when you HotSync.

- **Carry Over After Due** Use this item to make sure the task is still visible after its deadline has passed. On the Palm, though, To Dos are always carried over anyway, so the Palm ignores this option.

- **Remind** You can set up the Palm Desktop to remind you about upcoming tasks, but the Palm doesn't use this feature.

 *If you need to create a task exactly like the one you just made—complete with scheduling and priority information—use the Add Another button on the Task dialog box instead of clicking OK. The current task gets saved, and a new task is created in the same mold as the one you just made.*

Repeating a Task

You can create a task that, like the Repeating Events in the Date Book, occurs over and over on a schedule you determine. To do this, create a new task and click Repeat Task in the Task dialog box. Select the kind of repetition you want from the list menu and you can set the task to repeat indefinitely or to repeat until a date you specify.

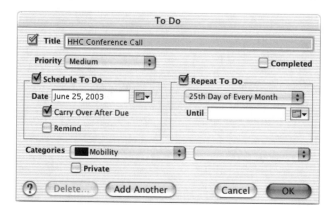

All the instances of a repeating task are transferred to your Palm when you HotSync, but they aren't related to each other on the Palm. This means if you later decide to change the series, the change occurs only to one task, not all of them. For this reason, use the Repeating Tasks with care.

Sorting and Filtering Your Tasks

You can customize the way your tasks are displayed by using the controls at the top of each column. If you want to see only some of the tasks, for instance, you can filter the display to show only certain entries. You can establish filters based on any column. To see only tasks with a priority of 1 (highest), for instance, choose Highest from the Priority column. Here's how:

1. Click the menu for the column you want to use as the filter criteria. You should see the filter and sorting menu.

2. If the criteria you want to sort appears on the menu, click it. If not, click Custom Filter. This displays the Custom Filter dialog box.

3. Choose the filter operator to accomplish what you want to do. If you want to display tasks that include the word "meeting," for instance, choose Contains and enter **meeting** in the field.

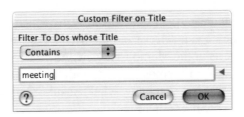

4. Click OK to close the dialog box and display the results.

7

Using the Memo Pad and Note Pad

As you've already seen, applications such as the Date Book, Address Book, and To Do List let you attach long notes to your entries. A note in the Address Book, for instance, enables you to list directions to the person's house, the names of all their kids, or 10 reasons not to visit them for Thanksgiving. But there's also an application designed to do nothing but create notes. These memos can be memory joggers, information you need to take on a trip, or anything not explicitly connected to an address, an appointment, or a To Do. The Memo Pad is your chance, in a sense, to color outside the lines and leave yourself any kind of message you want. And speaking of coloring, most Palm models also let you draw, sketch, doodle, and write notes in the Note Pad with "digital ink."

When should you use which program? Use the Memo Pad when you need to write a long note, but use the Note Pad when all you need to do is jot down a phone number you just heard on the radio, your hotel room number when you check in, or a street name you need to drive to later in the day.

The Saga of the Last Button

You know the drill by now; there are four buttons on the front of your Palm, and the last one should start the Memo Pad, right? Right.

Unless it doesn't. Depending upon which Palm model you own, it might be your new Palm is preprogrammed to launch the Note Pad. And some other models assign that button to something else entirely, like a Web browser. See Chapter 2 if you need a button refresher.

The solution, especially if you've already read about the To Do List, is obvious. After you get comfortable with your Palm and decide which apps you use most often, you can leave your Palm the way it is or reassign that program to launch the Memo Pad or Note Pad instead.

Viewing the Memo Pad

The Memo Pad has two views—the *Memo List* (which is, not surprisingly, a list of all the memos you created) and the *Memo View*, which shows you the contents of whatever memo you select from the Memo List. When you start the Memo Pad, it always starts in the Memo List view. As you can see in Figure 7-4, the Palm displays each of your memos in a list, with the first line of the memo visible as a kind of title that lets you know what's inside. Getting around is easy—just scroll up or down to see more memos.

FIGURE 7-4   The Memo List displays all of your memos.

   *If your memos are divided into more than one category, and if you have the Memo Pad assigned to one of the four buttons, every time you press the Memo Pad button, you'll switch categories. You can cycle through the first page of tasks in each category by repeatedly pressing the button.*

Cool Things to Do with the Memo Pad

Do you know what surprises us? Lots of things, actually. Dave is surprised Rick has no appreciation for the fine arts—specifically, bands such as *Pink Floyd,* the *Velvet Underground,* Kristin Hersh, and the *Throwing Muses.* (Inexplicably, Rick has an entirely different definition of "fine arts.")

More to the point, we're surprised at how many people can't seem to come up with good uses for the Memo Pad. They let it languish while they use the Address Book and Date Book all the time. To help you fully realize the potential of this cool little application, here are some helpful suggestions for how to use the Memo Pad:

- **A "Million Dollar Idea" memo**   Create a memo with a header that says **Million Dollar Ideas**. No matter when or where you come up with one of those incredibly amazing ideas to help you retire before you turn 50, pull out your Palm and jot it down.

- **Trade show category**   Got a lot of booths to visit at next month's lawn care trade show? Create a category and put all the memos for that event in the category. As you walk the show floor, you can reference your notes about the show in one easy-to-find set of memos.

- **Store passwords**   This one is dangerous, so make sure you make it private. But, if you have a lot of passwords you routinely need—for your ISP, Web sites, computer logons, and that kind of thing—you can store them all in one place in a memo for passwords. Note, we have to reiterate this is kind of dangerous—if your Palm is stolen, you can give all your passwords away if they're not protected properly. No IT department on Earth would sanction this particular tip, and we won't even admit to writing it down if questioned in court.

- **Meeting notes**   Take notes during a meeting and beam the memo to others when the meeting is over.

- **A "Phone Messages" memo**   Name a memo "Phone Messages" and when you check voice mail, jot down the notes in your Palm in this memo. If you're diligent about this, you won't end up with a million yellow stickies all over your desk after each VM-checking session. And names and phone numbers will be in your Palm where you need them, not splayed out all over your desk.

- **Store your new words**   Dave makes up new words in an effort to evolve the English language at a grassroots level. If you, too, make up new words frequently (and that's a beautiquious thing to do), store them in a "New Words" memo so you don't accidentally forget them. Chizzy! (Rick is working on a way to delete that particular memo from Dave's Palm, perhaps by using a large hammer.)

Creating New Memos

Sure, there's a New button at the bottom of the Memo List—but you don't need to use it. Start writing in the Graffiti area, and the Palm automatically switches from the Memo List View to the Memo View.

The memo can be as long as you want—up to 4,096 characters, or about 700 words. That's pretty long, and it should suit your needs most of the time. You can include blank lines and divide your memo into paragraphs—anything you need to make it logical and readable. If you need longer documents, consider getting an office suite, which we cover in Chapter 11.

> **TIP**   *You can't name your memos in the sense that you can save files on the PC with a specific filename, but the first line of the memo is what appears in the Memo List. To keep things neat and organized, you can write a brief description of the memo on the top line, and then start the memo itself on the next line.*

Using Editing Tools

The familiar cut, copy, and paste tools are available in every Palm app, but nowhere are they more important than in the Memo Pad, where you're likely to be writing more than a sentence or two. Remember, you don't have to create text from scratch all the time. Using these edit tools, you can move text from other applications and rearrange it to suit your needs.

Suppose, for example, you previously had a Date Book appointment that read

```
Meeting with Ted
```

Within that appointment, you might have created a note that looked like this:

```
Discuss performance review
Get feedback on budget for 2Q
Agree on approach for marketing plan
```

7

If you want to have a record of your meeting with Ted, take notes in a memo. Open the appointment note and select the three lines of text from the note. With the text selected, choose Edit | Copy from the menu (or you can use the Command gesture and write **C**). Then switch to the Memo Pad, create a new memo, and paste the text into the memo using Edit | Paste (or COMMAND-P using the Graffiti shortcut).

After pasting the text into the memo, you can use it as your agenda items—and insert notes as needed, giving you a complete record of the meeting. When you HotSync your Palm, you can paste that data into Word or some other application and generate a formal report.

Assigning Categories

After you accumulate a few memos, you might find the Memo List View getting a bit crowded. Clean it up with the Palm's ever-helpful category filing system. Assign a category like this:

1. Create a new memo.

2. Tap the Details button. The Memo Details dialog box appears.

3. Choose a category from the Category list.

4. Tap OK to close the Memo Details dialog box.

After your memos are arranged into categories, you can cycle through them easily by pressing the Memo Pad hard button on the Palm case.

Making a Memo Private

If you have private information stored in a memo, you can easily hide specific memos from prying eyes. The procedure is essentially the same as with other Palm applications. Do this:

1. In the Memo List, select a memo by tapping it.

2. Tap the Details button. You see the To Memo Details dialog box.

3. Tap the Private box to add a check mark. Now the entry is marked as private. Tap OK and you see this dialog box:

4. Tap OK to close the dialog box.

The memo probably isn't hidden yet—you still have one more step to go. To make your memo disappear, you need to enable the Private Records feature in the Security app. For details on how to do this, see Chapter 10.

Deleting Memos

No matter how much you like your memos, eventually you may need to delete some. To delete a memo, tap the memo you want to delete. Then choose Record | Delete Memo from the menu. The memo is then deleted from your Palm.

Arranging Memos in the Memo List

Computer users are, for the most part, fanatical organizers. We tend to spend hours straightening up the Desktop so icons appear in exactly the right place when the computer starts each morning. That said, we're sure you want to organize your memos. This isn't pointless busy work: if you need to open the same memo over and over, having the memo appear at the top of the list whenever you open the Memo List can help. At the very least, we're sure you'll want to understand how to take control of the way memos appear onscreen.

When you add memos to the Memo List, by default, the newest ones always appear at the end of the list. The default order of Memo List entries is essentially chronological, with the oldest entries at the top and the newest ones at the bottom.

It's a little more complicated than that, though. You can specify the sort order of memos by choosing Options | Preferences. You get two choices:

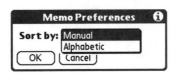

- ■ **Manual**   This is the default mode your Palm uses out of the box. New memos are added to the bottom of the list, but you can actually drag and drop memos to different positions in the list. Suppose you have a frequently used memo you want to appear at the top of the screen. Tap and hold the stylus on the entry, and then drag the stylus up to the position where you want it to appear. You should see a line move with the stylus, indicating where the memo will land if you release the stylus.

- ■ **Alphabetic**   This option sorts all entries into alphabetical order. If you select this option, the drag-and-drop method of moving memos won't work unless you revert to the manual method.

Blank Lines for Emphasis

Here's a trick you can try if you think the Memo List is too cluttered. If you use the manual ordering method and arrange your memos in a specific order in a near-fanatical way, you might be bothered by the fact that memo number 4 is "touching" memo number 5. Rick, for instance, is adamant about not eating his mashed potatoes if they come in contact with his peas. Maybe you suffer from the same kind of problem with your Palm.

Try this: Create a new memo with a blank first line. You have to enter at least one character on the second line, because the Palm doesn't let you create a completely blank memo. Close the memo and you see you've made a new memo with a blank header. Drag this memo between two memos you want separated and voilà—you've found a way to separate memos.

Working with Notes

The Note Pad is very similar to the Memo Pad. The major difference is this: instead of writing long messages in Graffiti, you're sketching or writing them directly on the screen, as if the stylus were a pen writing on paper. Though Note Pad gives you the freedom to write anything on the screen any way you like, keep in mind that you can't transform this "digital ink" into Graffiti. Your scribbles stay scribbles. When Note Pad starts, you'll see the Note List view (which looks a lot like the Memo Pad's Memo List view).

Creating a Note

To create a note, tap the New button at the bottom of the screen (you can also just start writing in the Graffiti area). Start your note by giving it a name. Unlike memos, all notes get their own unique subject line. By default, this subject begins with a "time stamp," though you can erase that if you want to.

When you're ready to draw, just write or sketch in the main part of the Palm display. Here are the controls at your disposal:

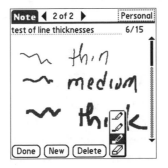

7

Alarming a Note

Unlike those yellow sticky notes you leave all over your office walls (clean up already—it looks like a pigsty!), the notes you leave in your Palm can actually buzz you at a certain time and date. Why on Earth would you want that to happen, you ask? Well, here's a good example:

You're stopped at a red light when you hear on the car radio that Diana Darby is playing a show in town in a few weeks. You'd love to go to the concert, so you whip out your Palm. The light will turn green in a moment, though, so you don't have a lot of time to write. Instead of trying your luck with Graffiti, you simply press the Note Pad button and scrawl "Call Joan" on the screen. Then you quickly choose Options | Alarm from the menu and choose Saturday at 10 A.M., which is when the tickets go on sale. Tap OK, and when Saturday morning rolls around, the Palm will turn on, bring your note to the front, and play the alarm. As you probably expect, you can accept the alarm or tap the snooze button:

Using Notes and Memos in Palm Desktop

You can create and review your notes and memos on the Palm Desktop. That's good, because many kinds of memos might come in handy on the desktop. If you took our advice from earlier in the chapter to create a Phone Messages memo, for instance, you'd appreciate the capability to type directly into the PC when the phone rings.

Using the Windows Memo Pad

Because the Palm has pretty limited real estate on the small screen, you have to switch between the Memo List and Memo View. But, on the Palm Desktop, you can see both at once. To see a memo, click the header on the left, and the memo's contents appear in the window on the right, as you can see in Figure 7-5. Double-clicking a memo opens the memo in its own window if you prefer to see it that way.

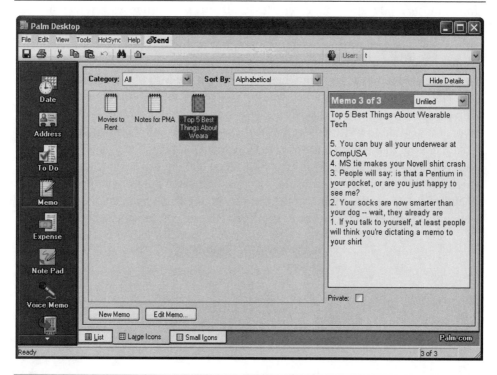

FIGURE 7-5   The Memo Pad lets you view your Palm's memos on the desktop, where you can edit them with your full-sized keyboard.

Most of the Memo Pad's operation is obvious. The controls aren't identical, though. Here are some things to remember:

■ You can't rearrange memos; you can sort them alphabetically or by the way they appear on the Palm. Use the Sort By drop-down menu at the top of the screen.

■ You can display memos in a list or by icons (like Outlook's Notes) using the tabs at the bottom of the screen.

Importing and Exporting Memos

You don't need to create memos from scratch. Heck, you don't even have to cut and paste to create a memo. The Palm Desktop lets you import text files from elsewhere on the computer. To import a text file, do this:

1. Choose File | Import. The Import dialog box appears.

2. Choose Text (*.txt) from the File of Type list box.

3. Find the file you want to import. It has to be a plain text file in ASCII format— no Word or other specially formatted file types are allowed. Select the file and click the Open button. You then see the Specify Import Fields dialog box.

4. The text file should be ready to import, with the text lined up with the Memo field. If it isn't, drag the Memo field on the left until it lines up like the one shown here:

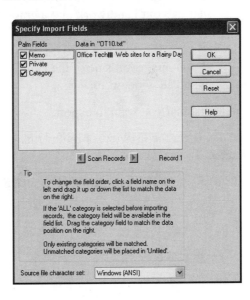

5. Click OK.

6. If your text file is too large to fit in a single memo, the Palm Desktop automatically divides it into multiple memos.

7. Click OK.

What about the other case—you have a memo and you'd like to get it into Microsoft Word? Piece of cake! Just right-click on a memo and choose Send To | MS Word from the menu. The text will automatically appear in a new blank document in Word.

 For the Send To feature to work, you need to have the Palmapp.dot template installed in Microsoft Word. Some folks delete that template and then are mystified when they can't send documents to Word. On the other hand, you can always get text into Word the old-fashioned way: copy and paste.

Using the Windows Note Pad

The Note Pad is a little more limited. You can't create notes on the desktop, for instance—all you can do is look at ones you created on your Palm. Notes won't alarm on the desktop, either, so if you want to be alerted when a note's time comes up, you'll have to have your Palm with you.

Besides looking at notes, you can also export them to a graphics program. Don't expect to stick one of these sketches into a high-resolution PowerPoint presentation, of course. A Note Pad image measures just 152×352 pixels, which is not enough to fill a computer screen. But getting your handiwork into a graphics program is easy. Just do this:

1. Press the Note Pad button on the left side of the Palm Desktop display. You should see the Note Pad window appear.

2. Find the note in the list that you want to export.

3. Right-click on the note (in the list view or on the image itself) and choose Copy from the menu.

4. Open your favorite image editing program and choose Edit | Paste from the menu.

Even if you synchronize your PDA with Outlook, you can still get your hand-drawn notes from the Note Pad section of the Palm Desktop—your PDA is smart enough to realize that notes aren't synchronized with Outlook, so it syncs them with Palm Desktop for you!

Using Memo Pad in Outlook

Outlook's Notes View is, like the Palm's Memo Pad, a place to store free-form notes of any kind. You can use it to record phone messages, jot down reminders, leave long-term documents (such as things to bring on a trip), or to remind yourself about Web sites you want to visit. It doesn't matter what you put in these notes. By default, Outlook's notes look like little sticky notes.

Quirks Between Outlook and Palm

Although the Outlook Notes View and Palm Memo Pad are perhaps the simplest of all the features in these two programs, there are a few things you should know to ensure everything works smoothly when you HotSync:

1. The Palm Memo Pad has a size limit—but Notes in Outlook don't. This means you can create a very long note in Outlook that doesn't transfer properly to the Palm. If you create a huge note in Outlook, only the first 4,096 characters appear in the Palm Memo Pad. You also see a warning saying this occurred in the HotSync log.

2. The Palm's categories aren't used by Outlook. This means your Palm memos, when they appear in Outlook as notes, are unfiled. The same is true in the other direction.

Look Ma, No Scroll Bar!

Outlook's notes have an annoying glitch—lacking scroll bars, it's hard to read a long note that trails off the bottom of the sticky note window. Don't know what we're talking about? Copy a long Word document into a new note. Or create a really long Palm memo and HotSync. You'll find the text extends beyond the bottom of the note window in Outlook and there's no scroll bar to scroll down to read it all.

The solution is deceptively simple: click in the note window to place the cursor in the note, and then use the down arrow key on the keyboard to scroll through the document. Or make the note's window larger, so it can show more text.

Why do we mention this? Rick didn't realize there was any way to scroll through the document at all—he thought anything that didn't fit in the sticky note window was totally inaccessible—until Dave showed him the keyboard arrow trick. So, if you were ever perplexed by the missing memo text, now you are at least as smart as Rick (fill in your own jokes here).

Creating Memos on Macintoshes

The Memo List is the Mac's unique version of the Note Pad. It's more flexible and powerful than the Windows version, but there's a downside—the Palm Desktop for the Mac does not have a conduit to sync Note Pad drawings. That means you can only transfer text notes—not sketched Notes—from the Memo Pad to your Mac.

Creating and Editing Memos

You can use memos on the Mac just like on the Palm—to track phone messages, leave yourself yellow sticky notes, or nearly anything else. To create a new note, you can use either one of these techniques:

- Double-click on a black space in the Memo List. The Memo dialog box appears, which you can fill in and close when you finish (there's no OK button to save the changes).

- Click the New Memo icon on the Palm Desktop toolbar.

To create a note, fill out the Title field, and then enter information in the body of the message. The title becomes the first line of the note on the Palm, not unlike the way we recommended you create a title for your note on the first line of the note, earlier in this chapter. In addition, watch for these other differences between the Palm and Mac versions of the note:

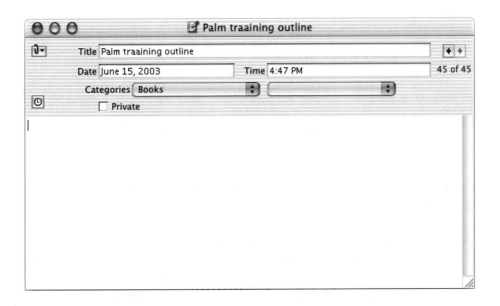

- **Date and time fields**   The date and time fields don't get transferred to the Palm because the Palm doesn't remember when you created a note.

- **Date stamping**   A date stamp icon in the Note dialog box inserts the current date and time in the body of the note. You can use this to create a log or a journal-like note. This data is stored in the body of the message, so it does get transferred to the Palm during a HotSync.

- **Categories**   Two categories are in the Mac's Palm Desktop, but only the first one is used by the Palm when you HotSync.

- **Length**   The Mac can accommodate extremely long notes, but only the first 4,096 characters are transferred to the Palm.

- **Attachment gripper**   You can drag the gripper to another item to attach the note—we discuss this in more detail soon.

Attaching Memos

Attaching memos is a bit different on the Mac than on the PC or Palm. Specifically, you're not limited to memos but, instead, you can attach any kind of item to any other kind of item. You can attach a memo to a contact, of course—that even works on the Palm and the PC Palm Desktop—but you can also attach an address to a memo or a task to a calendar appointment. There's no limit on how you attach stuff.

 *This may sound odd, but you can actually attach a memo to another memo. This can come in handy if you have related information in different memos and want to connect them to each other.*

This flexibility makes managing your life on the Mac easy, but an important caveat exists: most of those attachments won't get transferred to the Palm properly. Remember these rules about attachments and the Palm:

- The only kind of attachment that will HotSync to your Palm is a note attached to an item created in one of the other three primary apps (Address Book, To Do, or Date Book). Any other kind of attachment (such as a task attached to an appointment) is ignored during the HotSync.

- For the note to attach, you must name it exactly like one of these titles: "Handheld Note: Address Book," "Handheld Note: Date Book," or "Handheld Note: To Do Item." After you name the note with one of those titles, you can attach it to another item.

You can attach a note or other item in several ways on the Palm Desktop. Each way has its advantages—use the method that works best for you at any given time.

- **Drag an item onto another item**   If you can see both windows onscreen at once, then the easiest way to attach an item to another one is to grab the first item and drag it onto the second item, and then release the mouse.

- **Use the Attach To menu item**   Open the item you want to attach to something else, and then click the paperclip icon. Choose Attach To | Existing Item. You should see the Attach Existing Item dialog box appear at the bottom of the screen. Now, open the item you want to attach it to, and drag the item from the Attach Existing Item dialog box onto it. This might sound convoluted, but it makes sense when you can't easily display both items onscreen at once.

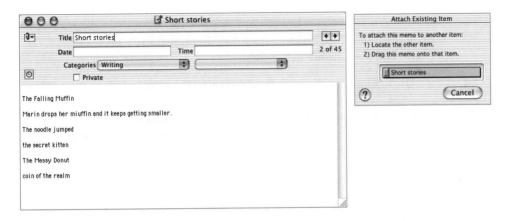

- ■ **Drag an item to the toolbar**   If you want to attach an existing item to one you haven't created yet, use this method. Grab the item and drag it to the Palm Desktop toolbar. As you move the item across the toolbar, you find it highlights the Create icons for each kind of item. Drop it on the icon that represents the item you want to create. The new item appears with the old item automatically attached. Or, you can achieve the same result by clicking the item's paperclip icon and choosing Attach To. Then choose the appropriate item, such as New Appointment or New Task.

Sorting and Filtering Your Notes

You can customize the way notes appear on the screen by using the controls at the top of each column. This feature works just like the filtering tools you've probably already seen in the Contact List and Task List. Essentially, this lets you hide note entries you don't want to see using a set of easy-to-use filters. Here's how it works:

1. Decide what basis you want to use to filter your notes. Suppose, for instance, you want to see only notes with a specific word in the title. You'd obviously want to use the Title column. Click the menu for the appropriate column. You should see the Sort and Filter menu.

2. If the criteria you want to filter appears in the menu, click it (if you were displaying only today's notes, for instance, there's an entry for that in the Date menu). If not, click Custom Filter, which displays the Custom Filter dialog box.

3. Choose the filter operator to accomplish what you want to do. If you want to display memos that include the word "home," for instance, choose Contains and enter **home** in the field.

4. Click OK to close the dialog box and display the results.

TIP   *You can create detailed filters by combining different columns. You can apply a filter to both the Title and Date columns, for instance. Anything that passes the first filter must then also pass the second filter to appear in the Memo List.*

The View menu includes another option you may want to use. As we already discussed, attached notes on the Palm look different and can get in the way. That's why the View menu features an option to display only Desktop Notes. If you choose this option, an entry that conforms to the Palm standard for attachments—that is, it starts with the words "Handheld Notes:"—won't appear in the list.

Chapter 8

The Rest of the Palm OS Team

How to...

- Access security features
- Set records as private
- Hide or show private records
- Set a security password
- Password-protect your Palm device
- Find third-party security measures for your Palm and data
- Use the Find feature
- Find third-party utilities that extend your search capabilities
- Use the calculator
- Find third-party calculators
- Decide whether or not to use the Mail applet
- Use a Palm device to track expenses
- Use the Expense auto-complete feature
- Use Expense to track mileage
- Make effective use of categories
- Synchronize your expenses with Excel
- Synchronize your expenses on a Macintosh
- Find other expense-management software and solutions

Now that we've looked at the stars of the Palm OS—the Address Book, Date Book, Memo and Note Pads, and To Do List—let's turn our attention to the supporting cast. We're talking about the Security program, which enables you to hide private records and "lock" your Palm device; the Find feature, a search tool that helps you quickly sift through all your data; the calculator, which, big surprise, calculates; and the potentially mystifying Mail program, which is used to send and receive e-mail— sort of. We also give you the full scoop on the often-ignored Expense program.

NOTE
We designed this chapter as a kind of catch-all, a place to cover programs that don't really fit into specific categories or require their own chapters. That said, there may be programs bundled with your handheld that aren't covered here—or anywhere else in the book. That's because different manufacturers bundle different software with different models, and it's impossible to cover everything. We do, however, cover the really important extras that are common to all models—and Security is foremost on the list.

Palm Security

At the risk of sounding like a spy novel, listen up, 007. If your data falls into the wrong hands, it could spell disaster for *M, Q,* and lots of other letters of the alphabet. Fortunately, we've outfitted your Palm device with foolproof security measures. Only you will have the access codes. Only you can view Heather Graham's phone number. (Can we have it? Please? Please?)

In all seriousness, it's not unlikely that you'll be storing some sensitive information in your Palm device—information that should be kept private. Important passwords, account numbers, meeting locations, contact data—these are among the items you'd be loathe to let a stranger see. Fortunately, the Palm OS offers two effective ways to protect your data: marking individual records as private and locking your Palm every time you turn it off.

In both scenarios, you—or anyone who's trying to access your Palm—must supply a password to gain access. It's a bit of a hassle to have to enter it over and over again, but at least you have the comfort of knowing your Palm and data are totally secure.

TIP
Although you may want to familiarize yourself with the Palm OS's built-in security capabilities, we prefer some of the third-party solutions you can download and install. See "Other Security Software" later in this chapter for the scoop on those appealing alternatives.

Security 101

To get started with Palm security, find and tap the Security icon.

NOTE
In Palm models such as the Tungsten C and Zire 71 (those with Palm OS 5.2 or later), there is no separate Security icon. Instead, the Security option is accessible from within Prefs (see Chapter 2). Other than that, everything's the same.

8

You'll see the screen shown in Figure 8-1 (or something like it—it may look a bit different depending on which version of the Palm OS you have). The first step is choosing a password. Notice that the Password box currently says "Unassigned"— meaning simply that you haven't entered your password yet. Before you do, read a little further.

What You Should Know About Passwords

The password you choose can be any combination of letters, numbers, symbols, and spaces. You can make it "Spock" or "H4T*Q" or "The quick brown fox." Ideally, it should be something reasonably short, because you'll probably wind up writing it frequently. Don't make it too obvious, like "123," but you could use something as simple as the last four digits of your Social Security number or your favorite *Star Trek Voyager* character.

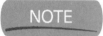

Capitalization doesn't matter. Even if you make a point to capitalize "Spock" when you enter it as your new password, you can write "spock" to unlock your Palm and it'll work just fine.

Whatever password you decide on, it's vital that it be something you can easily remember. If you forget it, you could wind up unable to access certain records—or your entire Palm device! Thus, if you have even the slightest concern that you might forget your password, write it down on a piece of paper and store it in a safe place. Better safe than sorry.

FIGURE 8-1   In Security, you select a password for use in hiding private records and locking your Palm device.

Working with Passwords

Okay, let's enter a new password on your Palm device. Just tap the "Unassigned" box, and then use Graffiti or the onscreen keyboard to enter your desired password.

At this time you're also asked to supply a hint. If you use, say, your mother's maiden name as your password, you should put "mother's maiden name" in the Hint field. This hint appears when an incorrect password is entered.

Note the warning that's included here: "If you assign a password, you must enter it to show private records." This sounds a little scary, but don't worry—none of your existing records will immediately be affected by your selection of a password. Only when you mark one as private, as we explain later, does your password enter into play.

After you tap OK, you'll be asked to verify the new password by entering it again. And you'll see another warning about what'll happen if you forget your password. The moral of the story is, *don't forget your password!*

Tap OK again, and notice that the Password box now reads "Assigned."

TIP *You can tap this box again at any time to change or delete your password, but you have to supply the original one first.*

Now, when you mark records as private, they become hidden from view, requiring your password to reveal them. Additionally, if you use the "Lock & Turn Off..." option (as detailed in the following section), you'll need to supply your password the next time you turn on your Palm.

SHORTCUT *If you tap the "abc" button in the bottom-left corner of the Graffiti area, the onscreen keyboard will appear. You can use this to enter your password!*

The "Lost Password" Button

Oh, the perils of the forgotten password. For the last time, just don't forget yours, okay? If you do, there's a scary but effective way to reestablish access to those records you've marked as private. In Security, when you tap the "Assigned" button under Password, you're prompted to enter your password. You also see a "Lost Password" button. Tap it, and your password will be deleted—and all your marked-as-private records along with it. Zoiks! However, those deleted records will be restored on your Palm device the next time you HotSync.

Password-Protecting Your Entire Handheld

If you really want to secure what's stored in your Palm device, you need to password-protect the entire thing, not just certain records. That's where "locking" comes into play. When activated, your Palm becomes locked the next time it's turned off. Translation: When the Palm is turned on again, a screen pops up requiring the password (see Figure 8-2). Without it, there's no getting past that screen.

Danger, Will Robinson, Danger!

The Palm Operating System's built-in security features are far too weak for the corporate environment. Consider the password, for instance. There's no mandatory length or required combination of letters or numbers: users can create a password from just a single character, sure to send any system administrator into heart failure.

Passwords are also easy to bypass. A free utility called *No Security,* for instance, can easily circumvent the Palm security application, erasing the Palm's password and exposing all of the private records on the device. It's billed as a way to recover data if you've lost your password, but the reality is that such programs make it all too easy for thieves to retrieve sensitive data on a lost, stolen, or unguarded PDA. There's no need even to HotSync the device to install the app; No Security can be beamed from another handheld.

No Security won't let someone turn on a locked Palm, but some Palm hardware vendors have customized the security feature to defeat even that slim measure of security. The Samsung I300 smartphone, for instance, lets users turn on a locked device by resetting the password to the default password, usually the I300's phone number. If you know the phone number, you can get in without a hitch.

The moral of the story? Be careful what kind of data you store on your handheld, and take extra measures to protect it if it's valuable. Read on to learn about the software and techniques you need.

FIGURE 8-2   When you "lock" your Palm, only the correct password will unlock it.

NOTE   *You can modify the information that appears on this "locked" startup screen by going to Prefs | Owner (see Chapter 2 for a refresher). We recommend including your name and phone number, and maybe even a reward offer—all so that anyone who might find your lost Palm device will have an easier time returning it (and an incentive to do so). What's a good reward? Considering how much a new Palm would cost you, we think no less than $20.*

Auto Lock Handheld

Palm OS 4.0 and later includes several automated locking options, all of them accessible by tapping the Auto Lock Handheld button in the main Security screen. Here's a quick rundown:

- **Never**   No automatic locking.

- **On power off**   The moment you turn your handheld off (or it shuts off after a few minutes of inactivity), it locks.

- **At a preset time**   Set the handheld to lock at an exact time. For example, if you use it a lot during the day, but rarely at night, you might set it to lock at, say, 6 P.M. That way, you won't have to keep entering your password all day.

- **After a preset delay**   This is our favorite option. It locks the handheld after a period of inactivity—ten minutes, three hours, whatever you choose.

The "Current Privacy" Menu

We've saved the Current Privacy option until last because it relates to the upcoming section on hiding and masking individual records. Simply put, when the Hide option is selected, all records you've marked as private will disappear from view. When you select Mask, private records are hidden but still listed. When you select Show, which you need your password to do, private records are made visible.

 *The Mask option was added to Security in Palm OS 3.5. If you have an earlier version, you may want to consider upgrading— masking is a far better solution than hiding.*

Hiding and Masking Your Records

In the main applications—Address Book, Date Book, Note Pad, Memo Pad and To Do List—any record can be marked private, meaning it suddenly becomes masked or invisible and, therefore, inaccessible. Here's how:

1. Select a record (just by tapping it) in any of the aforementioned programs.

2. Tap the Details button. (In Address Book, you have to tap Edit to get to the screen with the Details button.) You'll see a window containing some options for that record—and a box labeled Private.

3. Tap that box, noticing the check mark that appears. This indicates that the record will become private after you tap OK.

4. Tap OK.

Remember, marking a record as private has no effect unless you've chosen one of the two privacy options in the Security program. If it's set to Mask Records, records you've marked as private will turn into solid gray bars. If you choose

Hide Records, records will just plain disappear. (Don't freak out—they're still in memory, just not visible.)

The Difference Between Masking and Hiding

The Mask Records option provides a middle ground between the visibility of "shown" records and the total invisibility of "hidden" records (which appear to have been wiped from existence—great security, but awfully inconvenient). Masked records still appear in your phone list, memo pad, and so forth but appear as solid gray bars (see Figure 8-3). This remains a less-than-stellar solution, because there's still no way to know what lies beneath until you tap the record and enter your password.

The Hide Records option goes a major step further, removing marked-as-private records from view altogether. To make them visible again, you must return to Security and select Show Records. Naturally, you'll need to supply your password at this time.

Passwords on the Desktop

Security isn't limited to the Palm device itself. It also extends to Palm Desktop, working in much the same ways. Thus, you can hide certain records or password-protect the entire program. The same password you've selected for your Palm device will automatically be used in Desktop.

FIGURE 8-3   When you choose Mask Records, all records marked as private are hidden by gray bars.

Unfortunately, this is an area in which Mac users get the short shrift. Palm Desktop for Macintosh doesn't include any security features whatsoever. Although you can still keep your data protected on your Palm, anyone who has access to your computer has access to your info (unless you've installed some third-party security software).

 Only Palm Desktop is affected by masked and hidden records. If you synchronize with Microsoft Outlook or another third-party contact manager, records marked as private on your Palm device will still be visible on your PC.

Hidden Records

Whenever you HotSync, any records marked as private on your Palm will become hidden in Palm Desktop—and vice versa. To change whether private records are visible or not, click the View menu, and then select the desired option: Hide, Mask, or Show.

Password-Protecting Palm Desktop

Just as you can lock your Palm, so can you lock Palm Desktop. When you do, and then exit the program, your password will be required the next time it's started—by you or anyone else. Here's how to activate this setting:

1. Make sure Palm Desktop is running, and then click Tools | Options.

2. In the tabbed dialog box that appears, click the Security tab.

3. Click the box that says "Require Password To Access The Palm Desktop Data."

4. Click OK, and then exit Palm Desktop.

 This security setting applies only to your *data. If multiple users are sharing Palm Desktop on a single PC, they'll need to implement password protection for their own user profiles.*

Other Security Software

Although the Palm Operating System's built-in security features are fairly comprehensive, there's always room for improvement. Hence the availability of numerous third-party security programs, which generally offer greater versatility and/or convenience. Here we spotlight some of the more intriguing solutions.

How to ... Keep Others from Accessing Palm Desktop

Suppose you step away from your desk for lunch or a meeting. You don't want coworkers or corporate spies poking around through your records. Fortunately, there's an easy way to password-protect Palm Desktop for Windows (alas, the Macintosh version has no security features). Choose Tools | Options, click the Security tab, and check the box marked Require Password To Access The Palm Desktop Data. Now, whenever someone starts Palm Desktop, he must input the correct password (which is the one you created on your handheld) to access your data.

Passwords Plus

8

Your Palm can be a handy place to store account numbers, PIN numbers, passwords, and other secret codes, but stuffing them all into a memo isn't the most practical solution. DataViz's Passwords Plus, one of Rick's personal favorites, is designed expressly to organize and protect your important numbers and passwords. You need to remember only one password (different from the one used by Palm Security) to access all this neatly categorized information. Passwords Plus also has a Windows-based counterpart, so you can manage and access the information on your PC.

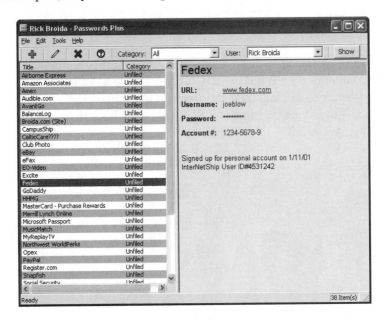

Rick is a fan of Passwords Plus, but Dave likes Chapura's Cloak—a similar product. It's worth checking out if you're interested in this kind of security. And these two are by no means the only choices. Visit PalmGear.com and search for "security software" to see some others.

OnlyMe

Like Security on steroids, OnlyMe locks your Palm device automatically whenever it's turned off. Your password is entered by tapping on a special six-button keypad, or by pressing the Palm's buttons in a particular sequence, or by entering certain letters or numbers in the Graffiti area. You can even create a password that's based on sliding your stylus over the special keypad. Best of all, OnlyMe lets you set a "lock delay," so that your Palm won't lock until after a designated period of time has elapsed.

Sign-On

Passwords can be guessed or discovered, but it's a lot harder to duplicate your signature. Communication Intelligence Corp.'s Sign-On automatically locks your Palm when it's turned off, and then requires you to sign your name—right on the Palm's screen—to unlock it again. This is a great choice for those concerned about forgetting their password.

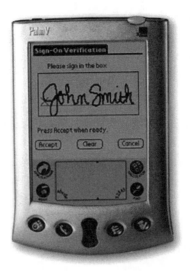

The Find Feature

The more you use your Palm device, the more data you're likely to wind up storing. And the more data you have, the harder it can be to expediently find what you're looking for. Some examples:

- A couple days ago, you set up a meeting a few weeks in the future, and now want to check the details of that meeting. Must you page through your calendar a day at a time to find the entry?

- You have dozens of memos and need to find the ones containing the word "sponge." Must you open each memo individually?

- You have 1,500 names in your address list and want to quickly find the record for that guy named Apu whose last name and company you can't remember. How will you locate him?

Using the Palm Operating System's built-in Find feature, you can unearth all this information in a snap. True to its name, Find sifts through your databases to ferret out exactly what you're looking for, be it a name, a number, a word, a phrase, or even just a few letters.

As we showed you in Chapter 2, Find can be found in the lower-right corner of the Graffiti area, represented by a little magnifying-glass icon. Using it couldn't be simpler: Tap it (at any time, no matter what program you're running), and then write in what you want to search for (see Figure 8-4).

Capitalization doesn't matter. Even if you're looking for a proper name like "Caroline," you needn't capitalize the first letter.

If you use your stylus to highlight a word or chunk of text (done much the same way you select text using a mouse), that text will automatically appear in the Find field when you tap the Find icon.

The search process should take no more than a few seconds, depending on how many records you have on your Palm device and the complexity of your search criteria.

How Find Works

When you execute a search, the Palm OS looks through all stored records (except those marked as private) for whatever text you've specified, starting with whatever program you were in when you tapped the Find icon. It looks not only in the main databases—those used by Address Book, Memo Pad, and so forth—but also in the databases associated with any third-party software you may have installed.

FIGURE 8-4   Looking for a specific word? Just write it in the Find box and the Palm will find it for you.

If you're looking for, say, a phone number, you can save a lot of time by loading the Address Book before tapping Find. That's because Find starts its search in whatever program is currently running.

Keep in mind that Find searches only the beginnings of words. Thus, if you look up "book," it will find "bookcase" but not "handbook." There are third-party programs that can perform much more thorough searches—we talk about some of them in the next section.

You can make your data a bit more "Find friendly" by using special modifiers. For instance, you might use the letters AP to preface any memo that has to do with Accounts Payable. Then, when you do a search for "AP," you'll quickly unearth all the relevant records.

Running a Search

After you've written the desired search text in the Find box and tapped OK, the Palm will get to work. You'll see items appear in a categorized list as they're found. If you see what you're looking for, you can halt the search immediately by tapping the Stop button. Then, simply tap the item to bring up the corresponding record in the corresponding program.

If the Palm finds more instances of the desired item than can fit on the screen at once, it will stop the search until you tap the Find More button. This essentially tells it to look up another screen's worth of records. There's no way to backtrack— to return to the previous screen—so make sure you need to keep searching before tapping Find More. (You can always run the search again if need be, but that's a hassle.)

Third-Party Search Programs

Many users find that Find isn't nearly as robust as it could be. If you want to maximize the search potential of your Palm device, one of the following third-party programs might be in order. They're a little on the advanced side, meaning they require the program X-Master (which we talk about in Chapter 12). That doesn't mean you should shy away from them, just that they might prove a little more complicated to install and operate.

Most Hacks don't work with Palm OS 5, and these are no exception.

FindHack

The Rolls Royce of search programs, Florent Pillet's FindHack lets you specify whether to search all the installed applications, just the main applications, or just the current application. It also remembers the last six searches you ran, lets you preconfigure up to four "permanent" searches, and supports the use of wildcards. Best of all, it's faster than Find.

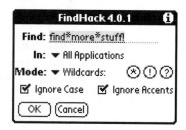

Find Ignore Hack

This simple Hack lets you select applications that should *not* be searched during the Find process. Why would you want to do this? E-books are a great example: if you have a few of them loaded on your Palm device, they can slow a search considerably. With Find Ignore Hack, you could exclude your e-book viewer.

 *While a potential lifesaver, Find Ignore Hack is an older program that is unsupported by its author, so use at your own risk. On the other hand, it's a free risk, because the software is freeware.*

IntelligentFind

Quite possibly the most sophisticated Find replacement ever, IntelligentFind allows you to ask questions in English ("What is Dave Johnson's phone number?") and displays the results ranked by the relevance to your questions. When in "simple" mode, IntelligentFind will search your handheld for multiple words and/or phrases at the same time, just like a Web search engine. We'd have to call this the power-user's "find" tool.

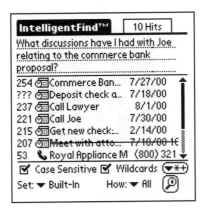

The Calculator

What's an electronic organizer without a calculator? Not much, so let's take a quick peek at the Palm's. Activated by tapping the Calc icon, Calculator operates like any other (see Figure 8-5). In fact, it's so self-explanatory that we're not going to insult your intelligence by explaining how to use it.

There are, of course, one or two features we feel obligated to point out. First, you can use the standard Palm copy option to paste the result of any calculation into another program. Second, you can review your last few calculations by tapping Menu | Options | Recent Calculations.

 *Calc's buttons are large enough that you can tap them with a fingernail, so save time by leaving the stylus in its silo. Just keep in mind that oil and dirt from your fingers will grubby-up the screen.*

The Palm Calculator functions like every other calculator you've ever used.

Third-Party Calculators

Whether you're a student, realtor, banker, or NASA engineer, there's no debating the value of a good scientific and/or programmable calculator. Your Palm device has ample processing power to fill this role, and the proof is in the dozens of third-party calculators currently available. Let's take a look at some of the best and brightest.

LoanMax

Think the car salesman is sharking you? Need an amortization schedule to maximize your house payments? At times like these, a good loan calculator is worth its weight in gold. LoanMax makes it simple to calculate payments based on interest rate, loan term, down-payment amount, and so on. It can also generate on-the-spot amortization schedules (though, unfortunately, you can't save or print them). Not bad for a $10 piece of software.

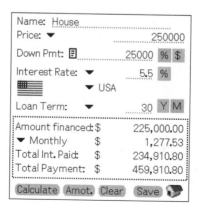

The powerOne Series

Infinity Softworks offers a series of task-specific calculators: powerOne Finance, powerOne Graph, powerOne Scientific, and so on. They vary in price and capability, so visit the company's Web site to see which one meets your needs.

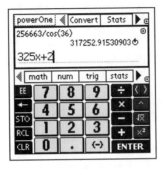

SynCalc

A fully algebraic calculator, Synergy Solutions' SynCalc offers a unique plug-in architecture that allows new functionality to be added. As it stands, SynCalc is already plenty powerful, with algebraic parsing of expressions, a full suite of trigonometric and logarithmic functions, and support for up to 100 macros that simplify the execution of complex calculations.

The Mail Program

An underrated member of the Palm's supporting cast of characters—er, programs— is Mail. We're going to teach you to use it in Chapter 10, but a brief bit of explanation is in order now. Specifically, Mail enables you to read, compose, and send e-mail, but not in the traditional sense. That is, Mail isn't capable of connecting to your

Internet service provider (ISP) via a Palm modem and conducting e-mail transactions. Rather, it merely synchronizes with your desktop e-mail program, such as Eudora or Outlook Express, absorbing copies of messages you've received and transferring outgoing messages you've written.

The Palm m100 doesn't come with the Mail program, and many other models don't have it preloaded. Instead, you must install it separately from the software CD, where it's sometimes called HotSync Mail. Some of the latest models, like the Zire 71, don't come with Mail at all. Instead, they have a product called VersaMail (see Chapter 10).

In practical terms, this means that your Palm serves as a kind of portable e-mail viewer. Here's an example: in the morning, before heading off to work or the airport, you HotSync with your PC. All the e-mail messages you received the night before are transferred to your handheld. Throughout the day, you read through those messages and reply to those that require it. You can even compose new messages if the need arises. Later, when you return home, you HotSync once again, and all the outgoing messages are transferred to your desktop e-mail program, and then sent. See Chapter 10 to learn all about Mail—when to use it, why to use it, and how to use it.

If you own a smartphone or a PDA that has some kind of wireless Internet connection, that obviously eliminates the need for Mail, because you can send and receive messages directly. You'll use a different program for that—Mail is designed to work solely via HotSync.

Expense Management

Expense is an often-overlooked but decidedly valuable addition to the Palm software arsenal. With it, you can track and manage all your expenses and mileage, whether for personal reconciliation or reimbursement from your company or clients. Although a bit on the rudimentary side, Expense does afford quick and easy item entry and direct synchronization with Palm Desktop. It can also export items to Microsoft Excel, creating detailed and attractive-looking expense reports that are ready to print.

Getting Started with Expense

Put simply, Expense is like an electronic folder for your receipts and a logbook for your mileage. Whenever you buy something, you simply add it to your expense list. Whenever you take a business-related road trip, you do the same. On the Palm side, using Expense is a piece of cake. (Using it with Palm Desktop is just as easy, but we'll talk about that a little later.)

Creating New Expense Items

Adding new expense records is a snap. Here's the basic process:

1. Tap "New" to create a blank expense item. You see a line appear with the date, the words "-Expense type-", and a blank field next to a dollar sign. Note that your cursor appears in that field.

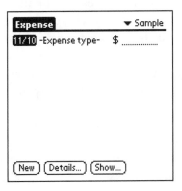

2. Write in the amount of the purchase or, if you're recording mileage, the number of miles driven.

3. Now, tap the words "-Expense type-" to see a predefined list of expense categories, and choose the one that most closely matches your purchase.

8

If you're recording mileage, select that option, noticing that the dollar sign changes to the abbreviation "mi."

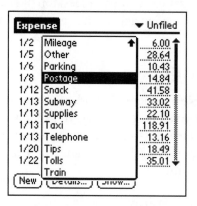

NOTE   *Unlike most lists that appear in Palm applications, the Expense list cannot be modified or expanded. In short, you're stuck with the categories provided. If you can't find one that fits the situation, there's always the "Other" category.*

   4. By default, any new expense is created with the current date. If, however, you're catching up on previous purchases, you can tap right on the date that's shown to bring up the calendar and select whatever date is appropriate.

There, wasn't that easy? You've just recorded a new expense. Now let's talk about recording the more specific details of that expense.

TIP   *You can save yourself a step when you create a new expense by not tapping the New button first. Instead, just start writing the dollar amount in the numeric portion of the Graffiti area. A new expense item is instantly created. This same practice also works in Date Book, Memo Pad, and To Do List.*

Modifying Expense Details

Obviously, any expense report worth its salt needs to have more than just the date, expense type, and amount. As you probably guessed, your next stop after entering these tidbits is the Details button.

NOTE   *Before tapping it, make sure you select the expense item you want to modify. You know when an item is selected because the date is highlighted and a cursor appears in the Amount field.*

The Receipt Details screen (see Figure 8-6) lets you specify the minutiae of your purchase, from the category to which it belongs to the type of currency used to the city in which it took place.

Expense in Palm Desktop

As with the other core Palm applications (Address Book, Memo Pad, and so on), Expense synchronizes its data with Palm Desktop every time you HotSync. Likewise, any additions or changes you make in Palm Desktop are reflected on your handheld.

> **NOTE**   *Older versions of Palm Desktop don't include direct synchronization with Expense—one more reason to upgrade. Visit Palm's Web site (www.palm.com/ us/software) to download the latest version of Palm Desktop.*

As you can see in Figure 8-7, Palm Desktop keeps your Expense entries in a neat list. If you click the tabs at the bottom of the screen, you can view the items as icons (large or small), which can help you get an at-a-glance overview of the kinds of expenses you've incurred. If you need a hard copy, just choose Print from the File menu. You can choose to print an expense summary, a list of expense details, or both.

From Expense to Excel

You can also export your Expense data to Microsoft Word or Excel, provided you have those programs installed on your PC. This can be helpful if you need to include your Expense data in a preformatted invoice or spreadsheet. To start the process, click Edit | Send To, then choose MS Word or MS Excel from the list that appears. That's all there is to it!

FIGURE 8-6   You can record any or all of the crucial details of your expense in the Receipt Details screen.

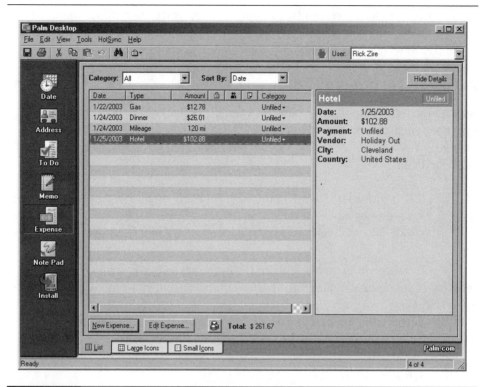

FIGURE 8-7   Palm Desktop displays and organizes your Expense data, just as it does with your addresses, appointments, and so on.

Just Don't Take Away My...

Most people come to have a single favorite program for their handhelds, be it the Address Book, the Expense program, or, in Dave's case, his beloved Hello Kitty game. In case you're wondering what else we'd be loathe to live without...

Rick: I'm a huge fan of e-books, and the combination of Palm Reader (see Chapter 14) and the Palm Digital Media e-bookstore allows me to read just about any mainstream book on my handheld. In fact, if there's a new book out that sounds appealing, instead of heading to Amazon, I'll visit Palm Digital Media and see if it's available. I can read an excerpt online or even download it to my handheld. You can take away my Calendar, Note Pad, and my Expense program—just don't take away my e-book reader.

Dave: As much as I can't do without Hello, Kitty—oh, wait, that's Rick making things up again—I am truly lost without AvantGo. Each and every day

I fire it up at lunch to read the Joke of the Day, The Onion, The New York Times tech articles, and other bits of news that help me while away my lonely existence as I eat lunch. Why, oh why, does Sandra Bullock ignore my letters?

Alternatives to Expense

Truth be told, Expense isn't the most robust expense-management program—especially relative to some of the software created by third-party developers. If your needs extend beyond what Expense has to offer—and for businesspeople who rely heavily on reimbursement reports, they probably do—you should definitely check out one of the many available alternatives.

We've spotlighted some of the major programs, but keep in mind that these are designed for expense-tracking only. There are other programs that manage billing as well as expenses, and that let you track your bank accounts and stock portfolios. So don't be discouraged if none of these packages fit your particular bill. Chances are good there's a program out there that will.

8

- ■ **ExpensAble**   ExpensAble began as a PC application and has migrated to the Palm. LandWare's software makes it a snap to record reimbursable, nonreimbursable, and personal expenses, and it supports split transactions. Also present is the ever-popular AutoFill feature, a Quicken staple that simplifies repetitive data entry. Naturally, the Palm version of ExpensAble integrates seamlessly with the computer version, the latter offering report submission via e-mail or the ExpensAble Web site.

- ■ **ExpensePlus**   One of the most robust and versatile expense managers available, WalletWare's ExpensePlus uses an icon-based interface to simplify the selection of expense types, and automation to fill in dates and amounts for things such as hotel stays and car rentals. More important, it can link directly to any existing company expense forms created in Excel or FileMaker (including the Mac versions), so you needn't contend with nonstandard forms. And, if your company's forms aren't based in Excel, WalletWare can design a custom link (for a fee) to other software programs.

■ **TimeReporter**   Iambic Software's TimeReporter is more than just a business-expense manager, though it offers plenty of power in that area. The program also tracks time, which is helpful if your business requires you to bill clients that way.

Where to Find It

Web Site	Address	What's There
Chapura	www.chapura.com	Cloak
CIC	www.cic.com	Sign-On
DataViz	www.dataviz.com	Passwords Plus
Handmark	www.handmark.com	MobileSafe
Iambic Software	www.iambic.com	TimeReporter
Infinity Softworks	www.infinitysw.com	powerOne calculators
IntelligentFind	www.intelligentfind.com	IntelligentFind
LandWare	www.landware.com	ExpensAble
PalmGear	www.palmgear.com	FindHack, Find Ignore Hack, and most other programs
Synergy Solutions	www.synsolutions.com	SynCalc
Tranzoa	www.tranzoa.com	OnlyMe
WalletWare	www.walletware.com	ExpensePlus
XiY Technologies	www.xiy.net	LoanMax

Chapter 9

Going on a Trip

How to...

- Organize your Palm's categories and data for travel

- Pack smartly so you're prepared for Palm trouble

- Make sure your Palm doesn't run out of power during the trip

- Prepare for HotSync opportunities away from home

- Enhance the core apps for life on the road

- View your coworkers' Date Book entries on your own Palm

- Load your Palm with essential travel phone numbers

- Use the Palm as an alarm clock

- Use the Palm as a subway map

- Communicate in a foreign language with your Palm

- Navigate your way around town and country with a Palm

- Use your Palm as a compass

- Get star charts on your Palm

- Read books on your Palm

Some people find their Palm so useful that—imagine this—they put it in their pocket and take it on trips away from the home and office! Daring, we know. And, as it turns out, the Palm is even designed for these kinds of "away missions." Its batteries mean you needn't plug it in, and because it synchronizes with your desktop PC, you can bring important information with you wherever you go. The Palm even has a built-in clock in case you forget your watch. What could be better?

Seriously, we know you already carry your Palm around town. But, if you plan to take it on an extended trip, you might want to read this chapter. We have all kinds of suggestions for how to prepare your Palm for a grueling business trip, as well as what kind of software you might need to make the trip a little smoother. Planning to go camping? Your Palm might not be the first accessory that springs to mind when you consider roughing it in the Rocky Mountains, but your trusty little handheld has a lot to offer in the wilderness, too.

Preparing Your Palm for the Road

When we go on a business trip, it's usually such absolute pandemonium—running around at the last minute, throwing power cords and HotSync cables in the travel bag—it's a wonder we ever make it to the airport in time. Because of our experiences with forgetting data, bringing dead batteries, and being unable to connect to the Internet in strange cites, we offer the following checklist to you for bringing your Palm on trips.

Setting Up Your Data

Make sure your Palm is ready for the details of your upcoming trip. Specifically, consider the kinds of data you need to create while you're on the road and prepare your Palm ahead of time. Here's how you can make sure you're ready:

1. In the To Do List or Memo Pad, consider creating a "trip checklist" and use it to enter everything you need to do before you leave, as well as what you need to bring with you. If you have a comprehensive checklist, you're less likely to forget something important before you go.

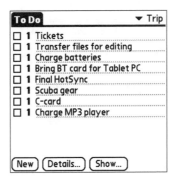

TIP   *You probably don't want to build your travel list from scratch each time. We recommend that you create a comprehensive list of travel tasks and leave it in the Memo Pad. You can copy the entire memo and paste it into a new memo before a trip, and then erase individual lines as you complete them. The master list is still safely stored in a different memo entry.*

2. Create a category just to store data related to your trip. If you're going to Chicago for a convention, for instance, create a category called Chicago. (If you want to call it something else, that's okay too.) By using a special

category on the road, you can find data related to your trip more quickly—both during the trip and after you return home. When you get back, you can recategorize the data any way you like.

3. If you use the Expense application to track stuff like car fares while you're away, you can make it much easier to file those T&E reports for your boss. But although you might be able to get by with lobbing all your To Dos or memos in the same Unfiled category, don't try that with expenses. After all, how are you going to distinguish among a dozen cab receipts? We don't want to see you up late at night with a calendar and your PDA, trying to figure out what city you were in when you paid $14 for a cab ride, especially if you don't fill in the details for each entry. A much easier way is simply to create a category for your upcoming trip and put all your expenses in there.

4. Enter your itinerary in the Date Book. If you're flying, enter each flight's number, departure, and arrival time in your Palm so it's available when you need it. An easy way to do this is to enter the flight number in the Date Book at the scheduled departure time, and note the arrival time there as well. That way, you can check your Palm in-flight to see how much longer you have to grit your teeth and eat peanuts.

 *You can block out the dates of your trip on the Palm using an untimed event. The trip appears at the top of the Date Book and still lets you schedule actual appointments during those days.*

Getting the Hardware Ready

When you leave on a trip, you should make sure your Palm is fully prepared to go the distance. There's nothing like being a thousand miles from home and remembering

Have a Backup Plan

Call us Luddites, but we don't like to rely 100 percent on a fragile piece of electronic gizmotry (and yes, that's a word. Don't look it up, just trust us). What if you drop your Palm in the airport and it shatters on the pretty marble floor? You'd better have a Plan B.

Dave: For me, the most important document to have access to on a trip is my flight itinerary. I always buy e-tickets—so I have no written record of my flight—and then I enter the flight information in my Palm. But, to be on the safe side, I also print a copy of my flight info and stick it in the back of my bag somewhere. That way, if my Palm batteries die before I finish my trip or if my Palm falls out of a five-story window, I can always refer to the piece of paper and get myself home.

Rick: If your Palm has an expansion slot, do yourself a favor and purchase a memory card and one of the many backup utilities available from PalmGear.com. With just a few stylus taps, you can back up the complete contents of your handheld's memory. Then, in the event that some catastrophe left you with a wiped handheld (it's been known to happen), you could pop the card in and restore everything in a matter of minutes. Well worth the $30 to 40 you'll spend for the card and software.

9

you forgot to bring some data from your desktop PC, or discovering you forgot an important cable.

To save yourself from calamity, remember these tips:

- *Always bring a stylus with a reset pin.* Most Palm models include a reset pin in the metal stylus—just unscrew the end to get to it—or let you reset the device with the pointy end, as in the Tungsten T. If neither of those options work for you, bring a paperclip or a thin pin instead. And test the pin before you go! Rick once traveled with a paperclip too thick to fit in the hole. D'oh! Bottom line: There's nothing worse than having your Palm crash when you're away from home and discovering you have nothing small enough to fit in the reset hole.

- *Perform a HotSync right before you leave.* This way, you're sure to have the latest info on your Palm, and you also have a current backup in case something unfortunate happens to your trusty handheld while you're away.

Real-Life Tragedy

A while back, Dave spent a week in sunny Florida in the dead of winter to see a photography trade show and do a bit of scuba diving. While there, his trusty Visor Prism held all his data—contact info, schedules, even flight information for the return trip. Well, thanks to a bitterly frustrating glitch in a wireless modem attachment, two days into the trip, the Visor performed a hard reset, erasing all the data on the device.

"I had thrown caution to the wind," Dave reports. "I thought I could trust my Prism, and I had no backup of any kind—no laptop, no backup module, not even a printout of my schedule."

In fact, Dave had to call home repeatedly to be updated on his daily schedule and to know what time to show up to the airport at the end of the trip. Frustrating? You bet. He's since learned to better heed his own advice and now travels with a data backup for his current PDA, a Tungsten T.

■ *Do you plan to do a lot of typing?* If so, pack a keyboard for the Palm. You have over a dozen options to choose from, from the fold-up Fellowes Stowaway to the cloth, flexible Logitech Key Case. See Chapter 15 for more details.

■ *Be prepared to restore.* Call us paranoid, but... hey, wait a minute, did you just call us paranoid? Sheesh, the nerve.... Anyway, if your Palm should lose all its data for some reason, you might want to have the capability to restore it while you're on the go. Depending on what model Palm you have, you can do that in a few ways. A HotSync cable can let you restore data from a laptop, for instance, but a better bet might be a backup on a memory card. Sony CLIÉ models come with a backup program that lets you create a perfect copy of the PDA's contents on a Memory Stick and recover your data at any time, even when you're far away from your PC. Any Palm model with an SD card slot (such as an m515, Tungsten T, or Zire 71) can take advantage of Palm's 64MB Backup Card Plus—available at Palm's online store in the Accessories section. It lets you back up your device as well.

Staying Powered

A dead Palm is no good to anyone. Take these steps to keep working when you're away:

■ *Recharge your Palm right before you leave.* More importantly, if you plan to be away for more than two days, bring some sort of charging solution with you. There are many options, from Electric Fuel's Instant Power system (available for most Palm models) to Tech Center Labs' Palm V Emergency Charger, which connects a 9-volt battery to your Palm's HotSync cradle port. Be sure to check out Palm's online store, which sells a variety of charging solutions, including USB chargers (which plug into laptops or desktop PCs for charging power), car chargers, and more. Other companies, such as Targus and Belkin, also specialize in charging solutions for PDAs. One of the coolest ways to stay charged is with the Power To Go, a "sled" that clips onto the back of most Palm devices and provides a very long run time via the integrated Lithium Ion battery. It's available at Palm's online store at palm.com.

■ *If your Palm takes replaceable batteries, check them before you go.* There aren't many of these kinds of PDAs left in the world, but if you have one, heed this advice. If you're going to be away for a week or more, bring a spare set of batteries with you—better safe than sorry. If you generally leave a spare set of batteries in your travel case, score 10 points for preparedness. But use a battery tester before each trip to make sure your backup batteries are still in good shape.

■ *Bring batteries for any Palm accessories you use.* This includes your modem, keyboard, cell phone, GPS receiver, and other gadgets.

Road Tips

We've done our share of traveling, and we've amassed a few handy tips for making the best use of your Palm on the road. Not all of these suggestions will appeal to you, but you're sure to find a few things to make your next trip a little more enjoyable.

■ If you're planning to stay at your destination for more than a few hours, reset the time on your Palm. Otherwise, all your appointments will alarm at the wrong time, and you'll show up late everywhere you need to be. The exact method varies from Palm to Palm, but most new devices work like this: tap the Prefs icon in the Home screen and choose the Date & Time page, as in the following illustration. Tap the Location menu and select your new city. Other models may require you to tap a Set Time Zone box, or—for really old models—you may have to simply change the time since pre–OS 5 PDAs didn't have a Time Zone selector at all.

- Some PDAs (especially the Palm V) can run their battery down easily if you're not careful. Why? Packing the Palm in your pocket or a crowded travel bag can result in things getting pressed against the power button and the scroll button, causing a constant power drain. There are two solutions. First, a number of software products can help keep the battery from draining. For older (pre–OS 5) Palms, you can use programs like PalmOffHack, StayOffHack, or Stay Off If Up Hack. These programs prevent inadvertent pressure on the buttons from accidentally turning your Palm on. Alternately, you can get a hard-shelled case to enclose your PDA, which keeps the power button from getting triggered accidentally. Worst case: you can cut a slot in the cover that prevents the power button from getting activated, but that's an ugly fix for the problem. Dave knows: his Palm V was once the laughingstock of taxi drivers all over the country.

- Your Palm may set off the metal detector at the airport. To save yourself time and hassle, go ahead and pop it into one of those little trays, along with all your change, time-travel portal control, roll of aluminum foil, and other personal items, right at the outset when you go through a metal detector.

- The Palm is considered a "portable electronic device" and you shouldn't use it at the beginning or the end of a flight. You probably already knew that, but your Palm can get you in trouble anyway if you're not careful. Specifically, don't enable any alarms for the start or end of the flight, or your Palm will come to life and start beeping during the Forbidden Times. If you want to be a real stickler for FAA rules, you should be sure to turn off any wireless features in your Palm, such as Bluetooth or WiFi. You can find the master toggle for these functions in the Prefs application—look under the Communication category.

■ You might need to print something stored on your Palm while you're on your trip. There are several ways to print. The easiest solution is to get a print driver for your Palm such as PalmPrint, PrintBoy, or one of the print solutions from IS/Print, especially if you have access to a portable printer. If that's the case, just aim your Palm and print. If you do a lot of printing, get a portable model and carry it with you (see Chapter 11 for details). If you can get to a printer, but it isn't IR capable, you still have options. First, if you have a few extra bucks, you might want to carry the PrintBoy InfraReady Adapter from Bachmann Software. This is a little device that fits in your pocket (or your travel bag) and plugs into the parallel port of any printer. Its infrared port lets you instantly convert almost any printer into an IR-ready printer for your Palm. When you're finished printing, remove the adapter and put it back in your travel bag. It's a very cool solution for printing anything anywhere you can find a printer when you travel. The next best thing is to carry a serial cable for your Palm and a serial-to-parallel converter (this is available from Stevens Creek, the company that sells PalmPrint). As a last resort, you might install a fax program such as Mark/Space Fax. Equipped with a Palm modem, you can fax to your hotel's front desk, and then pick up the printout.

Software to Bring Along

Don't rely on the software that comes with your Palm to get you through your extended trips away from home. Most of the software we discuss in this next section is available from PalmGear.com. Experiment and see what applications are useful.

CAUTION *Don't install a new application as you're walking out the door to go to the airport. Some applications might cause your Palm to misbehave. Others can change the way your Palm functions or make it hard to access data you've already created. You don't need to discover those kinds of things after you're already on an airplane bound for Topeka. Bottom line: install and experiment with new software well in advance of a trip.*

Address and Date Book Enhancements

Sure, you love the Address Book and the Date Book. But, by enhancing these core applications, you might find you can significantly improve the way you work when you're away from home.

Synchronize with the Web

Believe it or not, you can synchronize your Palm's Date Book and Address Book with Web-based information managers. Why would you want to do that? Well, when you're on the road, you might want to access your schedule and contacts from a PC that isn't yours. And, if you can get to any Web-enabled PC, you can log on to a Web-based calendar and address book. Here are some cool reasons to try this:

- Send e-mail from a Web-based e-mail system using contact information culled from your Palm.

- Add calendar appointments on the PC and synchronize it to the Palm later.

- If something happens to your Palm on a trip, access all your data from a PC that's connected to the Internet.

The Web site Yahoo! offers the best Palm synchronization support on the Internet. By installing a small utility on your home or office-based PC, you can sync the Palm's Date Book, Address Book, and To Do List with equivalent applications on the Yahoo! site. Because Yahoo! also offers free e-mail, you can use the Palm Address Book to send messages without re-entering any data.

To get started with Web synchronization, visit www.yahoo.com. If you don't already have an account there, create one. You'll need to find the site's synchronization tools, which are actually buried a few layers deep. Click on the link for Yahoo!'s Address Book or Calendar, then click on the Options link (at the top-right corner of the page). You should then see a list of links; click the Sync link to be taken to your Sync options. Follow the instructions to download and install TrueSync for Yahoo!.

TIP   *Once you've installed and synchronized, you may find that you can't see entries on your Palm that were created in Yahoo! That's because, by default, Yahoo! marks its records private. You have to display private records on the Palm to see them. For details on how to do that, see Chapter 5.*

Get Common Phone Numbers

The Palm can hold lots of phone numbers, so why not take advantage of this?
Several databases of phone numbers exist to services like rental car companies,
airlines, and hotels. Here are some examples of what you can find at
PalmGear.com:

Topic	What You'll Find
Rental cars	You can find a handful of downloads at PalmGear that include all the major rental car companies. Check out programs called Palm Rent-a-Car and Travel Telephone Numbers.
Golf courses	Believe it or not, we found a slew of downloads at PalmGear.com that pour phone numbers to golf courses in locales such as L.A., New York, and Florida into your Palm, so you can easily find the numbers you need when you travel. Search for "phone numbers" at PalmGear for the whole bunch.
Restaurants	Want a guide to restaurants in major cities? You'll find that online as well— The Finer Life Restaurant Guide is available at PalmGear for cities such as San Francisco and L.A. Of course, if you want a really good guide to local restaurants when you travel, you'll want a city guide, which we cover later in this chapter.

9

TIP *If you have a Palm with wireless Internet capabilities, don't forget about
Web clipping applications. A number of clipping apps were custom designed
for on-the-go reference. Check out Chapter 10 for details on these wireless
wonders that can help you order a taxi, find a gas station, get airline
information, or satisfy nearly any other travel need.*

Itinerary Tracking

Although you can certainly store your itinerary information in the Date Book,
using a specialized program is more efficient for many people. There are many
applications at a site such as PalmGear that fit the bill. Some of our favorites
include TravelTracker and TravelPal, both shown here:

In Search of the Ultimate Alarm Clock

You can set alarms with the Palm, but the somewhat-anemic alarm system built into the Date Book isn't terribly useful in a lot of situations. Instead, you may want to download a copy of a specialized clock application. A program just to tell the time? When your Palm already comes with a clock? Surely we jest.

We don't, and stop calling us Shirley.

Note to selfs: That joke simply doesn't work in print.

The Palm software universe is filled with some excellent clocks and alarm clock applications. These programs tend to offer more advanced features than those that come with the Palm itself, such as multiple alarms that aren't tied to specific Date Book events, snooze buttons, countdown and stopwatch modes, and world time displays. Here are some programs worth investigating:

- **BigClock** BigClock is the granddaddy of alarm clock apps for the Palm. It's free, yet has a wealth of useful features. Not only does it display the time, but it has a timer and four independent alarms. It also lets you easily change time zones—a boon if you're still using an older Palm device without OS 5's easy time zone adjustment. It also allows you to change the look of the program and display your own favorite background images behind the clock using the program's themes feature.

- **WorldMate Professional** This gorgeous program isn't just great for travelers, it's eye candy for your PDA as well. At its core, WorldMate lets you compare four world clocks to your local time and features a beautiful map display that animates the day/night terminator. It also synchronizes the Palm with an online atomic clock at each HotSync, retrieves weather forecasts, and includes a currency converter.

■ **MegaClock**   This is a must-try. MegaClock is a multifunction clock app that has a huge collection of alternative views; you can see the time in a variety of analog and digital clock faces, display a world globe with day/night terminator, and more. It has no fewer than 20 alarms and four programmable daily timers.

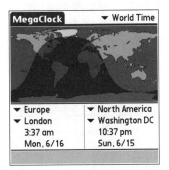

9

■ **CityTime**   Like WorldMate, CityTime has a gorgeous color display that graphically shows the day/night terminator as it moves across the globe. CityTime displays four world clocks and lets you change your location and time easily without entering the Prefs app. It displays sunrise and sunset times, moon phase information, and performs time and distance calculations between locations.

■ **Time 2.0**   For those who want a simpler, calendar-based view, Time 2.0 shows the time and a calendar along with a second time zone and upcoming appointments.

Finding Your Way Around

Many Palm tools can help you find your way around in a strange place. In fact, you can actually connect your Palm to a GPS navigation system (see "PDA Survival Tools," later in this chapter)! Most people need more mundane assistance, though, so we've collected a few interesting applications for you here.

Have a Better Time with City Guides

City Guides have become virtually indispensable for frequent travelers. These programs deliver up-to-date, trustworthy information about things to do in cities you travel to—such as restaurant, nightclub, shopping, and sightseeing advice. Here are a few to check out:

- **Vindigo** We list Vindigo first for a reason: it has become the single most popular city guide in the world. It supports over 50 cities and has categories for food, shops, services, museums, movies, essential services such as banks and ATMs, and more. The program has maps and provides directions to wherever you're trying to go; it also features reviews to help you make good choices about where to go. Alas, it's not a one-time fee; Vindigo costs $25 per year.

- **Zagat To Go** The popular Zagat restaurant guide is available for the Palm. Its database includes about 65 cities and has reviews of dining and nightlife in the same familiar form as the paper version.

- **Qvadis Envoyage** Looking for a free city guide? Live or travel in Canada? Try Envoyage, which has some of the same features as Vindigo and Zagat for a handful of cities, such as Toronto, Vancouver, Montreal, and Ottawa.

Get Metro and Subway Routes

Do train, bus, and subway routes leave you scratching your head? Those maps they put in the train stops aren't exactly intuitive, and finding the best route from one end of Paris to the other can be a nerve-wracking experience. That's why you might want to search a site such as PalmGear for metro aids—these programs help you find your way around strange towns when you travel. The best ones let you enter two stations and simply tell you what train to get on. Others include digital maps and displays to help you navigate. To get started, search PalmGear for terms like "metro" and "subway" to locate apps that interest you. Here are some of the better ones we dug up:

Region	Service	Program Name
200 cities worldwide	Displays best routing information for finding your way by subway or bus.	MetrO
Paris 3.1P	Metro paths between monuments, museums, and stations.	Paris
Versions available for New York, Boston, London, Paris, Chicago, and others	Map that plans the best route between metro stops; combined with a street map for easier route planning.	TUBE
Databases available for select cities in California, Washington, New York, and others	Comprehensive bus and train schedules.	Transit
19 cities, including New York, Paris, and London	Computes the best route between any two stations.	Route Expert
New York	Enter a Manhattan address and program provides the nearest cross street.	X-Man
Southern California	MetroLink schedule.	MetroLink

Language Translators

In the past, traveling abroad often resulted in serious communication difficulties. Do you know how to ask for the bathroom in French? If not, try one of these applications.

- **Small Talk**   This program is a real-time, two-way translator. Hold the Palm up to the person you want to communicate with. Small Talk presents you with complete sentences organized into situation-based categories such as Basics, Lodging, Emergency, Food, and Entertainment. Select a phrase in English and it's translated into the target language, as you can see in Figure 9-1. The person you are communicating with can then select a response from a menu, which is translated back into English. Small Talk supports French, Italian, Spanish, German, and Japanese.

- **TourMate** Available in several versions (including English–Spanish and English–Italian, English–French and English–German), TourMate is easy to use. Choose a common greeting, expression, or question in English, and read the phonetically spelled foreign-language equivalent expression to the person with whom you're trying to communicate.

- **Translate** This application enables you to enter a word and instantly translate it among 18 languages. The translator works in both directions, so you can go from English to Italian or Italian to English, for instance.

Unit Conversions

If you're an American in Europe, you need to contend with an alien set of measurements: not only is the currency different, but even the length, weight, and volume of common items are unusual. Heck, unless you're a scientist or an engineer, you may not know if 40 degrees Celsius is hot or cold. Try Conversions (see Figure 9-2), a calculator utility that lets you instantly make conversions among measurements such as currency, temperature, length, area, and volume.

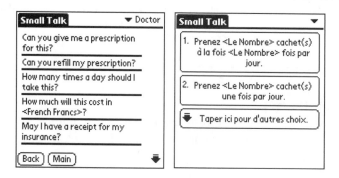

FIGURE 9-1 Choose a phrase from a list, divided by topic (left), and your associate can choose a response (right) that is translated back into English for you.

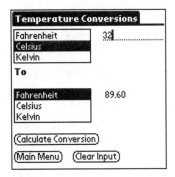

FIGURE 9-2   Conversions makes it easy for an American to get by in a metric world.

PDA Survival Tools

It's not surprising to walk into a fancy hotel and see a dozen executives standing around in fancy suits, checking their schedules via the Palms. But how often do you go camping in the middle of the woods and see people bring their Palms? Not that often, we're willing to bet. And that's too bad, because the Palm is a handy survival tool. It does almost everything, except open cans of beans or start campfires.

Navigating with Your Palm

Have you ever gotten lost in a strange town or some deserted stretch of highway? Have you wished you hadn't seen the *Blair Witch Project* because it reminds you of exactly how bad you are at navigating in the wilderness? If so, you might benefit from a GPS navigation system. Combined with a GPS system, your Palm is perfectly capable of telling you exactly where to go.

There are several popular GPS solutions for the Palm and other Palm-powered PDAs. The Navman is a GPS solution that's available for "m-series" Palm models such as the m125, m500, and m515. It's a sled design that clips onto the back of the PDA. Delorme sells the Earthmate Road Warrior package, which is a stand-alone, palm-sized GPS receiver that attaches to the PDA via a serial cable that plugs into the HotSync port. There's also the StreetFinder GPS from Rand McNally, another sled that snaps onto the back of older Palms such as the Palm III and Palm V.

If you have a Bluetooth-enabled PDA such as the Tungsten T, you can use Emtac's Bluetooth GPS antenna—it's a tiny gadget that you can place anywhere, like under the windshield of your car, and then use the GPS data on your PDA anywhere up to 30 feet away. It's a great solution because you don't have to keep the PDA itself in view of the satellites or tether it to an external antenna via a cable. It's all wireless and very convenient.

Sony CLIÉ owners may eventually be able to use a GPS Memory Stick, but when we wrote this, Sony showed no sign of offering one. If you have a CLIÉ and want GPS, your best bet is the Holux GPS bundle from Mapopolis.

Not all GPS receivers give you the same level of control—if you don't know what you're buying, you might be disappointed by your GPS system's performance.

- Some GPS solutions come with software that lets you plan a door-to-door route. Once the route is on the Palm, you can follow these directions to find your way to the destination. Better GPS systems even recalculate the route on the fly if you miss a turn. With the GPS receiver attached to your Palm, it uses satellite data to alert you about each upcoming turn. GPS systems from Delorme and Navman do this kind of duty.

- Other GPS systems don't do routing. Instead, they show only your position on a map, which is updated constantly as you move. Solutions that use Mapopolis software do this.

What Is GPS?

GPS stands for Global Positioning System, and it's comprised of 24 satellites flying around the Earth in semi-synchronous orbit (each trip around the Earth takes 12 hours). These satellites transmit extremely precise timing signals toward the Earth.

On the ground, an inexpensive GPS receiver simply listens for these timing signals. At any given moment, the time broadcast from each satellite in the GPS system's field of view is slightly different because the satellites are at different distances from the receiver and, consequently, some signals take longer to reach the receiver from the satellite. Because the orbit of each GPS satellite is very, very precisely known, the GPS receiver can process the different timing signals and determine its own position through simple triangulation.

The bottom line is this: through this process, a GPS receiver can narrow its position to an accuracy of about 100 feet—not bad for a system that works anywhere on Earth.

For GPS to do its magic, though, you must be able to see enough satellites. You need to see no less than three satellites for accurate position data, which isn't a problem in clearings. In a skyscraper-infested metropolitan area or in a forest with lots of tree cover, though, GPS can have trouble working. Even obstacles like trees can block the GPS signal.

Using Your Palm as a Compass

Although we're quite sure you know a Palm won't open a can of beans, we suspect you wouldn't believe it could be a compass, either. But you'd be wrong. Using a program such as Sun Compass, you can get an immediate onscreen indication of north any time, anywhere (during daylight hours).

Unfortunately, Sun Compass comes with virtually no documentation, which may make it confusing for new users. To use Sun Compass, all you need to do is input a few pieces of information:

- **Tz** This is the time zone you are in currently. Time zones are calculated from –12 to 0, and then on up to +12. Your time zone value is simply the number of hours away from Greenwich, England (home of Greenwich Mean Time) you are located. GMT is a time zone of 0. New York is –5, and California is –8. You can find a complete list of time zones in Windows by opening the Date/Time Properties dialog box (in the Control Panel) and looking on the Time Zone tab.

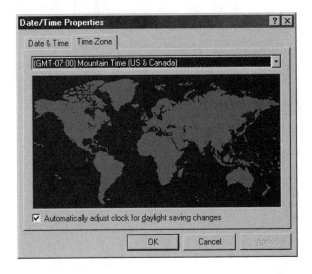

- **La**   Enter your latitude. Latitude is measured from 0 degrees (the equator) to 90N and 90S.

- **Lo**   Enter your longitude. Longitude is commonly measured from 0 (at the longitude line that cuts through Greenwich, England) to 180E and 180W.

TIP   *Looking for your latitude and longitude? Visit www.census.gov/cgi-bin/ gazetteer. Enter your city or ZIP code to find out your lat/long.*

- **DSI**   DSI stands for daylight saving time, and it needs to be set either on or off, depending on the time of year. Daylight saving time is on between the first Sunday in April and the last Sunday in October.

TIP   *A few locations in the United States don't observe daylight saving time at all. These include Arizona, Hawaii, and parts of Indiana.*

Once you enter these values, point the front of your Palm at the sun (keep the Palm level with the ground), and the compass indicates which way is north. That's all there is to it!

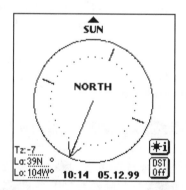

Finding Stars

You can also use Sun Compass to find the North Star. Choose Misc | Polarstar from the menu and you see a dark screen with the Big and Little Dipper constellations. By aligning them with what you see in the sky, you can find the North Star, and thus get a northerly orientation even at night.

That's great, but you can also use your Palm for some real star gazing. Here are a few programs you can try the next time you're far away from city lights with your Palm:

■ **Planetarium**   This program calculates the position of the sun, the moon, the planets, and over 1,500 of the brightest stars and deep sky objects in the sky. You can enter any location and any time period—you needn't use the present system clock. In addition to using this program for stargazing, it can also be used as a compass when the sun or moon is visible (much like Sun Compass).

■ **Star Pilot**   This program lets you specify your location, and then see the planets, the moon, and 500 stars in a compact star map. You can identify objects by clicking them and search for celestial objects by name.

Reading Late at Night

When all of your tent buddies are trying to sleep while wondering if that odd sound is an approaching bear, you can relax in your sleeping bag and read a good book— with your Palm. The Palm's efficient backlighting makes it easy to read both in total darkness and in bright sunlight. What you need is a document reader. You can see Chapter 14 for details on electronic books and document readers, but we think it's worth pointing out right now that there's nothing like curling up with a good e-book on a camping trip. You can store lots of reading on one Palm, so you can travel light and still have a lot of things to read on those quiet, lonely nights.

Where to Find It

Web Site	Address	What's There
Tech Center Labs	www.talestuff.com	Battery chargers
Electric Fuel	www.instant-power.com	Instant Power Charger
RGPS	www.rgps.com	StayOffHack
BigClock	www.gacel.de/palmpilot.htm	BigClock
Mark/Space	www.markspace.com	Mark/Space Fax
Stevens Creek Software	www.stevenscreek.com	PalmPrint
Bachmann Software	www.bachmannsoftware.com	PrintBoy
IS/Complete	www.iscomplete.com	BtPrint and IrPrint
Yahoo!	www.yahoo.com	Web-based information management that HotSyncs to the Palm
SilverWare	www.silverware.com	TravelTracker
Delorme	www.delorme.com	Earthmate GPS

Web Site	Address	What's There
Rand McNally	www.randmcnally.com	StreetFinder GPS
Navman	www.navman.com	Navman GPS
Magellan	www.magellangps.com	Magellan GPS
Mapopolis	www.mapopolis.com	GPS for CLIÉ and other PDAs; also sells Emtac Bluetooth GPS
Vindigo	www.vindigo.com	City guide software

Chapter 10 Unwire Your Palm

How to...

- Choose a smartphone or connected organizer

- Decide between landline, wireless, and cell phone connections

- Connect your cell phone to your handheld

- Configure your handheld for Web and e-mail access

- Find and download Web clipping apps

- Work with the wireless e-mail programs

- Access America Online

- Use AvantGo to take the Web with you

- Choose and work with handheld Web browsers

- Work with Bluetooth technology

The world it is a' changin'. A few years ago, when PDAs were the hot new thing, it was enough to be able to check your schedule from an electronic organizer kept tucked in your pocket. These days, "connected" organizers are the new thing, and everyone, it seems, wants one. A connected organizer is simply a PDA that has some sort of wireless connectivity. Such a gadget can retrieve e-mail, let you surf the Web, and perhaps even make phone calls. The possibilities are staggering.

There are all kinds of ways to get your Palm online. You can connect your PDA to a cell phone with a connection cable and let the phone act like a modem. If you're a bit more adventurous, you can connect your phone and Palm wirelessly with infrared or Bluetooth. Of course, one of the most exciting trends in PDAs is the smartphone—a combination of PDA and cell phone that does it all in one smart little box. With so many options at your fingertips, this chapter is here to help you figure out how to connect your Palm and join the fast-growing world of the Internet. (For a brochure on how *you* can make money on the Internet, send $5, cash only, to Dave or Rick. Allow 6 weeks for delivery.)

A lot of the information in this chapter, particularly the stuff about e-mail and Web clipping, is applicable to all wireless Palm devices and configurations. Whether you have an Earthlink Minstrel for your Palm m515 or want to connect your Tungsten T to a Bluetooth mobile phone, you're likely to find some worthwhile stuff in these pages.

Wireless PDAs

It's too expensive. It doesn't do real Web browsing. It forces you to work with a special e-mail account. The monthly service plans are too limiting and too expensive. It'll be Palm's first flop.

Those were some of the things that people said about the Palm VII, Palm's first wireless-enabled PDA. Yet it eventually sold so well that it led the entire PDA industry to make wireless PDAs. These days, Palm, Kyocera, Samsung, and Handspring have all released wireless PDAs. How to choose? For starters, we should probably explain that there are really two kinds of wireless PDAs out there:

- ■ **Smartphones**   A smartphone combines aspects of a PDA with a mobile phone. You can use a smartphone like a regular cell phone to place calls, but it also has all the guts of a Palm. That means you can track your schedule, dial the phone directly from the Address Book, and even run Palm applications and games. Smartphones are designed to be phones, first and foremost, like the Treo shown in the following illustration. They are for people who want to carry one device, not two, and have all the advantages of both.

10

■ **Connected organizers**   Not all Palms with Internet access can place phone calls—some are just designed for data, such as e-mail and the Web. These gadgets are for folks who think that two devices are better than one; they principally use their PDA for data, so they want it to be really good at that. A typical connected organizer is the Tungsten C, shown in the following illustration:

The Three Body Solution

Just when you think you understand how the world works, new technology comes along to change everything. In addition to smartphones and connected organizers, there's a third class of device out there that is part of what is sometimes called a "three body solution." A PDA like the Tungsten T has integrated Bluetooth. That means it can connect to a mobile phone up to 30 feet away. Imagine leaving your mobile phone in your pocket or briefcase, dialing a number on the phone from the Tungsten's Address Book, and automatically taking the call on a Bluetooth headset. Such solutions will get increasingly popular— especially among folks who already use a headset for their mobile phone anyway, and would like to get rid of the clumsy wire that connects the two.

The good news is that no matter what your preference, you can find a device to satisfy your needs. There are several excellent models to choose from today, and the following table outlines the most popular ones:

Model	Style	Features
Palm i705	Connected organizer	Always-on Internet access using a nationwide cellular-like radio network. It's designed for e-mail and Web browsing. The i705 comes with 8MB of memory and is fully compatible with Palm's universal connector and SD memory cards.
Tungsten C	Connected organizer	A powerful OS 5 device with a high-speed processor, 64MB of internal memory, SD card slot, and integrated 802.11b (Wi-Fi). You can use the Tungsten C to access the Internet whenever you're in a Wi-Fi hotspot.
Tungsten W	Smartphone	Palm's first shot at a smartphone, the Tungsten W is a GSM/GPRS mobile phone and Palm device rolled into one. It does not have a traditional handset microphone/earpiece—instead, you need to use a plug-in headset or a leather cover that has a headset/microphone built in.
Tungsten T	Bluetooth device	A seemingly ordinary PDA, the Tungsten T has integrated Bluetooth, which means you can use it to connect to a mobile phone for data access (see the preceding sidebar, "The Three Body Solution").
Handspring Treo	Smartphone	Voice, e-mail, and Web access. Available in several models, you can get it with GSM/GPRS or CDMA service plans and in a flip-cover, PDA-style, or a more traditional mobile phone handset form. It comes with 16MB; some models have an SD memory slot and integrated digital camera.
Kyocera 7135	Smartphone	Voice, e-mail, and Web access. Color screen, 16MB of memory, SD slot, MP3 player. Supports newer CDMA2000 1X network.
Samsung I330	Smartphone	Voice, e-mail, and Web access. Comes with color screen and CDMA service plan. 8MB of RAM, and no memory slot.

10

Choosing a Handheld

Before you pick a wireless Palm, you should play with them a bit. All of these models are popular enough that you can find them on display in office supply stores, computer shops, and cellular provider outlets. Here are some things to consider:

- **What you want your wireless device to do**   The most important criteria is to decide if you want a data device that also makes occasional calls, or a voice device that you'll sometimes use to access data. The distinction is important, because a voice device should work naturally, simply, and elegantly as a phone. If it's a great PDA but making phone calls is a pain, then you'll be frustrated. On the other hand, you might want to mainly interact with the data aspect of the device—in which case, a large, high-resolution display and a convenient data entry system is probably more important than great phone features. And with the advent of WiFi and Bluetooth devices such as the Tungsten C and Tungsten T, you can pick a PDA for data-only Internet access as well, without regard for voice capabilities.

- **Coverage areas**   There are two major kinds of service offered by cell phones today: GSM and CDMA. CDMA is significantly more popular and has broad coverage throughout the US. It's an aging technology, though, and newer smartphones use GSM service, which is the same network used in Europe. The advantage of GSM is that it is an international standard, allowing you to use the same phone almost worldwide (though, because of regional differences in the way GSM works, you need a "tri-mode" GSM phone to get service both in the U.S. and Europe). For now, though, you may have difficulty getting coverage outside of major metro areas with GSM phones. If you're looking at a Wi-Fi device such as the Tungsten C, on the other hand, consider the fact that it'll only connect when you're in a hotspot. Does your home or office have Wi-Fi? Do you frequent public places that have Wi-Fi networks installed? These are questions you should ask yourself before investing in the C.

- **Size and shape**   How does it fit in your hand and against your head? The Treo 300, for instance, has a clamshell cover that folds open to fit the contour of the human head quite well. The Samsung I330 is a flat, brick-like device that may not be as comfortable without using a headset.

- **PDA features**   This is an important consideration. Do you want a color screen? What about 16MB of internal memory or memory cards? Some smartphones are built on a rather closed PDA base that doesn't let you back up your data on the road or expand past 8MB. Fortunately, most of the newest models offer some form of expansion capability, usually in the form of a Secure Digital slot.

■ **Price** There are some excellent deals to be had on older models. The now discontinued Palm VIIx routinely shows up in online auctions for a steal, for instance, and the older Kyocera smartphone sells for under $100. Don't forget to compare the monthly service plan costs. Factor in data access— you may have to pay your ISP to "dial up" your e-mail account from your smartphone, for instance. Of course, the i705's monthly fee is for data since it doesn't have voice capabilities.

Connecting Other Handhelds

So you've already invested in a nonwireless handheld. Does that mean you have to toss it out the nearest window and buy something new if you want wireless Internet access? Of course not! This is the Palm universe we're talking about. There are a number of ways to get your handheld connected, including landline modems, wireless modems, and cell-phone cables.

Landline, Wireless, or Something Else?

There are two kinds of modems available for Palm devices: landline and wireless. The former are similar to what most computers have, and make their connections via standard telephone lines (or *landlines*, as geeks like us call them). *Wireless* modems require no wires at all, relying instead on cellular and/or radio towers to make their connections. Naturally, there are pros and cons to each technology— and some alternatives to consider as well. Here's what you need to know.

Landline Modems

Landline modems clip onto (or into) your Palm device, then plug into a phone jack using traditional RJ-11 cable. Unfortunately, they're getting harder to find for PDAs, since fewer people want to deal with the hassle of connecting one to a phone line for Internet connectivity. Here are the most common choices available:

Modem	Compatible With
PalmModem Connectivity Kit	Most Palm models
Card Access Thinmodem/Thinmodem Plus	Handspring Visor
Sony PEGA-MD700 Modem	N and S series Sony CLIÉ

Wireless Modems

Wireless modems rely on existing cellular and radio technologies to transmit and receive data through the ether. Keep in mind that there are several different kinds of wireless options for Palm devices, including mobile phones and dedicated modems. In this section, we focus on the latter.

If you're shopping for a dedicated wireless modem for your handheld, you'll probably find you have relatively few choices. In fact, only Earthlink sells a wireless modem (made by Novatel) for select Palm models. If you don't have one of these, you'll probably have to upgrade to a connected organizer.

Cell Phones

You probably already own a cell phone—most people do. And it's already wireless, so wouldn't it be great if you could link it to your handheld for Web browsing and e-mail? You can, and it's easier than you might think. Here's what you need:

- **A phone that supports data calls** Most modern phones do (those that work with CDMA and GSM networks), but check with your service provider to be sure. You may also have to pay extra per month to make data calls, though some companies build the cost into their standard service plans.

- **Cable, infrared, or Bluetooth** You can use a cable to link your handheld to a phone, or connect the PDA to the phone with an infrared port, if your phone has one. For many folks, using a cable is the best bet, because it gives you greater flexibility in positioning the two devices. (With an IR connection, the phone and handheld need to lay on an even surface and point at their respective IR ports so they can communicate, as in the following illustration of the Zire 71 and Nokia 3650.) On the other hand, the cable is one extra thing to carry and lose—so if your phone is IR-capable, you might want to try it and see if you like it. One last option: if you have a Bluetooth-capable Palm and a Bluetooth-capable mobile phone, you can connect wirelessly, without the line-of-sight restrictions imposed by infrared.

■ **Palm OS 3.5 or later** That version of the operating system includes the necessary components (known as the Mobile Internet Kit) for data communications via cell phone. Keep reading to learn how to install these components and start using your cell phone with your handheld.

Finding Connection Cables Unless you're lucky enough to have an IR-equipped phone, you'll need a cable to make the connection to your handheld. We know of two good sources for them:

Site	URL
Purple Data Cables	www.pcables.com
SupplyNet	www.thesupplynet.com

You may also be able to find cables at your local computer or office superstore, or at one of your cell phone company's outlet stores.

Configuring Your Palm with a Cell Phone Now that you have all the parts, it's time to set up your Palm to actually connect to the Internet via your mobile phone. Here's what you need to do:

1. Make sure that the data services on your phone are enabled (you may need to call your service provider to be sure).

2. Connect the cable between the Palm and phone, or point the IR ports at each other if you're going the infrared route.

3. On your Palm, tap the Prefs app in the Home screen and choose Connection (it may be in the Communication category if you have a newer Palm).

4. Create a new connection by tapping the New button.

5. Give your connection a handy name (like Phone or Cable). Set the Connect To option to Modem, and set Via to Cable or Infrared, as appropriate. If you have an older Palm, this screen is a bit different, and you may need to select an option such as Serial to Modem. Dialing should be set to TouchTone.

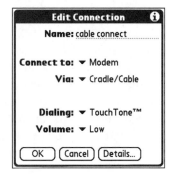

6. Tap the Details button and set the Speed to 19,200 for starters. If this setting works, you can later try increasing the speed to 57,600 and testing it again.

7. Tap OK twice, then tap Done to return to the main Preferences screen.

8. Open the Network Prefs.

9. Create a new network by tapping New, then enter a descriptive name for this service (such as ATT or Sprint). Set the Connection to the new connection you created back in step 4.

10. Enter the username and password, then add a phone number to dial. Make sure you enter the number properly; some phones require nine-digit dialing.

11. Test your connection by using the Connect button. If all is well, tap Done. It's complete!

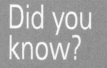

How to Connect Your PDA and Cell Phone via IR

Here's a little-known secret about many cell phones—well, those that have infrared ports, anyway. Many IR-equipped phones can receive contact info beamed from your handheld, and can also beam their own address book entries to your handheld. Although you're limited to sending one contact at a time, this can be a timesaving way to transfer important phone numbers into your phone (much quicker than entering them manually). Consult your phone's instruction manual for information on beaming (it's a little different on each phone). We've tested this on Nokia and Sony Ericsson phones, and it works like a charm—on the Sony Ericsson T68i, for instance, just turn on the phone's IR port in the Connections prefs, them beam. The phone receives the address info automatically and files it in its own phone list.

Introduction to Web Clipping

Some wireless-capable Palm devices—such as the Palm VII, Tungsten W, and i705—can access the Internet two different ways: with a standard Web browser, or using a more efficient Palm-invented technology called *Web clipping*. The concept behind Web clipping is simple. Most of us turn to the Web for specific bits of information. We look for news, sports scores, stock quotes, airline flight information, weather reports, and so on. But when we visit sites that provide this information, there's always "fluff" that goes with it: big splashy graphics, banner ads, tables, and links to other sites. These flourishes are time-consuming to download and typically work best with a large display.

Web clipping dispenses with Web fluff, pulling down only the raw information that's needed. Thus, connection speed becomes less of an issue, because only tiny amounts of data are actually being transmitted. And because the data is mostly text, screen size becomes largely irrelevant.

Web clipping also dispenses with the Web browser, instead employing specialized programs called Web clipping apps. These little gophers pull specific bits of information from the Internet, then present that information to you on neatly formatted screens. They're used to obtain everything from news and weather to movie times and traffic reports (see Figure 10-1).

Web clipping was originally limited to models like the Palm VII, but with the arrival of Palm OS 3.5 and the Mobile Internet Kit, it's now available for almost all Palm Powered handhelds. In fact, if your handheld comes with OS 4.0 or later, everything you need for Web clipping is already installed. You just need to download a few Web clipping apps and get online (using either a modem or cell phone, as described in the previous sections).

Finding and Installing Web Clipping Applets

Hundreds of Web clipping apps are available from third-party developers. You can get news from ABC and ESPN, stock quotes from E*Trade, driving directions from MapQuest, and so on. Most of these apps are free, but some cost a few dollars up front or have subscription-related fees.

Web clipping apps are as easy to find and install as any other Palm software. We suggest starting with Palm (www.palm.com/wireless/apps or www.palm.net), which boasts a collection of over 500 Web clipping apps. You can also find them on software sites such as Handango (www.handango.com) and PalmGear H.Q. (www.palmgear.com). Once you download a clipping app, you install it exactly as you would any Palm application (as detailed in Chapter 4).

FIGURE 10-1   With Web clipping apps, you can access a wide range of information and services.

E-Mail and Your Palm

It's hard to remember life before e-mail, isn't it? Imagine, having to actually pick up the *phone* every time you wanted to communicate with someone. Now we just fire off e-mail messages.

Many Palm models come with a simple e-mail application called Mail. It's not a wireless e-mail program; instead, it's designed to allow you to write messages on your Palm, then send them later when you get back to the office and HotSync.

Mail links to the e-mail program on your desktop computer. Just as Memo Pad, Address List, and the other apps synchronize with Palm Desktop, Mail synchronizes with Outlook Express, Eudora Pro, and various other e-mail programs. The end result is that Mail becomes a portable extension of that program, allowing you to view, delete, and reply to messages and write new ones.

What if you have wireless connectivity? Then you won't want to use Mail. Instead, most wireless devices typically come with some sort of e-mail application you can actually use to send and receive messages while away from the desktop. Palm includes a program called VersaMail with most new wireless Palms; Sony includes CLIÉ Mail. Handspring has its own Treo Mail application.

All of these programs have a few things in common. In general, you can use them to retrieve e-mail from one or more POP3 accounts (that's the standard kind of Internet mail most people have). They tend to include all the basic features you'd expect from any e-mail application—the ability to reply, reply all, and forward messages; attach signatures to the end of messages; and filter e-mail. But most Palm-based e-mail programs give you other controls as well. When you set up your e-mail, be sure to look for these features:

- **Leave mail on server**   This is an important setting, since it lets you leave the mail on the server, where your desktop e-mail client can later retrieve it. In most cases, you'll want to be able to get your messages a second time on the desktop—but if not, the option is usually there to delete it as it's downloaded to the PDA.

- **Get Subjects Only**   Since online time is expensive for many wireless devices, most Palm e-mail programs allow you to download just the subject lines for starters—and you can decide which e-mails to download based on that. It saves you the trouble of retrieving 100 spams. Some programs let you choose to download a few lines of the e-mail as well as the subject line.

- **Download attachments**   Most desktop-oriented attachments won't do you much good on a PDA, so some people disable this feature. But it's getting easier and easier to download and use Word, Excel, and PowerPoint files on a PDA, so you may want to enable this feature if you have the right Office-compatible applications on your Palm.

E-Mail Alternatives

You don't have to stick with the e-mail client that comes with your Palm. There are many alternatives available—most of which are commercial applications that cost a small amount of money. This table lists some of the best options currently available:

E-Mail Client	Company	Features
Aileron	www.corsoft.com	This outstanding e-mail client's best feature is the capability to send and receive attachments in common word processing and spreadsheet formats.
Basejet	www.basejet.com	An e-mail client that behaves a lot like a desktop program, with lots of cool tap-and-hold menus, 3-D buttons, and drop-down menus. Basejet doesn't access your mail server directly; it redirects your PC's desktop e-mail to the PDA, keeping both in sync all the time.
SnapperMail	www.snappermail.com	Our favorite third-party e-mail client, SnapperMail has a great interface and can easily handle a wide variety of attachments thanks to "plug-in" applications. It can display JPG images using JpgWatch and sends Word and Excel files to Quickoffice Pro, for instance.

Accessing America Online

At last count, America Online (AOL) had something like 70 billion subscribers. Okay, we may be off by a few billion, but there's no debating the popularity of the service. With AOL for Palm OS, you can access your e-mail account(s) as well as some of the service's more popular areas. Get it from within AOL at keyword Anywhere, or on the Web at www.aol.com/anywhere.

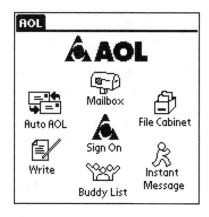

 *Hey, guess what! AOL for Palm is available for both Windows and Macintosh. Way to go, America Online!*

Web Browsing with the Palm

Typically, Palm Powered PDAs don't come with any built-in Web browsing software (the exception is Palm smartphones and connected organizers, which include browsers because they're wireless devices right out of the box).

Essential Web Sites

There are a bunch of Web sites that are dedicated to the Palm OS family of handheld devices. If you're surfing for good Palm-related content, give some of these sites a try:

- The best collection of downloadable Palm software on the Internet can be found at www.PalmGear.com.

- There are lively discussion forums, news, feature stories, and reviews at www.pdabuzz.com, a site that caters to all kinds of handheld PCs.

- Call it a plug if you like, but we can't help recommending Handheld Computing and Mobility, two magazines you can find at www.hhcmag.com. Yeah, we're the editors, but we also think these two magazines give you the definitive word on all things Palm.

- You can find news, product reviews, software, and other Palm stuff at www.handango.com.

- Thanks to news and message boards, www.palmpower.com is an interesting place to stop for Palm information.

- Your home for Web clipping apps is www.palm.net.

10

That's okay—you can add your own. There are several browsers available for the Visor. The most popular browsers include Eudora Internet Suite, AvantGo, Blazer, and Xiino. All of them are available for download from PalmGear.com. Some—such as AvantGo and Eudora—are free, but Blazer and Xiino offer more features.

Surfing Limitations

Once you have a browser installed and some sort of modem (either wired or wireless) attached, you're ready to start surfing. Surfing with your PDA is radically different than surfing with your PC, though. Keep these limitations in mind as you start exploring the Internet with your Palm:

- **Much more limited graphics**   It doesn't take a rocket scientist to deduce this one, but you don't have a lot of room to work with. Most browsers can squeeze large graphics to fit on the small screen, but it can make them hard to see clearly.

- ■ **Color** Unless you have a color model, you'll be looking at everything in shades of gray. The good news? Most browsers support color, so armed with the right handheld model, you can surf the Web in full color.

- ■ **Much lower connection speeds** Your overall Web surfing experience may be a lot more sluggish than you're used to, especially if your desktop PC has a corporate T1 line or some other form of high-speed surfing. Palm modems—especially wireless ones—are quite slow and it can take minutes, not seconds, for a Web page to display.

- ■ **Don't download** The Palm isn't really equipped to handle ordinary Mac or Windows applications or data files—so don't bother trying to download anything. (One exception: you can download Palm apps and Web clipping apps by using the Xiino browser.)

Channel Surfing with AvantGo

Buy all the modems you want—the Web just doesn't fit on a two-inch screen. Enter AvantGo, a free service that not only delivers Web-based content to your

Palm, but also formats it to look pretty (and readable). With every HotSync, the software downloads your preselected channels—everything from news and stock reports to driving directions and movie showtimes—using your computer's modem to ferry the data. Pretty slick—and did we mention it's free? You get 2MB of content—that can be as many as a dozen channels, depending upon how much data is included in each. Want more? You can upgrade to 8MB of AvantGo service for $20/year.

Setting Up AvantGo

To install the AvantGo software, visit the AvantGo Web site and download the software. Install it as per the directions in the package and configure your AvantGo account. You'll need to set up an AvantGo account, complete with username and password.

NOTE   *AvantGo is included on the installation CD-ROM with some Palm devices, but you're better off visiting the AvantGo site and installing the newest software, since it is occasionally updated with new features.*

To set up the channels you want to transfer to your Palm, go to the AvantGo Web site and log in. The AvantGo site should look something like the one shown in Figure 10-2, in which your currently selected channels appear on the left in a column called Your Channels. You can browse the AvantGo Web site and click on any channel you like to add it to your personal AvantGo hot list.

Editing Your Channel Content

Most AvantGo channels are configured to work well on a handheld device with limited memory. Sometimes you might want to customize the way channel content is delivered to your Palm, though. Take *The Onion,* for instance—Dave loves to read this news parody Web site each week while eating lunch, but the site is so large that many of the stories often aren't downloaded to the Palm in their entirety.

10

Wireless Channels

AvantGo is mainly known for its offline browsing capabilities, but it also supports both real-time browsing in the form of Web page access and wireless channels. Several channels are interactive when used with a wireless device; you can request real-time stock quotes, find movies playing in your area, get map data, and more. Here are some of our favorite wireless channels:

- **MapBlast! Maps**   Need to find your way around a strange town? MapBlast displays street-level maps and driving directions of the requested location—just enter an address to get a detailed map of the area.

- **Hollywood.com**   This channel lets you find movie listings, theaters, and showtimes for movies wherever you happen to be.

- **Trip.com**   Want to know details about a flight—such as its airspeed, flight path, and arrival time? This channel lets you find that data.

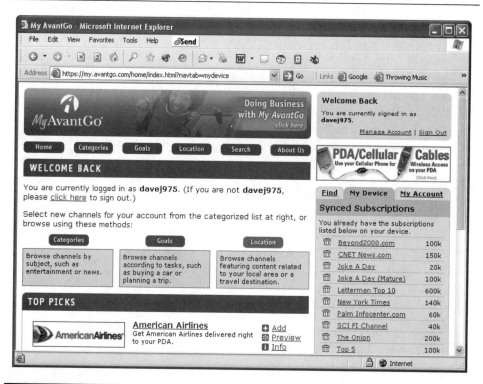

FIGURE 10-2   AvantGo lets you transfer Web "channels" to your Palm for offline reading.

The solution? Dave increased the Maximum Channel Size from the default of 100KB to 500KB so it all fits on his Palm. To edit your channels as cleverly as Dave, open the AvantGo Web page, log in, and click on a channel in the My Device tab. You should see the Channel Properties, as shown in Figure 10-3. Make your changes and click the Save Channel Changes button.

Low on internal memory? You can store your 2MB or so of AvantGo channels on your PDA's memory card, preserving precious RAM in the Palm. To do that, start the AGConnect application (it's AvantGo's configuration program) on your Palm and tap the Settings button at the bottom of the screen. The last option lets you store your channels on the memory card.

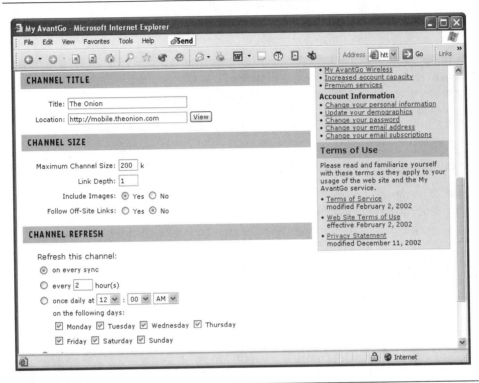

FIGURE 10-3 You can modify the amount of data contained in each channel from this page.

Using AvantGo on Your Palm

Ready to read some news on your Palm while you eat lunch? Start AvantGo and you should see all the channels that you selected and configured on the Web.

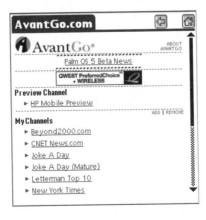

NOTE *If you don't see any channels in AvantGo, it's probably because you haven't HotSynced yet.*

To use AvantGo, just tap on one of the channels in the My Channels list. You can read text, view pictures, and drill deeper into the channel by tapping on links. There are several navigational tools built into AvantGo:

- Tap the navigational arrows to move forward and backward through the current channel.

- Tap the Home icon to return to the My Channels list.

- The newest versions of AvantGo also let you navigate using whatever special navigation controls are on your Palm—such as the Navigator on the Tungsten models or the thumb scroll on the Sony CLIÉ.

In addition to reading cached channels on your Palm, AvantGo can also be used to open live Web pages if you have a modem attached. To do that, follow these steps:

1. Start AvantGo.

2. Choose Channels | Connect from the menu. This tells AvantGo to activate your modem.

3. Choose Channels | Open Page from the menu. Enter the URL you would like to visit and tap OK.

NOTE *AvantGo isn't your only option. Some users prefer HandStory or Plucker (available at PalmGear.com, of course).*

All About Bluetooth

As you've no doubt gathered by now, Bluetooth is a short-range wireless technology that allows devices to communicate with each other up to a distance of about 30 feet. That's really just a fancy way of saying that Bluetooth is a technology designed to replace connection cables. By using Bluetooth, handheld gadgets such as your Palm and cell phone can communicate with each other without wires and without even getting in line-of-sight with each other.

That said, Bluetooth is a new technology that is just starting to hit the streets. That's obvious from the overall lack of Bluetoothness in the world; only the Tungsten T and a few Sony CLIÉs ship with Bluetooth built in.

Adding Bluetooth to Your Palm

Interested in Bluetooth? There are a number of Bluetooth peripherals that enable older, non-Bluetooth Palm devices for wireless communication. These are the most common:

■ **Palm Bluetooth Card**   This $129 device is an SD card that fits in any Palm with the standard SD memory card slot. It's available directly from Palm.

■ **BlueM**   TDK sells a sled-style Bluetooth adapter for Palm m-series PDAs (any device with the Palm universal connector).

So, suppose you have a Tungsten T or a Palm m515 with a Bluetooth adapter. What can you do with it? Right now, the killer app is connecting your Palm to a Bluetooth mobile phone to get Internet access. That means you need to get a phone with built-in Bluetooth. When we wrote this chapter, these phones were available with integrated Bluetooth; by the time you read this, no doubt there will be more:

■ Sony Ericsson T39

■ Sony Ericsson T68i

■ Nokia 6310i

■ Nokia 3650

Once your Bluetooth adapter is installed, here are some of the things you can do with your Palm:

- **Dial the phone**   Just tap on a phone number to dial the phone from your Palm's Address Book.

- **Access the Internet for Web and e-mail**   Once you configure PDA to recognize your Bluetooth cell phone, you can use your Bluetooth connection like any PDA modem to access the Internet.

- **Print**   Armed with a Bluetooth-aware printer driver from Bachmann Software (PrintBoy) or IS/Complete (BtPrint), you can print to a Bluetooth-enabled desktop or portable printer. Epson, MPI Tech, and HP all sell Bluetooth adapters which work with desktop printers and the Pentax PocketJet 200 portable printer.

- **Chat**   The Palm Bluetooth Card comes with whiteboard and chat software that lets several people collaborate from up to 30 feet away from each other.

Pairing Devices

Ready to try your hand at Bluetooth? Once configured, it's very easy to use—but you need to begin by "pairing" the two devices that need to communicate with each other. The pairing process is Bluetooth's built-in security. When devices are paired, both know that they have permission to communicate with each other. It's pairing that prevents you from walking down the street and connecting to a total stranger's Bluetooth device.

Typically, you'll start by pairing your Palm with a mobile phone. The process varies depending upon which Palm and Bluetooth solution you have:

- **Tungsten T**   Your Tungsten T comes with an excellent utility called Phone Link. It's a wizard that steps you through the process of pairing your Palm and phone as well as setting up the PDA to use whatever wireless service you have subscribed to. It's easy and painless, though you may want to check the Support section of the Palm Web site for updates if your new Bluetooth phone is not in the wizard's list.

- **CLIÉ**   If you have a Sony CLIÉ with Bluetooth capabilities, you need to download the Sony Mobile Connection Wizard from the Sony Web site's Service & Support link. This utility runs on the desktop—use it to choose your phone and wireless service, then HotSync to transfer the settings to your PDA.

If you don't have access to one of these wizards because you're using a
Bluetooth card, or you're trying to pair a device other than a phone, the process is
straightforward. Do this:

1. Make sure both devices are discoverable. On the Palm, go to Prefs and tap
on the Bluetooth option. Then make sure that Discoverable is set to Yes.
For the other device, you may need to read its user guide to find out how to
temporarily turn on its Discoverable status.

2. On the Palm, in the Bluetooth Prefs, tap on Trusted Devices and you
should see a list of all the devices that your PDA is set to trust as paired
(if you haven't paired anything yet, this list will be blank).

3. Tap Add Device. After a few moments, your Palm will display a list of all the
Bluetooth devices in the room. Select the one you want to pair and tap OK.

4. The Palm will ask you for a passkey or pairing code. Enter the code preset in the other device according to the user manual. If there is none, you can create your own. Enter a four-digit code into your Palm. You'll immediately be asked to enter the same code into the other device—do so.

5. The Palm will appear in the list of paired devices on the other gadget, and that device will be added to the Trusted Devices list on the Palm. You're done; you can now use the two gadgets together.

Where to Find It

Web Site	Address	What's There
Palm.Net	www.palm.net	Service coverage maps, additional Web clipping apps, instructions on creating clipping apps
Handango	www.handango.com	Web clipping apps (and lots of other Palm software)
PalmGear H.Q.	www.palmgear.com	Web clipping apps (and lots of other Palm software)
MPI Tech	www.mpitech.com	Bluetooth printer adapter
Epson	www.epson.com	Bluetooth printer adapter
IS/Complete	www.iscomplete.com	Bluetooth printer driver
Bachmann Software	www.bachmannsoftware.com	Bluetooth printer driver

Part III

Beyond the Box

Chapter 11

Your Palm as a PC Replacement

How to...

- Use your Palm as a complete business application computer
- Read and edit Word and Excel documents on your Palm
- Distinguish between Palm Doc and Word .doc files
- Import Palm documents into Microsoft Word
- Generate graphs and charts on the Palm
- View Adobe Acrobat files
- Project PowerPoint slides via your Palm
- Print to wireless printers
- Print to serial and parallel printers

The core applications that come with your Palm are fine for many people—they offer all the basic functionality you need to stay on top of contact information and schedules while on the go. But, as you've already seen in this book, your Palm can do so much more. In fact, it's possible to use your Palm as a full-fledged alternative PC, capable of running applications as varied as a word processor, a spreadsheet, and a database program.

Why on Earth would you want to do that? Well, which would you rather carry around—a Palm that fits in your pocket or a seven-pound laptop? Which is easier to store in a hotel room? Which is more easily stolen? Which lasts longer on a set of batteries? We think you get the idea. Obviously, using a suite of "office" applications on your Palm isn't for everyone and won't work all the time. After all, a Palm has a limited amount of storage space, so you can't fit a whole lot of documents on it. Most Palm document editors don't support an extremely extensive array of formatting options, either; so even if you exchange documents with your desktop apps, your text and format options may be somewhat limited. But, if you're intrigued by the thought of leaving your PC at home and traveling only with a Palm, then read on. This chapter is all about creating the perfect Palm office.

Building the Perfect Beast

No, we weren't really big fans of that 80s-era Don Henley solo album either. But that does describe your Palm if you want to outfit it to be a mobile office, complete with office applications.

The name of the game when it comes to creating a Palm office is convenience and compatibility. What good is it, for instance, to generate documents on your Palm if they're not readable by the word processor on your PC? And why bother trying to do office-style work on your Palm if you can't do it easily, efficiently, and in all the apps and formats you're accustomed to on your desktop? With this in mind, here's a list of products you should have if you plan to do serious work on your Palm:

- **Your Palm**   Have plenty of memory. Working with Word documents, databases, and spreadsheets soaks up memory, so you should invest in a Palm with plenty of memory or the capability to upgrade to more, or you might get stopped short. If you still have an old 2MB Palm, consider upgrading to a modern device with 8MB, 16MB, or even more. The Tungsten C comes with 64MB of system memory, and devices with 32MB or more will get increasingly popular as people find how useful they are for working with desktop-style applications and their document files. We highly recommend investing in expansion memory—such as an SD card or Memory Stick—if your PDA is compatible. Equipped with a large expansion card, you can store lots of files on your PDA without running out of memory. How much memory does your Palm have? Find out by choosing App | Info from the Home screen.

11

- **A keyboard**   As much as we love Graffiti, the fact remains you'll hate writing long documents or entering data in a spreadsheet with the stylus alone. Invest in a Palm keyboard. There are a lot of compact, yet comfortable keyboards available for Palm-powered PDAs; see Chapter 15 for a rundown of the best ones.

- **Document reader**   If you mainly need to read documents on your Palm and don't care about creating or editing them, then you can get by with a document reader such as the Palm Reader, TealDoc, or iSilo. These programs let you read large documents that don't fit in the Palm's Memo Pad. Thousands of books and other documents are in the Doc format, which you can download and read on your Palm. Although certainly a popular use for the Palm, this isn't all that interesting from an office-application point of view. What you probably want is a full-featured office application—or, in other words, a document editor. And that's in the very next paragraph...

- **Office suite**   If you want to create new documents or edit files you've already made in Microsoft Word, then a simple document reader like Palm Reader won't be enough. You should try an office suite instead. Though these applications for the Palm are not quite full-featured suites—at least not in the sense that Microsoft Office on the desktop is—some programs deliver sophisticated tools such as spell checkers, rich text formatting, charting tools for your spreadsheet, and more. Most importantly, these programs break through the file-size limit imposed by the Memo Pad and let you edit documents of almost unlimited length that can be shared with Word and Excel.

- **Adobe Acrobat**   If your office makes extensive use of PDF files, you should have Adobe Reader on your Palm so you can view those documents on the go.

- **Database**   Yes, database applications are available even for the Palm. There are a slew of popular programs available for the Palm that let you create new databases from scratch, and most even let you import existing databases from programs such as Access, FileMaker, and other ODBC-compliant applications. Some of the most popular database engines for the Palm include HanDBase, JFile, MobileDB, ThinkDB, and dbNow. FileMaker also has its own PDA "companion" to FileMaker, called (not too surprisingly) FileMaker Mobile. If you're a FileMaker user, FileMaker Mobile may be all you need.

Top Ten Reasons to Use a Palm

Dave: With all the really neat office-like applications available for Palm devices, it got us thinking. What are the top ten reasons to use a handheld computer? So, here it goes (and if you imagine us reading this off blue cards at your local book store, you've pretty much experienced a *How to Do Everything with Your Palm Handheld* book signing):

10. New excuse at work: I was writing the weekly status report, but I dropped it and it broke.

 9. Something new to lose!

 8. Makes you look like a spy.

 7. It's smarter than your dog. Wait—that's also true of houseplants and silverware.

6a. As a *Star Trek: The Next Generation* fan, you like to pretend you're an Enterprise crewmember on an away mission.

6b. As a *Star Trek: The Original Series* fan, you like to pretend you're an Enterprise crewmember in a landing party.

You know, for me, the funny thing is you have to be a *Star Trek* fan to even appreciate the difference between those last two items.

Rick: For me, it's funny to hear Dave describe any of his half of the list as "funny."

 5. Gives you a great pickup line: "Hey, let's HotSync!"

 4. When tipping the pizza guy, now you can calculate 15 percent of $36.87 to the exact penny.

 3. No one can tell you're reading Monica Lewinsky's biography.

 2. You can look busy in a board meeting when you're actually playing a game of SimCity.

 1. They don't put a single penny into Bill Gates' pocket!

Dealing with Documents

If you're like most business travelers, you're used to carting a laptop around with you to edit Word documents. If you have a 14-inch or 15-inch display, then you know what it's like trying to get the laptop screen open in the cramped space on an airplane seat. Heck, sometimes we can't get it open far enough to read what we're typing.

Thankfully, there's an easier solution. Your Palm—combined with a keyboard—can take the place of your laptop for text entry. You can even synchronize specific Word documents with your Palm, edit them on the road, and update your desktop PC with the latest versions of your work when you get home.

Using an Office Suite

Pocket PC users have one small advantage over Palm users—a Microsoft-branded office suite that includes Pocket Word and Pocket Excel. People can trust those apps to be very compatible with Microsoft Office on the desktop.

What a lot of people don't realize, though, is that there are several excellent Office-compatible suites for the Palm as well. Most Palm models come with one

Understanding the Doc Format

All Doc files are not created alike. Specifically, when Palm users talk about Doc files—text documents in the Doc format—they're usually not gabbing about Microsoft Word's .doc format but, instead, about a text format originally popularized by a program called AportisDoc. These days, programs such as TealDoc (from TealPoint) and Palm's own Palm Reader are generally considered the de facto standard among Palm text readers today. Although any Doc file can be read by almost any Doc reader/editor for the Palm (and vice versa), the Doc format is totally incompatible with the version used by Microsoft Word. On the plus side, you can generally get converters for most of these readers that convert desktop .doc to Palm Doc files and back again.

right in the box, in fact: Documents to Go, from DataViz. If your Palm-powered PDA didn't come with an office suite—or you want to try another, you'll be happy to know that there are three popular suites to choose from:

■ **Documents to Go** (www.dataviz.com)   Documents to Go is quite popular by virtue of the fact that Palm has chosen to put it in the box of every new Palm model it sells. In addition to a word processor (Word to Go) and spreadsheet (Sheets to Go), the Professional edition of Documents to Go includes the capability to view PowerPoint slides and Adobe Acrobat (PDF) files.

■ **Iambic Office** (www.iambic.com)   Comprised of FastWriter and TinySheet, these programs offer Word and Excel connectivity for your Palm. In addition, the suite includes Iambic Mail, an e-mail client that lets you synchronize messages with your desktop e-mail program or check mail on the go with a modem. Iambic Mail uses FastWriter and TinySheet to let you read Word and Excel attachments in e-mail.

■ **Quickoffice** (www.cesinc.com)   This suite includes Quickword and Quicksheet for reading and editing Word and Excel documents. Quickword has its own thesaurus and spell checker, and you can install custom fonts as well. Quickoffice also allows Palm users to collaborate wirelessly on documents via cell phones and modems—so you can invite other people to view and make changes to a document even if you're in different cities.

NOTE *Very old versions of Documents To Go don't support document editing; they simply provided the capability to view Microsoft Office files. If you don't have Documents to Go 3.0 or higher, consider upgrading to a newer office suite so you can actually edit files.*

TIP *If you don't want the entire suite, you can usually buy the word processor and spreadsheet separately by visiting the vendor's Web site. Cutting Edge Software sells Quickword all by itself, for instance, if you don't need Quicksheet.*

Transferring Documents Between the Palm and Desktop

No matter which suite you choose, they all work more or less the same way: you use a desktop application to manage the documents you want to work with on the Palm. That's because most office suites don't read and write Microsoft Office documents directly. Instead, they need to convert Word and Excel files, for instance, into file formats that can be understood by the Palm software. That means there's an intermediate "conversion" step to get going.

Just drag the document you want to move into the suite manager (you can see several of them in the following illustration), and it'll be copied to the Palm at the next HotSync. When you make a change to the document on either the Palm or the desktop, it'll be synchronized after the following HotSync, keeping the two documents exactly the same.

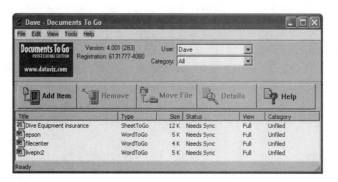

<table>
<tr><td>TIP</td><td>Bachmann Software's FilePoint is a file management program for the Palm that lets you install documents from the desktop as well. So if you have several different Office-style applications, you can transfer files on the Palm to all of them by using just one program—FilePoint—instead of loading each office suite's desktop component separately.</td></tr>
</table>

If you prefer not to synchronize your Palm documents with their cousins on the desktop, that's fine as well. In each suite manager, you can disable synchronization and select familiar options such as Handheld overwrites, Desktop overwrites, and Do nothing.

What if you create a new document from scratch on the Palm? No problem. On the next HotSync after you create the document, you'll find that it has been synchronized with the desktop. To find it, just open your suite manager software and double-click on the new file; it'll automatically open in Word.

Editing Native Office Files

There's one important exception to this file conversion process. The newest versions of both Documents to Go and Quickoffice Premier support native Microsoft Office files. That means you just need to drag and drop the original

Word, Excel, and PowerPoint files onto your PDA to immediately begin using them—no need for a desktop conversion at all. Even better, you can get Office documents as attachments in e-mail programs and edit them on the PDA:

- **Documents to Go**   In order to receive and edit Office e-mail attachments on your Palm, you need Dataviz Inbox to Go. It interfaces with Documents to Go to provide seamless document viewing and editing.

- **Quickoffice Premier**   If you use Quickoffice and want to edit Word and Excel files you receive via e-mail on your Palm, use SnapperMail (shown in Figure 11-1), from Snapperfish.com.

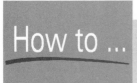

How to ... Work with Palm Documents

In a nutshell, here's what you need to know to work with text documents on the Palm:

- To create or edit long documents on your Palm, you need a program such as Documents To Go, Quickoffice, Iambic Office, or WordSmith.

- On the desktop, open your office suite's manager application.

- Click the button to add a file, or just drag and drop a document into the suite's manager's window.

- Close the program and then HotSync to transfer the files to the Palm.

- Edit the files on your Palm.

- HotSync to carry the changes you made to the Palm back to the desktop versions of the affected files.

FIGURE 11-1   New e-mail programs such as SnapperMail and Inbox to Go allow you to get native Office files—such as Word and Excel—as attachments and edit them right on your PDA, then forward the completed documents via wireless e-mail back to someone's desktop.

Working with Documents and Spreadsheets

If you want to leave your laptop at home and just carry a PDA, it's absolutely essential to be able to read and edit Word and Excel files on the go. Any of the suites we've already mentioned will work, and if all you care about is text, you have a fourth excellent option as well—a program from Blue Nomad called WordSmith (shown next). WordSmith doesn't come as part of a suite with a spreadsheet. Instead, it's a stand-alone word processor for the Palm that, like Quickoffice, includes font support, a spell checker, thesaurus, and sophisticated formatting controls. Many users choose WordSmith as their word processor of choice, especially if they don't also need a spreadsheet.

11

Although most Palm word processors try very hard to preserve all of the formatting in your document, keep in mind that these programs do it with varying levels of success. You may find, for instance, that group annotations or graphics such as "boxes" around text may be stripped out when the files are synchronized back to the PC. As a consequence, word processing on the Palm is often best reserved for documents that have fairly conservative levels of formatting. In addition, some word processors have more formatting features than others. Documents to Go, for instance, may be popular, but it can't hold a candle to WordSmith and Quickword when it comes to embedding formatted text in your documents.

Bottom line: since all office suites have a free trial period, we recommend installing all of them and seeing which one you like best.

Many word processors on the Palm don't support some advanced formatting features, and they're stripped away when you synchronize documents. When we tested these programs, Documents to Go did best with wacky stuff like text with Track Changes; Quickoffice and TinyWriter sometimes made a real mess out of the text. Documents to Go keeps the desktop version of the document intact even when it has truly unusual formatting elements (such as images) that don't display on the Palm.

Better Software for Bigger Screens

If you feel constrained by the anemic width of the Palm screen, you're not alone. That's why virtually all new Palm devices offer dramatically higher resolutions, either 320×320 or 320×480. And because most of the office suites support these higher resolutions (at the time that we wrote this, only Iambic Office didn't), along with a variety of fonts and font sizes, you can pack a lot more data on the screen— provided you have strong enough eyesight to see all those little letters.

Charts and Graphs on the Palm

Spreadsheets are often reported to be the most popular PC-based application in the history of computers (we're not sure who they talked to—personally, we'd vote for games). And like milk and cereal or guitars and rock 'n' roll, nothing goes with spreadsheets quite like charts and graphs. It makes sense, then, that you might want to view your spreadsheet data visually in the form of charts and graphs even on your Palm. You're in luck: both Iambic Office and Quickoffice come with their own spreadsheet graphing tools. As you can see in the following illustration, you can make some very attractive graphs using these programs.

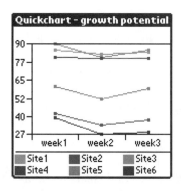 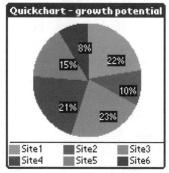

Adobe Acrobat on the Palm

In most offices, Word and Excel pop up pretty often—but Adobe Acrobat files, also known by their file extension as PDF files, are incredibly popular as well. That's because PDFs are self-contained, fancy-looking, text-and-graphic documents that display exactly the same no matter what kind of computer you view them on. They also can't be edited, so you can distribute a PDF secure in the knowledge that some clown in room 234 won't make changes to your handiwork.

That's great, but until recently you couldn't view them on the Palm. Today, there are several ways to display Adobe Acrobat files on your PDA. Two of the better ones are

■ **Documents to Go Professional**   This has its own PDF viewer. On the downside, this viewer strips out graphics, so it's only useful for documents that are text-based.

11

■ **Adobe Reader for Palm**   This is a free program from Adobe that lets you download PDF files to your Palm. This program lets you choose to include or strip out graphics, so you can save memory on your PDA by leaving out non-essential graphics or leave them in if they're needed to understand the document.

In our humble opinion, these are the best—but you can find other programs that do this as well. If you want to experiment, check out programs such as Microbat Reader, Ansyr Primer PDF Viewer, RichReader, and PDF2Doc.

PowerPoint on Your Palm

The last piece of the puzzle is PowerPoint. If you lug your laptop around so you can deliver slideshows on the road, well, we have some good news for you. Your Palm is capable of pumping slides directly to a projector—in their entire 1024×768, full-color glory.

Actually, depending upon your needs and which PDA model you own, you have a few choices:

■ **Documents to Go Professional**   This program just won't go away! It seems like we've mentioned it a dozen times in this chapter alone. The professional version of DTG includes a PowerPoint viewer. You can't broadcast these slides on a projector or even edit them once they're on your device, but you can use this viewer to view the slides in both a text-only and graphic mode.

■ **Margi Presenter-to-Go**   If you want to plug your Palm into a projector, get Presenter-to-Go. This product is available in several versions, including one for the Handspring Visor, as a CompactFlash card for the HandEra 330, for the Palm m-series (which uses the Palm's standard SD memory slot), and as a Memory Stick card for the Sony CLIÉ. You can fit hundreds of slides in memory, they project in high-res and full-color, and you can avoid all of the hassles that go with setting up, booting, carrying, and managing a laptop.

■ **iGo Pitch**   Like Margi's line of PowerPoint projectors, Pitch lets you
display PowerPoint presentations stored on your PDA directly on a VGA
screen. Pitch is a small, PDA-sized gadget that connects to your Palm via a
HotSync cable (you can use a HotSync cable or the entire cradle) or even
wirelessly via Bluetooth (if you have a Bluetooth-equipped Palm). The
Pitch hardware also has a standard VGA connector for attaching it to a
monitor or projector. It's shown here with the optional Bluetooth adapter:

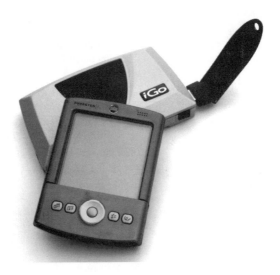

Printing from Your Palm

The ultimate handheld PC would probably look a lot like the Palm, but with one important difference: it would have a paper-thin printer embedded inside, enabling you to print anything you see on the screen. Although that's mere science fiction for the time being, this doesn't mean you can't print stuff from a Palm. Quite the contrary: armed with a print driver, you can send a wide variety of documents from your Palm to a desktop printer or to a portable, pocket-sized printer.

In order to print anything from your Palm, you need to add a print driver. There are several available, and selecting one isn't as easy as it sounds. You need to consider three ingredients:

- **Your operating system** Some print drivers require at least OS 4.0.

- **What you want to print** Some print drivers only print data from the Palm's four core apps, whereas others can print documents from certain office suites.

- **What kind of printer you want to print to** If you have your eye on a compact, battery-operated portable printer, you'll need to find a print driver that works with that printer.

This chart outlines some key data for the most common Palm print drivers:

	Printers	Software
InStep Print	Prints to almost all portable and desktop printers	The broadest range of document types, including Documents to Go, Quickoffice, WordSmith, and the Palm's own built-in applications.
IrPrint	Prints to almost all portable and desktop printers	Supports Documents to Go, WordSmith, and other apps. Has some problems printing from Handspring Visors, though.
PalmPrint	Supports most portable and desktop printers	Prints from the Palm's core apps, as well as a few third-party programs, including Quickword.
PrintBoy	Prints only 8.5×11-inch pages, which means it doesn't work with very compact printers such as the Sipix Pocket Printer	Largely prints only from the Palm's core applications.

As you can see, getting a good match among your Palm device, the software you want to print, and the printer you want to use can be tricky. Be sure to visit the Web site of each of these print-driver vendors to check their latest list of compatible programs and printers.

Did you know?

What IR Is All About

Technically, IrDA stands for the Infrared Data Association, which is just a bunch of companies that make IR-enabled products. More important, though, IrDA represents the industry-standard infrared port you can find on most laptops, handheld PCs, and printers with IR ports. If you find a printer with an IrDA port, chances are excellent it'll work with one of the Palm's print drivers.

Infrared Printers for Your Palm

The easiest way to print from your Palm to a nearby printer is via infrared. Your Palm's IR port (the same one that you can use to beam apps and data to other PDAs) can communicate directly with compatible printers. A small handful of lightweight portable and IR-enabled printers are around. If you like the idea of printing wirelessly from your Palm, or if you travel frequently and want to print from wherever you happen to be, look into one of these:

Manufacturer	Printer	Comments
Desktop Printers with Infrared		
Hewlett-Packard	LaserJet 6P	Desktop laser printer
	LaserJet 6MP	Desktop laser printer
	LaserJet 2100	Desktop laser printer
Portable, Laptop-Oriented Printers		
Canon	BJC-55	Lightweight mobile printer
	BJC-85	Lightweight mobile printer
Handheld-Sized Portable Printers		
Brother	Mprint	Handheld thermal printer
Citizen	PN-60i	Point-of-sale printer
Pentax	PocketJet 200	Handheld thermal printer, compatible with IrDA adapter
Sipix	Pocket Printer A6	Handheld thermal printer

11

Bluetooth Printing

If you have a Bluetooth adapter for your Palm (or you have a model with Bluetooth built in), you can print wirelessly to a Bluetooth-enabled printer. As we wrote this chapter, our Bluetooth options in the printing world were quite limited, but we expect that will slowly start to change over the next few months.

The best example of an honest-to-goodness, working Bluetooth printer is Epson's C80 inkjet printer. It's Bluetooth compatible, and by adding the Epson Bluetooth Adapter (a small gadget that plugs into the back of the printer), you can send print jobs to the printer from up to about 30 feet away.

If you don't want to buy the C80, you might also consider a Bluetooth print adapter. Several companies, including Epson (www.epson.com), Bachmann Software (bachmannsoftware.com) and MPI Tech (www.mpitech.com) sell affordable adapters that plug into the parallel port of your existing printer and make it Bluetooth-ready.

Of course, if you get a Bluetooth printer, you'll need a Bluetooth-aware print driver for your Palm as well. There are two, and both worked great in our testing:

- PrintBoy Anywhere (bachmannsoftware.com)

- BtPrint (iscomplete.org)

Printing to a Parallel or Serial Printer

What if you don't have access to an infrared printer? That's when things can get dicey. If you own a serial port printer (such as any Apple ImageWriter), plug the Palm's HotSync cradle into the printer and, with the Palm docked, send jobs to the printer.

Most Windows users don't have serial printers, though. They use parallel printers. In that case, you need a special serial-to-parallel converter (available from Stevens Creek, the manufacturer of PalmPrint).

You have another option as well. The PrintBoy InfraReady Adapter from Bachmann Software is a small plug that fits into the parallel port of any printer. A small IR port turns the printer into an IR-ready device that you can use with your Palm. It's small and light, so you can carry it with you when you travel.

NOTE *It doesn't make any difference if you print via the PC or via your Palm—the print quality is identical, and everything prints out fine on standard 8.5×11-inch paper. If it's more convenient to print via your Palm, go for it!*

Printers for Your Pocket

If you expect to do a lot of printing and want to have easy access to a portable printer, you have a few excellent choices. Forget about having to track down a desktop printer when you're on the road—just carry your printer in your pocket. Here are three models we highly recommend:

- The Brother MPrint. This thermal printer measures 4×6.4×.7 and weighs just 10 ounces—yet it holds 50 sheets of 3×4-inch paper in an internal tray and gets about 100 sheets on a single charge of its Lithium-Ion battery. It comes with IS/Complete's IrPrint software.

- The Sipix Pocket Printer A6. This is a lightweight printer that measures just 6×4×1 inches. It uses a thermal process to print on a roll of paper at about 400 dpi. The Pocket Printer runs on four AA batteries and has both a serial interface and an IrDA port, which means you can print wirelessly.

- The Pentax PocketJet is a bit longer—it's 10×2×1 inches and uses thermal imaging to print 300 dpi on either sheets or rolls of paper. The Pentax may be bigger, but it lets you print real letter-sized documents. It, too, uses serial and IrDA, and it uses AC power or internal rechargeable batteries for power.

11

> ■ The Monarch 6015 is a clever thermal printer that actually wraps around the Palm III, giving you a complete Palm and printing solution in one handheld package. It runs on four AA batteries and prints at 200 dpi on 2-inch-wide rolls, much like a restaurant receipt.

Where to Find It

Web Site	Address	What's There
Brother	www.brother.com	MPrint
Stevens Creek	www.stevenscreek.com	PalmPrint
DataViz	www.dataviz.com	Documents To Go
Blue Nomad	www.bluenomad.com	WordSmith
Cutting Edge Software	www.cesinc.com	Quickoffice
Iambic Software	www.iambic.com	Iambic Office
IS/Complete	www.iscomplete.com	IRPrint and other print drivers
InStep Print	www.instepgroup.com	InStep Print
Bachmann Software	www.bachmannsoftware.com	PrintBoy and the InfraReady Adapter
SnapperMail	www.snappermail.com	SnapperMail

Chapter 12

Hacks and Other Handy Utilities

How to...

- ■ Install and use Hacks
- ■ Make capital letters the easy way
- ■ Automatically correct spelling errors
- ■ Drag and drop text
- ■ Use the hard buttons to load multiple applications
- ■ Automatically remove duplicate entries from your databases
- ■ Access "hidden" Palm memory
- ■ Manage and beam applications
- ■ Choose a launcher
- ■ Create your own Palm OS software
- ■ Improve Graffiti recognition
- ■ Replace Graffiti with a different handwriting recognition engine
- ■ Write anywhere on the Palm's screen
- ■ Write faster with word-completion software

When you hear the word "utilities," you probably think of your monthly electric bill or those four worthless Monopoly properties (hey, $150 isn't gonna break anybody's bank). In the world of computers and Palm devices, however, utilities are software programs that add capabilities and fix problems. They're power tools, though not necessarily limited to power users.

In this chapter, we tell you about some cool and worthwhile Palm OS utilities. When we're done, you'll find yourself with a reliable backup that can overcome any data-loss disaster, a way to drag and drop text, a timesaving way to write capital letters, and lots more. Utilities may sound boring and technical, but they're actually fun, easy to use, and extremely practical.

X-Master

The mother of all Palm utilities, X-Master is what separates the men from the boys, the women from the girls. It's a tool Tim Allen would love, as it allows Palm devices to reach beyond their limits, to achieve "more power!" And, it's a tool many users come to find indispensable.

 Hacks don't work on the Zire 71, Tungsten C, Sony CLIÉ NX/NZ series, and other Palm Powered handhelds equipped with OS 5. However, some software developers have introduced OS 5–compatible versions of their products. See the section "OS 5 Hacks" for some utilities specific to your operating system. In the meantime, don't install X-Master (or any Hacks) on your device—it could cause major problems. That said, TealPoint Software's TealMaster does offer an OS 5 compatibility mode, but that might be more trouble than it's worth—unless there are some Hacks you absolutely cannot live without.

What X-Master Does

Technically speaking, X-Master is an "operating system extension manager." By itself, it serves no function. But it enables the use of *Hacks*—little programs that extend the capabilities of your Palm device. Forget the negative connotations usually associated with "hacking"—these programs are here to help, not harm.

And if you want to run them, you must first download and install X-Master. See Chapter 4 for information on installing programs like this—it's applicable to the Hacks you'll be downloading as well.

 *Because Hacks tinker directly with the Palm OS, they can create the occasional glitch. And the more Hacks you have installed and running, the greater the likelihood of some sort of problem. The most common is your Palm device crashing, which is usually more of an annoyance than anything else.*

12

As you venture out into the world of Palm software, you may discover other Hack managers. For instance, there's HackMaster, the granddaddy that started this whole crazy Hack business. There's also TealMaster, the most robust and feature-rich of all the Hack managers. But we're partial to X-Master because we've used it extensively and it has just the features we need. Plus, it's freeware—unlike TealMaster, which costs $9.95 (still a great deal).

How to Use It

Launching X-Master is no different from launching any other program—you just tap its icon. But, as previously noted, the software is useless without any Hacks loaded. Therefore, to help you learn to use this utility, we're going to walk you through the installation of one of our favorite Hacks.

It's called *MiddleCaps,* and it saves you from having to write the Graffiti upstroke every time you want to create an uppercase letter. Instead, you simply write the letter so it crosses the invisible line between the letter and number sides of the Graffiti area. We find this enables us to write much more quickly and naturally.

 *If your handheld has Graffiti 2, you don't need MiddleCaps. That's because Graffiti 2 works exactly the same way when it comes to uppercase letters: they appear automatically when you write across the middle.*

MiddleCaps is freeware, as many Hacks are, so you can download and use it free of charge. (A note of appreciation e-mailed to the author is always nice.) You can find MiddleCaps at PalmGear.com, among other sites. Let's get it running on your Palm device.

1. Download MiddleCaps and install it on your Palm. You won't find an icon for it in the Home screen. The only real evidence of Hacks appears in X-Master.

2. Tap the X-Master icon to load the utility, and you'll see MiddleCaps listed.

3. Notice the empty box to the left of the name. Tap it with your stylus and you'll see a check mark appear. That means the Hack is now enabled. If you want to disable it, just tap the box again. (For purposes of our tutorial, please leave it enabled.)

4. Notice the Configure button at the bottom of the screen. Tap it to set up MiddleCaps (a one-time procedure).

5. You're now in the MiddleCaps Preferences screen, where you can tweak a few of the program's settings. For now, check the box marked Caps On Crossing. This means a capital letter will appear whenever you write a character that crosses between the letter and number sides of the Graffiti area. You can test it by tapping to place your cursor on the line near the bottom of the screen, and then doing some sample writing.

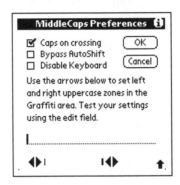

Tap OK to return to the main X-Master screen. That's it! MiddleCaps is now enabled and will work in all Palm applications—even third-party ones.

What about those other two buttons at the bottom of the X-Master screen? You can tap Details to get version information and other notes about the Hack or tap Info to get the Hack's "splash screen."

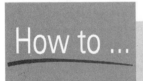 **Beam Hacks to Other Users**

X-Master has the enviable capability to beam Hacks directly to other users (see Chapter 4 for more information on beaming). But before you start, make sure the recipient has X-Master (or HackMaster or another Hack manager). If he doesn't, you'll need to beam a copy of X-Master before you beam any Hacks. However, X-Master doesn't include the option of beaming itself. For that, you must return to the Home screen and tap Menu | App | Beam. Choose X-Master from the list, and then tap the Beam button. Now you can return to X-Master and beam some Hacks. Highlight the one you want to share, and then tap Menu | Extensions | Beam.

12

Important Notes About Hacks

You need to abide by a few rules of thumb when using X-Master on your Palm device, all of them intended to keep things running smoothly:

■ If you ever decide to delete a Hack from your Palm, make sure you disable it first! If you try to delete a Hack while it's still running, it could cause errors, crashes, or even data loss.

■ If you install two or three Hacks on your Palm, don't enable them all simultaneously. Instead, enable one at a time, making sure each works properly before enabling the next one.

■ If you have to reset your Palm device for any reason, a message pops up asking if you want to "reinstall your formerly active collection of system Hacks." Tap Reinstall (the equivalent of "yes") only if you're sure it wasn't a Hack that forced you to have to reset in the first place. Otherwise, tap Cancel. Then you can go back into X-Master and manually enable your Hacks again.

World's Greatest Hacks

If you were impressed by what MiddleCaps did for your Palm, wait 'til you get a load of some of our other favorites. Rather than list them by name, which doesn't always express what they do, we're going to list them by function. You can find all these Hacks at PalmGear.com H.Q.

Automatically Correcting Spelling Errors

Giving Graffiti a helping hand, CorrectHack works like the AutoCorrect feature in Microsoft Word, automatically correcting words you frequently misspell. Alas, it doesn't have a database of its own; you have to supply both the words and their correct spellings. But as you compile your list over time, you'll wind up with far fewer mistakes. And you can also use CorrectHack as shorthand for commonly used words. For instance, you write your initials, and the software automatically plugs in your full name.

Fonts...Lots and Lots of Fonts

The Palm OS comes with a whopping three fonts: regular, bold, and large. That's not nearly enough for those of us who grew up with Arial, Century Gothic, Times New Roman, and other font faves. You can have access to a boatload of typefaces if you install *FontHack 123,* which lets you replace the system fonts with fonts of your choosing. FontHack comes with just one—you'll find 20 more in the Alpha Font Collection 1.71. Both products are freeware. Beat that!

```
On the 5th of july in 1963 some quick
foxes jumped over lazy dogs.
brown foxes jumped over lazy dogs.
On the 5th of July in 1963 quick
On the 5th of July in 1963 quick brown Dogs.
On the 5th of July in 1963 quick
quick brown Foxes jumped
ON THE 5TH OF JULY IN 1963
On the 5th of July in 1963 quick
1963 quick brown Dogs are
On the 5th of july in 1963
On the 4th of August in 1982 quick brown Dogs
```

Dragging and Dropping Text

Although you can select snippets of text by tapping and dragging your stylus, you can't drag that text to another spot and drop it in (as you can with any word processor). TextEditHack adds that capability to text-oriented applications such as Memo Pad and even makes it easier to select text. You can double-tap to select a single word, triple-tap to select a sentence, and quadruple-tap to select all the text on the screen. Very handy.

Launching More than Four Programs with the Application Buttons

The more software you have loaded on your Palm device, the harder it becomes to hunt for the desired program icon. Enter AppHack, which uses two sequential presses of the application buttons to launch up to 24 programs. You needn't remember the combinations you set up—AppHack displays a cheat-sheet when you press the first button, so you can see which program will load when you press the second one.

12

This Hack is a little confusing to work with, especially because no instructions are provided, but it sure can save time.

Enhance the Find Feature

FindHack turbocharges the Palm's Find function, remembering the last six searches you performed and letting you define up to four default searches. What's more, you can choose whether to search all installed applications, just the core apps, or only the currently loaded program. It even supports the use of wildcards—searching for "book*" would return "book," "bookmark," "bookstore," and so forth.

Improving Your Graffiti Accuracy

One of our all-time favorite hacks is TealEcho, which lets you see your Graffiti strokes as you write them. This "visual feedback" helps you improve your writing speed and accuracy, because it lets you see how your characters really look, as opposed to the way they're supposed to look. TealEcho (www.tealpoint.com) costs $11.95, but we think it's well worth the money.

Livening Up Those Sound Effects

Getting tired of your handheld's boring old beeps? TechSounds comes with a handful of nifty audio snippets you can assign to various system functions, and enables you to download even more sound effects (www.ecamm.com). It also supports startup and shutdown screens, if you're into that sort of thing.

OS 5 Hacks

Just because Palm OS 5 doesn't support the use of Hacks doesn't mean you can't add some worthwhile utilities. In this section, we spotlight some Hack-like programs no OS 5 user should be without. We found all of them at PalmGear.com.

- **CrossingOver**   If you own a Tungsten T or another model that has Palm OS 5 but *not* Graffiti 2, you'll appreciate this invaluable utility. Like the aforementioned MiddleCaps Hack (and Graffiti 2), CrossingOver creates capital letters when you write in the middle of the Graffiti area.

- **Fonts4**   OS 5 doesn't offer much in the fonts department. If you'd like to change the way text looks on your PDA, check out these nifty font collections. Make sure you get the one specific to your model, such as Fonts4NX (for the CLIÉ NX series), Fonts4TC (for the Tungsten C), and so on. Just search for "fonts" on PalmGear.com and you'll find all the collections.

- **PowerOn for OS 5**   It's a common scenario: you slip your PDA into a pocket or purse, only to find it dead a few hours later when you pull it out. The cause? Something was pressing against one of the buttons, causing the unit to power on and the battery to drain. PowerOn reduces the chance of

12

that happening by disabling the hard buttons. Or, more accurately, by requiring two quick presses of one of them to turn the unit on.

- **QLaunch** Your handheld has just four hard buttons, but there are probably a lot more than four programs you use regularly. QLaunch lets you launch up to three applications from each button. You can also use it to access special functions, such as the built-in keyboard or the Bluetooth radio (if your model has one).

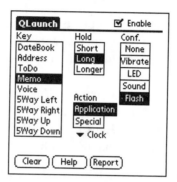

- **ToneDial** Because OS 5 devices have enhanced audio capabilities, they can dial a phone for you by generating the necessary tones. This can come in handy if you're standing at a pay phone trying to juggle kids, luggage, the phone itself, and so on. ToneDial integrates with the Palm OS Address Book, thus enabling you to dial any number in the contact list just by tapping it. Of course, you have to hold the PDA next to the telephone headset, but it's still easier than punching in the numbers by hand. It doesn't work with cell phones, though.

Two Great Utilities for Tungsten T Users

Much as we like the Tungsten T's cool sliding design, it's kind of a hassle to open the unit every time we want to access the Graffiti area. Fortunately, we found a pair of utilities that virtually eliminate the need:

- **Graffiti Anywhere** This handy utility frees you from the Graffiti area, enabling you to write anywhere on the screen. It's a freebie, too!

- **SlideFree** When you draw a special stroke on the screen, SlideFree pops up a command bar containing all the icons found in the Graffiti area—Favorite, Find, Brightness, and so on.

Other Utilities

X-Master works minor miracles, but it isn't the only tool you should consider owning. No Hacks can create reliable backups of your data, or give you greater flexibility in beaming software to other users, or remove duplicate entries from your databases. And there's certainly no Hack that digs up extra memory for you to use. So read on to learn about some of the other highlights of the Palm OS utility world.

> NOTE   *Most of the utilities listed here can be purchased and downloaded from PalmGear.com.*

Backup Utilities

One of the really cool things about the Palm OS is the way it keeps a complete copy of your data on your PC. Every time you HotSync, it's like you're making a backup of your important info. If something terrible befalls your handheld—the batteries die, or it gets lost, stolen, run over, sat on, or inexplicably wiped clean—at least you know your data lives on your PC.

Of course, what happens if you're a thousand miles from home and your PDA piffles? To reduce the chance of a major crisis, consider using a backup utility and a memory card. Most current Palm OS handhelds have expansion slots that can accommodate such cards, and there are numerous utilities that can make backups of absolutely everything. If your handheld gets wiped, you simply insert the card, run the backup utility, and hit "restore."

Memory Cards

First things first: you need a memory card. If you need a refresher on what memory cards are and how to use them, see Chapter 4. Just make sure you have a card with at least as much storage space as your Palm has RAM. That is, if your Palm has 16MB of internal memory, you need a memory card that holds at least 16MB. (Of course, you'll probably wind up with a 128MB or 256MB card, as they're the best deals—so you should be more than adequately covered.)

The card you use for your backup needn't be used for that exclusively—you can still use it to store extra applications, MP3 files, photos, and other stuff. You just need to be sure there's enough space available to store a copy of the contents of your PDA's internal memory.

> NOTE   *Palm offers two Secure Digital memory cards designed expressly with backup in mind. The 16MB Backup Card and a 64MB Backup Card Plus come with a backup utility already installed, so they're effectively plug-and-play solutions. Just pop the card in, run the software, and you're on your way.*

Backup Software

Once you're outfitted with a memory card, you need a backup utility to go with it. (A few handhelds come with backup software already installed or included in the software bundle, so check yours before you buy anything.) There are several programs that get the job done with a minimum of fuss. Usually it's just a matter of tapping Backup, then waiting a few minutes for the process to complete. If you need to restore your data, tap Restore and wait again.

That said, you may want to look for certain features when choosing a backup utility:

- **Scheduled backups**   Some programs can make backups for you automatically at predetermined times. This can be quite helpful if you're the forgetful sort, because it insures you'll always have an up-to-date backup at the ready.

- **Partial backups**   Although it's nice to have a backup of every single bit of data in your PDA, you may want to save time (or storage space) by backing up a select few files. Some programs let you pick and choose which files to copy; others make it an all-or-nothing proposition.

- **Incremental backups**   Making a complete backup of everything in RAM takes time. If your software supports incremental backups, only those files that have changed will be copied during subsequent backup sessions. That can save you a ton of time and storage space.

A search of PalmGear.com reveals a multitude of backup utilities. We recommend Botzam Backup, a full-featured program that supports not only all the features mentioned previously, but also Palm OS 5. At $14.95, it's also very reasonably priced.

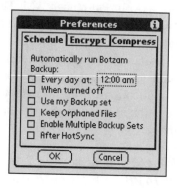

The Problem with Prequels

Palm, schmalm. . . let's talk about the really important stuff—namely, treasured sci-fi franchises that have been ruined by prequels.

Rick: First, there was the colossal disappointment of *Enterprise,* the blandest, most uninteresting *Star Trek* series ever. Now, George Lucas continues to make a mockery of the *Star Wars* trilogy by serving up pabulum like *Attack of the Clones.* Maybe I'm too old, maybe I'm jaded, maybe I just expect fresh writing and decent acting, but these prequels have left me colder than a polar bear in January. They're just not *fun.* The magic is gone. And I think this is a problem inherent to the prequel formula—when you know the outcome, there's no suspense. I *know* Anakin will turn into Darth Vader in *Episode III.* For me, there's no excitement in watching it happen. And don't get me started on all the ways *Enterprise* has violated *Star Trek* canon. . . .

Dave: You, my friend, have been abducted by mind-controlling body snatchers. First, *Enterprise:* it's fresh, fun, and engaging. I enjoy the show immensely, though I'm sometimes disappointed that the stories are too "*Next Generation*-ish." It's always with the time travel, and there's often not enough "gee whiz, Batman! We're in outer space!" As for Lucas's *Episode II,* you're just off your rocker. Are you too cool to like stuff anymore? All the million-dollar book royalties gone to your head? What do you expect? To be knocked off your feet like you were watching *Star Wars* when you were 12? Not going to happen—that film is a classic, and you were lucky enough to see it for the first time at the perfect age. *Episode II* is a good film in its own right, though, and it may eventually be judged as the second best of the lot. . . unless *Episode III* really knocks our socks off, that is. Check back in the fifth edition to see what we thought of *that* movie.

12

"Free" Extra Memory with JackFlash

Psst! Don't let this get around, but your Palm device has been holding out on you. It has extra, hidden RAM that's just sitting around doing nothing. You see, in addition to its 2 to 64MB of main memory, it has a couple megabytes of Flash memory (a.k.a. the Flash ROM) where the operating system (OS) is stored. But the OS occupies only some of that space, leaving idle upwards of 4MB (the actual amount varies depending on your model). Brayder Technologies' JackFlash lets you tap into that memory, using it to store programs, data, even backups of your primary databases.

Some Palm devices either don't have Flash memory or don't have enough free to make JackFlash worthwhile. Among them: the Palm IIIe, Palm VII series, m100 series, and Handspring Visor series.

Given that it ventures deep into the guts of your Palm device, JackFlash is admirably easy to use. It provides a list of the contents of main RAM and Flash memory. To move a program or database from one to the other, you simply tap the menu next to it, select RAM or Flash, and then tap the Update button.

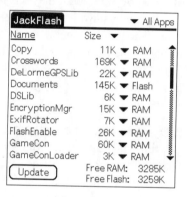

How to ... Beam Software to Another Palm User

Suppose you're enjoying a game of Vexed (one of our favorites), and a fellow Palm user says, "Hey, I'd like to try that!" Generous sort that you are, you agree to beam a copy of the game (which is perfectly legal because Vexed is freeware). To do so, return to the Applications screen, and then choose Menu | App | Beam. Find Vexed in the software list, tap to highlight it, then tap the Beam button. Point your Palm device at the other person's Palm device, and then wait a few seconds for the transfer to complete. Presto! You've just shared some great software—wirelessly! Just one caveat: some copy-protected programs (which will have a little padlock icon next to their name) can't be beamed.

Extending the Clipboard with Clipper

Like most computers, Palm devices make use of a "clipboard" for copying and pasting text. And, like most computers, Palms can hold only one selection of text at a time in that clipboard. Clipper turns it into a repository for multiple selections, thereby expanding your copying-and-pasting capabilities. Everything you copy is retained in Clipper (where you can even go in and edit the text). When you want to paste something, you simply make a special Graffiti stroke to bring up the Clipper window, and then choose which snippet of text to paste.

This can come in extremely handy if you frequently write the same lengthy words or phrases. Doctors could use Clipper to create a little database of diagnoses, lawyers to maintain a selection of legal terms, and so on. Sure, you could use the Palm's own ShortCuts feature (see Chapter 2) to do much the same thing, but then you have to remember the shortcut abbreviations.

Removing Duplicate Entries with UnDupe

If you routinely work with ACT!, Outlook, or some other third-party contact manager on your computer, it's not uncommon to wind up with duplicate entries on your Palm device. This can also happen if you import additional databases into Palm Desktop. Whatever the cause, the last thing you want to have to do is manually delete these duplicates from your records. UnDupe does it automatically, ferreting out duplicate entries in Address Book, Date Book, Memo Pad, and To Do List, and then eliminating them in one fell swoop.

Managing (and Beaming!) Your Files with FileZ

The more you work with software, the more you need a good file manager. FileZ lets you view, edit, copy, move, delete, and beam virtually any file on your handheld. It's not the most user-friendly program of its kind, but it does have one feature that makes up for it: it's free.

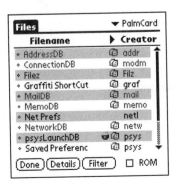

Beaming is one of FileZ's most admirable capabilities. As you may recall from Chapter 4, beaming programs and data to other Palm users isn't only practical, it's just plain fun. But the Palm OS is a bit limited in terms of what it can beam. Specifically, it can't beam Hacks or e-books or certain kinds of databases. That's where FileZ comes in—it can beam just about anything.

> **TIP**   *If you're an advanced user, you can use a program like FileZ to find and delete the extraneous files that are sometimes left behind when you delete an application. The standard Palm OS Delete tool usually doesn't show these "behind-the-scenes" files. Of course, you should take caution when deleting files, because you could accidentally remove something important. Make a complete backup first so you can restore files if necessary.*

The Wonderful World of Launchers

As you know from poring over Chapter 2 (you did pore, didn't you?), the Palm OS enables you to assign applications to different categories—the idea being to help keep your icons organized and more easily accessible. However, a variety of third-party programs take this idea to a much higher level and with much better results. In this section, we introduce you to a few of our favorite launchers—programs that organize your apps, simplify certain features, and, in some cases, slap on a much prettier interface.

What should you look for when choosing a launcher? Here are a couple key features to consider:

- **Support for memory cards**   If your handheld has an expansion slot (as most do nowadays), your launcher should have direct support for memory cards. That means you can install applications on a card, but still organize them as you see fit from within the launcher.

- **Support for color and/or high-res screens**   A good launcher should take full advantage of your screen's capabilities, meaning it should offer a colorful visage and let you tweak the colors to your liking. If you have a handheld with a high-resolution screen, choose a launcher that supports it directly. You'll be able to fit more icons on the screen at a time (if you desire to) and enjoy a nicer-looking interface.

- **Support for themes**   Part of the fun of using a launcher is customizing your handheld's interface. Some launchers let you install themes (or "skins," to use MP3 parlance) that dramatically alter their appearance (while maintaining the same basic layout and functionality). The standard Palm OS interface looks downright stark in comparison to these nifty themes, which are usually free to download (though the launchers themselves cost a few bucks).

■ **Support for jog dials and navigators**   If you have a handheld with a jog dial or navigator, make sure to choose a launcher that supports it. That way, you can still enjoy the benefits of one-handed operation.

A Few of Our Favorite Launchers

We've tried most of the launchers out there, including the one that attempts to re-create the—horrors—Windows desktop on your handheld's screen. Rest assured, that one isn't among our favorites (but if the idea intrigues you, by all means check it out— it's called GoBar). Here are our favorites:

> TIP   *As with most Palm software, you can try demo versions of these launchers before plunking down your hard-earned cash. We recommend you use each one for at least a week so you can really get to know it.*

■ **Launcher X**   This update of one of our all-time favorites, LauncherIII, organizes your icons into tabbed windows, thus enabling you to switch categories with a single tap of the stylus. Plus, you can drag and drop your icons between tabs—no irksome category menus to deal with. Launcher X is packed with other helpful features, ranging from onscreen memory and battery gauges to a built-in file manager. It's also one of the most expensive launchers, priced at $24.95.

■ **MegaLauncher**   In addition to its crackerjack support for memory media and high-resolution color screens, MegaLauncher offers a wealth of advanced features (including one-tap beaming, deleting, and copying) and comes with a handful of attractive themes. It costs $19.95.

- **SilverScreen**   Dave's launcher of choice, SilverScreen, offers the most glamorous interface of any launcher and a growing library of way-cool themes. It's also the only launcher to replace the core-app icons with icons of its own, thus creating an even more customized look. In short, if you're big on bells and whistles, this is the launcher for you. However, we should point out that SilverScreen is a bit on the slow side—the unfortunate by-product of its graphics-laden interface.

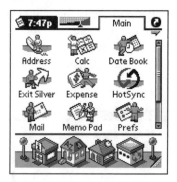

Palm Anti-Virus Utilities

Unless you've been living under a rock, you know that computer viruses can wreak havoc on a PC and even propagate from one system to another without users' knowledge. Viruses are an unfortunate fact of computer life. They aren't, however, a part of Palm life, at least not at press time. Although a few companies have introduced virus-protection software, do yourself a favor and don't bother wasting any money or energy on them.

Creating Your Own Palm Programs

Ever wonder why there's so much third-party software available for Palm devices? Maybe because it's so easy to write programs for the platform. Although the more sophisticated applications do require programming experience and professional development tools, utilities are available that enable you to design basic Palm software with ease. Indeed, if you're willing to tackle a short learning curve, you can create customized applications for your personal or business use.

NOTE   *If you're looking for software to create databases, see Chapter 11.*

Here's a quick rundown of some of the tools available to budding Palm software developers:

- **AppForge**   A powerful development tool (available in Standard and Professional editions), AppForge lets you write for the Palm OS, using Microsoft Visual Basic 6.0.

- **CodeWarrior**   Reputed to be the most popular Palm OS-development package, CodeWarrior (available for both Windows and Macintosh) requires extensive programming knowledge. It's based on the C and C++ programming languages.

- **NSBasic/Palm**   Remember that BASIC programming class you were forced to take in high school or college? Now you can put the knowledge to practical use. NSBasic/Palm (see Figure 12-1) lets you create Palm OS apps with everyone's favorite programming language. Okay, show of hands: who remembers what BASIC stands for?

- **PDA Toolbox**   Formerly known as PalmFactory, PDA Toolbox doesn't require much in the way of programming knowledge. Rather, the software employs a graphical interface and makes software design as easy as dragging and dropping elements onto a simulated Palm screen. You can even create your own icons for your programs.

12

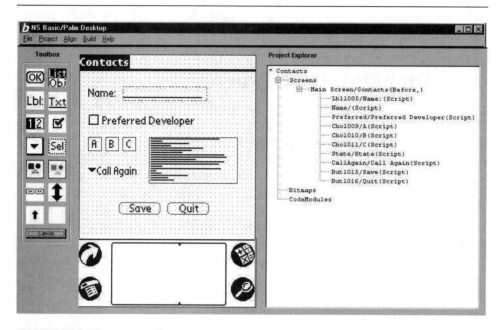

If you can remember your BASIC training, you can program for the Palm OS with NSBasic/Palm.

- **Satellite Forms MobileApp Designer**   Suppose you have an idea for a Palm program and want to create a prototype before hiring a programmer. Or, you want to design a special order form for your outside-sales team, one that links to your company's inventory database. Puma Technology's Satellite Forms can handle all this and more. It's a robust software-development package that can create sophisticated Palm programs. Although it uses a graphical environment—not unlike PDA Toolbox's—some database and programming knowledge is necessary.

- **SuperWaba**   Okay, we don't pretend to understand Java but, if you do, SuperWaba is a "Java Virtual Machine" that runs on the Palm OS (among other platforms). It's free, it supports OS 5, and it gives you the opportunity to say "waba" a lot.

Graffiti Enhancements and Alternatives

Many of us have a love/hate relationship with Graffiti, the handwriting-recognition software used by all Palm OS devices. Some users take to it right away, finding it a speedy and convenient method for entering data. Others just plain don't like it or can't get the knack. For those folks (who have absolutely nothing to be ashamed of, really), we present this section on Graffiti enhancements and alternatives.

> **NOTE**   *This section deals primarily with "Graffiti 1," which at press time was still predominant in Palm OS devices. If you have a Zire 71, Tungsten C, or another model that has Graffiti 2, you may still want to check out the products mentioned herein. Many of them may be updated to support Graffiti 2 by the time you read this.*

Suppose you don't mind Graffiti, but find it too slow to keep up with your thought processes—or too inflexible to recognize your particular style of handwriting. The answer could lie in one of many available "Graffiti assistants," which can not only speed data entry, but also make your handwriting more recognizable.

Maybe you've been using the onscreen keyboard as an alternative to Graffiti, but find it too small or cumbersome. There are keyboard alternatives as well, some of them quite radical. And maybe you're just ready to give Graffiti the old heave-ho and try some other means of data entry. Full-blown replacements are out there, and they let you say goodbye to Graffiti forever.

We divided all these products into four categories: overlays, which actually cover the Graffiti area; assistants, which give Graffiti a helping hand; keyboards, which substitute for the stock onscreen keyboard; and replacements, which send Graffiti packing.

> **NOTE**   *In this chapter's discussion of keyboards, we're talking about software options. We look at actual keyboards in Chapter 15.*

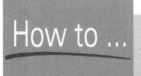

Add a Graffiti Area to a PDA That Doesn't Have One

If you own a Handspring Treo, Sony CLIÉ TG50, Palm Tungsten W, or another model with a built-in keyboard, you may find yourself wishing for a handwriting-recognition option. Some of these models, like the TG50 and Tungsten C, already have one—you can input Graffiti strokes directly on the screen. For those models that don't, however, consider installing a utility such as Graffiti Anywhere or Jot.

The former is designed to let you write anywhere on the screen, just like some keyboard-equipped models do already. The latter replaces Graffiti with a more natural character set, but has the added advantage of allowing you to write anywhere (that is, no Graffiti area required). See "Graffiti Replacements: A Software Solution" for more information on Jot.

Overlays: Wallpaper for the Graffiti Area

One of our favorite tips for Palm users is to apply a piece of Scotch 811 Magic Tape to the Graffiti area. This not only protects the area from scratches, it also adds a tackier writing surface that many people find preferable to the slippery screen. A new breed of plastic overlays takes this idea several steps further, redefining the Graffiti area's functionality and protecting it at the same time.

How do overlays work? The entire Graffiti area—buttons and all—is sensitive to pressure. That's why when you tap a button or write something with your stylus, your Palm responds. The overlays simply take advantage of this fact, using special software to reprogram the Palm's responses to your taps and strokes. The products take different approaches to this, as you see in our overview of each one.

Introduction to FitalyStamp

Before we talk about Textware Solutions' FitalyStamp, we have to tell you about Textware Solutions' Fitaly Keyboard—an onscreen-keyboard replacement discussed later in this chapter. It's a fairly unusual product, but with practice it can increase your data-entry speed.

The problem with pop-up keyboards like Fitaly (and the standard keyboard, for that matter) is they occupy a major chunk of the viewable area of the Palm's screen. FitalyStamp offers a solution: an overlay that moves the keyboard from the screen to the Graffiti area.

As you can see, the key layout is quite unusual. The idea is to minimize the distance your stylus needs to travel (more on that later in this chapter, when we look at the Fitaly Keyboard). But FitalyStamp also provides cursor-control buttons, numbers, symbols—even the Palm's ShortCut and Command functions. Thus, while there's a learning curve involved with the keyboard itself, there's also a lot

The Virtual Graffiti Area

A number of Palm Powered handhelds, including the HandEra 330 and Sony CLIÉ NR/NX/NZ series, take a unique (and very cool) approach to Graffiti. These models employ a virtual Graffiti area, one that appears in the bottom portion of the screen. The difference is that this Graffiti area is part of the operating system—it's software, not hardware. Thus, Graffiti pops up when you need it, but disappears to give you more reading area when you don't. Ingenious! (The Sony screens also make possible the use of "skins" for the Graffiti area, which are just about the coolest thing ever.)

of convenience. And FitalyStamp is a colorful, attractive addition to your Palm device—an important consideration for those who prize aesthetics.

Having Your Keyboard and Graffiti, Too

If you're often hopping between Graffiti and the built-in keyboard, and wishing you had an easier way to do so, Softava's Silkyboard is the answer. This overlay covers the Graffiti area with a large, easy-to-read QWERTY keyboard that enables full-time tap-typing, but also lets you use Graffiti without having to change modes.

Silkyboard's key advantage is it provides access to a keyboard without sacrificing any screen estate. Its secondary advantage is protection of the Graffiti area. Working with the overlay is as simple as tapping on the letter or number you want to enter, and holding down your stylus for a "long tap" when you want a capital letter or punctuation mark. Accessing Applications, Menu, Calc, and Find requires a stroke instead of a tap, but that's just a matter of simple memorization. Indeed, Silkyboard's learning curve is slight. And, if you get mixed up, you can go back to using Graffiti just by drawing the strokes on top of the letters. (The overlay even has the two little arrows that divide the letter and number areas.)

Given that different Palm devices have slightly different Graffiti areas, Silkyboard is available in several varieties. Make sure you order the right one for your model. A simple calibration routine is all that's required to set up the driver software, and a handy applicator strip is provided to make sure the overlay is applied without any air bubbles.

NOTE *At press time, Silkyboard was not available for any Palm OS 5 models.*

If you prefer to write with a keyboard but don't want to give up Graffiti entirely, Silkyboard is a great best-of-both-worlds solution.

Making Graffiti Smarter

One of the most ingenious overlays is TapPad, which doesn't try to replace or revamp Graffiti, but merely gives it a boost. TapPad extends the full length of the Graffiti area, thus providing total protection.

TapPad's benefits can be summed up thusly:

■ Protection of the Graffiti area and a tackier surface that makes handwriting more comfortable.

■ The addition of a keypad in the numeric half, thus enabling you to enter addresses and phone numbers much more quickly (and more easily, in our opinion).

■ One-tap buttons for six commonly used commands: undo, cut, copy, paste, delete, and backspace. The Undo button alone is worth the price of admission.

- Left–right and up–down scroll buttons for easier cursor movement and document navigation. If you ever tried to place your cursor between two letters or at the beginning of a line, you know what a struggle it can be. The left–right buttons move your cursor one space at a time, greatly simplifying its placement. And the up–down scroll buttons are a major improvement over the Palm's skinny scroll bars and tiny arrows.

- A host of shortcut and pop-up tools designed to simplify data entry. Space doesn't permit us to list them all, but we think they're outstanding.

If you want superb protection for the handwriting area along with some Graffiti-related perks, you're likely to love TapPad.

Graffiti Replacements: A Software Solution

Love the idea of Graffiti, but don't like Graffiti itself? We understand—some of those special characters are just plain tough (Dave can't make a *j* to save his life, and who can remember the stroke for the percent sign?). CIC's Jot, born for Windows CE devices but eventually ported to the Palm OS, replaces Graffiti with a more natural—and familiar—character set.

NOTE   *A derivative of Jot was used in the creation of Graffiti 2.*

12

Our Favorite Graffiti Aids

Rick: Although I never travel without my Stowaway Keyboard, most of the time I prefer to use plain old Graffiti. But my accuracy could always use improvement, which is why I've become a big fan of TealEcho. It reproduces my Graffiti strokes in digital ink as I make them, so I can see what my characters look like (and make sure they're drawn correctly). Best $11.95 you can spend on your Palm, if you ask me.

Dave: Personally, I don't use any Graffiti enhancements (my Jedi Master won't allow me to take the easy way out of any situation, lest it weaken my mind and allow the Dark Side to gain a foothold). I use my Graffiti zone just the way God intended it, but I always have a keyboard with me on trips so I can write long documents on airplanes and in my hotel room. I mainly use the Stowaway keyboard, though I've also been experimenting with Logitech's KeyCase, which is a flexible, cloth-based keyboard.

And that's only one of Jot's advantages. It also frees you from the Graffiti area, enabling you to write anywhere on your Palm device's screen. Even better, it leaves a trail of "digital ink" beneath your stylus tip, so you can see what you're writing as you write, as with a pen and paper. Finally, Jot recognizes a variety of cursive characters (see Figure 12-2), handy for those who mix script with print. Tricky Graffiti letters such as *q, v,* and *y* are much easier to make with Jot.

Not sure this is the Graffiti alternative for you? Try before you buy. As with most Palm software, you can download a demo for a test drive.

If you own a Handspring Treo that has a keyboard instead of the traditional Graffiti area, you can add handwriting-recognition capabilities by installing Jot.

Keys, Please

Like to tap-type? Many users prefer the onscreen keyboard to Graffiti, if only because it has no real learning curve. Of course, some software developers think they can do the keyboard one better, as evidenced by Textware Solutions' Fitaly Keyboard and an interesting Hack.

QWERTY, Meet Fitaly

The Fitaly Keyboard (so named for the layout of its keys, like QWERTY) proceeds from the assumption that the Palm's own built-in keyboard requires too much hand movement. Because it's so wide, you have to move your stylus quite a bit, leading to slow and often inaccurate data entry. The Fitaly Keyboard arranges letters in a tightly-knit group designed to minimize stylus travel. Hence, you should be able to tap-type much more quickly.

Now write like you normally do and not be confined to special characters. Jot recognizes all these forms.

FIGURE 12-2	Jot can recognize five versions of the letter *A* alone, meaning it's more accommodating to your style of writing.

Clearly, Fitaly represents a radical departure from the standard QWERTY keyboard, and therefore has a high learning curve. Make that practice curve: it could take you several days to master the layout, and even then you might decide you don't like it. The moderate speed gain may not offset the difficulty in learning an entirely new keyboard.

On the other hand, Fitaly is much more practical than the stock built-in keyboard, in part because it makes most common punctuation marks readily available, without the need to shift modes (or even tap the SHIFT key). And when you do access the Numeric mode (done by tapping the 123 button, as with the standard keyboard), you gain access to a number of extended characters (including fractions, the Euro symbol, and more).

If you like the idea of Fitaly but hate sacrificing a big chunk of the screen, check out FitalyStamp—a plastic overlay that moves the keyboard right on top of the Graffiti area. It's covered earlier in this chapter.

12

Hacks

Earlier in this chapter, you learned all about X-Master and the little OS enhancements (Hacks) that work with it. Let's talk about one that's expressly related to the Palm's onscreen keyboard.

If you've spent any time with the Palm's standard onscreen keyboard, you've probably been frustrated at having to switch modes to access numbers and punctuation. Horace Ho's Keyboard Hack solves the problem by replacing the standard keyboard with a slightly modified one. His keyboard sports 69 keys, including a numeric keypad and a row of punctuation keys. It also has left/right keys for moving your cursor a space at a time.

NOTE   *The latter feature, the cursor-control keys, was suggested by a Keyboard Hack user. The author of the program incorporated it into the next version. This is part of what makes the Palm community so great: so many software developers are just regular folks who are happy to hear from regular users. You can have a voice in the evolution of Palm software!*

Giving Graffiti a Helping Hand

Here's a novel idea: Rather than trying to build a better Graffiti than Graffiti, why not simply cut down on the number of letters necessary to write a word? Or make it so you can write anywhere on the screen, instead of just in the Graffiti area? How about tweaking the recognition engine so it's more accommodating to your handwriting? These are among the goals of Graffiti assistants—software tools that just make life with Graffiti a little easier.

Was This the Word You Were Looking For?

Remember the old game show *Name That Tune?* The host would describe a song, and the contestant would say, "I can name that tune in three notes." Imagine if

What About a Real Keyboard?

Thumbs, overlays, styluses—whatever you use to enter data on your Palm device, it won't be as fast as an actual keyboard. Fortunately, actual keyboards do exist for Palms—lots of them. To find out all about them, see Chapter 15.

How to ... **Improve Graffiti Recognition**

For all its quirks, Graffiti is actually an excellent handwriting-recognition tool. If you plan to stick with it, you can use these tips to improve accuracy. By the way, if your handheld has Graffiti 2, the first three tips still apply.

- **Write big.** If your characters fill up the bulk of the Graffiti area, they're more likely to be accurately recognized.

- **Don't write on an angle.** Many of us do just that when writing with pen and paper, but that's poison to Graffiti. Keep your strokes straight.

- **Take advantage of the built-in Graffiti Help application.** This provides a graphical cheat sheet for all Graffiti strokes. Go to Prefs | Buttons | Pen, then choose Graffiti Help from the list of available options. Now, whenever you draw a line from the Graffiti area to the top of the Palm's screen, the Help applet appears.

- **Draw the letter V backward.** If you're having trouble with the letter *V*, start from the right side and end with the left. You needn't add the little tail (as with the standard Graffiti *V*) and the letter will come out perfectly every time.

- **Write the number 3 for the letter B.** Forget trying to draw a *B* Graffiti's way—write the number 3 instead. Similarly, writing the number 6 gives you a good *G* every time, and the number 8 creates the perfect *Y*. Naturally, you should still make these characters on the letter (that is, left) side of the Graffiti area.

- **Start your R at the bottom of the letter instead of the top.** That initial downstroke often produces the ShortCut symbol instead of an *R*.

12

Graffiti could adopt that precept, guessing the word or phrase you're writing as you write it. By the time you entered, say, the *e* in "competition," the software would have figured out the rest of the word, thereby saving you six additional pen strokes.

That's the appeal of CIC's WordComplete, a Palm utility that helps you write faster by helping you write less. As you enter characters, a box containing possible word matches appears. If you spy the word you're after, just tap it. The more letters you enter, the closer you get to the correct word (if it's in the software's database).

Obviously, for little words like "the" and "to," the program won't help much. But for longer words, it can indeed save you some scribbling. And WordComplete lets you add your own words and/or short phrases to its database, which can definitely save you time in the long run.

Goodbye, Graffiti Area!

Ever notice that the Graffiti area is kind of, well, small? Most of us aren't used to writing in such a confined space, and that alone can be a source of Graffiti contention. Fortunately, a pair of virtually identical utilities can liberate your stylus from that tiny box, effectively turning the entire Palm screen into one big Graffiti area.

Graffiti Anywhere enables you to write—using Graffiti characters—anywhere on the screen. What's more, it leaves a trail of "digital ink" beneath your stylus tip, which goes a long way toward helping you produce more accurate characters. You see what you write as you write it, just as you would with a pen on paper. Plus, it's free!

The Best Little Graffiti Tweak in Town

Part of the challenge in learning and mastering Graffiti is that you can't see your characters as you write them. (Actually, if you have one of the Sony CLIÉ models with the virtual Graffiti area, you can—the input area leaves a trail of digital ink beneath your stylus. Very cool.)

That's where TealEcho comes in. This simple utility displays your pen strokes on the main screen as you make them in the Graffiti area. As a result, you can gauge just how accurate (or inaccurate) your characters are. Sounds like no big deal, but trust us when we say TealEcho goes a long way toward improving Graffiti accuracy.

Graffiti, Your Way

Finally, we come to the one product that really manhandles Graffiti, that says, "Look, can't you just learn to understand *my* writing?" It is TealPoint Software's TealScript, a utility that lets you tweak Graffiti so it's more responsive to your hand, or replace it altogether with a customized character set.

If you're willing to battle one of the steepest learning curves we've encountered in a piece of Palm software, the benefits are truly worthwhile. TealScript works its wizardry through the use of custom profiles, which contain the Graffiti character set as you define it. In other words, you teach TealScript how you like to write, and it teaches Graffiti to accommodate your penmanship.

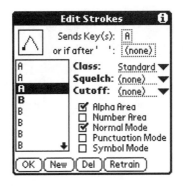

The letter *v* is a good example of how this works. Your profile can include the standard character—the one with the little tail we always forget to add—and a regular *v* you added yourself. Similarly, instead of always having to write capitalized versions of letters like *R* and *B,* you can add lowercase versions.

As confusing as TealScript can be to work with, it's not totally out of the question for novice users. That's because it comes with an already-built profile that helps you overcome the most commonly miswritten Graffiti characters. So, right out of the box it's useful. And even though TealScript may not be the friendliest program around, it's by far the best way to make Graffiti an ally instead of an obstacle.

TIP *If you've upgraded to a Palm OS handheld that has Graffiti 2, but you miss good old Graffiti 1, TealScript lets you switch back.*

Where to Find It

Web Site	Address	What's There
AppForge, Inc.	www.appforge.com	AppForge
Botzam	www.botzam.com	Botzam Backup
Brayder Technologies	www.brayder.com	JackFlash
CIC	www.cic.com	Jot, RecoEcho, WordComplete
Linkesoft	www.linkesoft.com	X-Master, ToneDial
Metrowerks	www.metrowerks.com	CodeWarrior
NS Basic Corp.	www.nsbasic.com	NSBasic/Palm
PalmGear	www.palmgear.com	The vast majority of the Hacks and utilities mentioned in this chapter
PDA Toolbox	www.pdatoolbox.com	PDA Toolbox
Puma Technology	www.pumatech.com	Satellite Forms

Web Site	Address	What's There
Softava	www.silkyboard.com	Silkyboard
TapPad	www.tappad.com	TapPad
TealPoint Software	www.tealpoint.com	TealEcho, TealScript, and other great utilities
Textware Solutions	www.fitaly.com	Fitaly, FitalyStamp

Chapter 13 Playing Games

How to...

- Adjust your handheld's volume for games
- Install new games
- Control games on your handheld
- Play action, board, and card games
- Play sports, strategy, and word games
- Play two-player games on two handhelds
- Play interactive fiction games
- Use your PDA as a substitute for dice

Spreadsheets, databases, document readers, and memos are all well and good. If that's all you ever plan to do with your PDA, that's fine—you're just unlikely to ever get invited to one of our parties.

Your PDA is a miniature general-purpose computer, and, as a result, it can do almost anything your desktop PC can do—including games. Sure, there are limitations. The display is pretty small and the processor isn't nearly as fast, but the fact remains your Palm OS device is a great game machine for passing the time in an airport, on a train, in a meeting (where it looks like you're taking notes), or any other place you're bored with doing productive activities. In this chapter, we discuss what you should know to get the most out of your handheld as a gaming machine, and we recommend some of the best games for you to try.

NOTE   *As Palms have evolved, so have their capabilities. Some have color screens, some have high-resolution color screens. Some have limited audio hardware, some have rich audio hardware. Some have Palm OS 4, some have Palm OS 5—and so on. As you look around for games (and even check out those we recommend), make sure they're compatible with your particular model. Some games require OS 5; others are optimized for HiRes+ screens like you find on the Garmin iQue and Sony CLIÉ NR/NX/NZ. A lot of games are universally compatible, but you should always check the system requirements before installing anything on your PDA.*

Prepping Your Palm for Gaming

No, playing games isn't exactly rocket science, but before you get started with them, you should learn a few things that'll come in handy. You should know, for instance, how to control your Palm's volume, install applications, and enable beaming (some games let you play against other handheld users via the IR port).

Controlling Game Volume

At the top of the list is the Palm OS sound system, which includes a control for how loud to play game sounds. Logic dictates you'll want to set this loud enough to hear what's going on in your game, but this might not always be the case. As much as we like to play games, we don't always want others to know that's what we're doing. Fortunately, it's possible to set the game sound level low or even off completely. This means you'll play your games without sound (which, if you're at work, is probably a wise decision).

To tweak game sounds, do this:

1. Tap the Prefs icon to open your Preferences application.

2. Switch to the General category by tapping on the category menu at the top-right corner and choosing General. (If you have an OS 5 device, look for the Sounds & Alerts option instead.)

3. Find the Game Sound entry and choose the volume level you're interested in.

13

 *If you find that a game still squeaks and squawks even if the Palm OS volume setting is set to off, the game must have its own sound preferences. Check its options menu for a control to set the sound volume. Indeed, many games have built-in volume controls that eliminate the need to futz around with the settings in Prefs.*

Enabling Beaming

If you know other Palm OS handheld users, you might want to try your hand at some head-to-head games, which are made possible thanks to the devices' infrared ports. It's fun and addictive, and very nearly sociable. For two games on different handhelds to "find" each other, though, you need to make sure the Beam Receive setting in Prefs is enabled.

1. Tap the Prefs icon to open your Preferences application.

2. Switch to the General category by tapping the category menu at the top-right corner and choosing General. (If you have an OS 5 device, choose the Power option.)

3. Look for the entry called Beam Receive and make sure it's set to On. (By default, it is.)

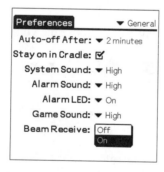

Installing Games

Installing games is a snap. We discussed how to install applications on your handheld in Chapter 4, and working with games is no different. After all, a game is just another kind of Palm application. Need a refresher? We won't make you go all the way back to Chapter 4. Turning pages is such a drag.

Let's assume you're dealing with games you want to download from the Web. (Some computer and office-supply stores sell game bundles, most of which have

Game Packs

Occasionally, you may find game compilation discs in the store or online. They promise to deliver hundreds of unbeatable Palm OS games for just 10 or 20 bucks. Should you invest in one of these packages?

Our opinion: probably not. The collection may sound promising, but anyone with a halfway decent Internet connection can get all of the games they like from a site like PalmGear.com or Palmgamingworld.com just as easily, without spending a dime. Remember: Palm games are tiny compared to games for the PC, and they download in seconds.

Also, keep in mind that you won't get the full, registered version of shareware games even though the disc itself cost you cash. Instead, these discs are sort of like samplers for folks who want a guided tour of someone else's idea of the "best" games for the Palm. If you like a game you find on the disc, you'll still have to pay to keep playing it, just as if you downloaded it from the Internet.

their own installation programs. You don't need us for those.) If you're new to downloading, you need to know that most apps come compressed in one of two popular formats:

- **Zip**   This is the standard way of managing files in Windows. To install a Zipped file, you need a program capable of unzipping it first. Typically, this means using a utility such as WinZip. (Windows XP can automatically extract the contents of Zip files.)

- **SIT**   Macintosh files are compressed in the SIT format, which can be uncompressed with a program such as Aladdin Stuffit Expander 5.0.

Once you expand the compressed file, you'll probably end up with a folder containing several files. Installation instructions typically come in one or more file formats:

- **Plain text files**   These are usually called something clever like readme.txt or install.txt. These will tell you which file(s) to install.

- **HTML pages**   These will probably have an Internet Explorer icon (or whatever Web browser you use), and usually contain the game's instructions. Double-click them to see the instructions in your Web browser.

13

- **PDF files**   You need Adobe Acrobat Reader to read these files, though it's probably already installed on your computer. If not, visit adobe.com to get this popular document reader.

- **Files with a PRC extension, and possibly PDB as well**   These are the actual game files that need to be installed on your Palm. Open the Install tool and use the Add button to mark these files for installation during the next HotSync.

SHORTCUT   *If you use WinZip, a faster way to install the games is simply to double-click the PRC and/or PDB files from within WinZip. That will save you the extra step of having to unzip the files first. Alternatively, if you have a Tungsten C, Zire 71, or any other newer Palm handheld (one that has Palm Desktop version 4.1 or later), you can just drag Zipped files directly into the Install Tool window.*

CAUTION   *If you reset your Palm while a game is paused, the game session you were playing will be lost and you'll need to start over.*

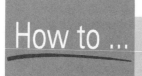

How to ... Control Your Jet/Race Car/ Submarine/Spaceship

Now you're all set to start playing some games, but where's the joystick? There isn't one, silly (unless you have a Zire 71). Many games use the handheld's buttons to control the action. While the game is running, the Date Book, Address Book, Memo Pad, and To Do List buttons are typically diverted to game controls and won't switch you to the usual apps. To find out which buttons do what in a given game, you can experiment (our favorite way) or check the game documentation. In most games, you can find basic instructions by checking the game's built-in Help screens (tap Menu to find them). A handful of newer games take advantage of the Navigator control found in newer Palm handhelds.

Gone But Not Forgotten

Rick: Frogger, Galaxian, Pac Man—these were household names back in my youth, and they're just a few of the arcade classics that have been resurrected for Palm OS handhelds. Of course, a Palm's buttons don't compare too favorably with traditional coin-op controls, so longtime favorites like Spy Hunter, Joust, and Sinistar are a bit tricky to control. Still, it's a blast to revisit my youth with these favorites of yesteryear—and I don't even need to pump quarters into my PDA.

Dave: I love the old arcade classics as much as the next geek, but it's time to move on, dude! It's the 21st Century! I've put childish games like those well behind me and today, I play mainly just the mature, modern classics. Like Bejeweled.

Rick: Don't call me "dude."

A Few (Dozen) of Our Favorite Games

Games account for a pretty healthy chunk of all software sold for Palm OS handhelds, so it should come as no surprise that you can find hundreds upon hundreds of titles spanning every genre. Card games, action games, puzzle games—you name it, it's out there. Of course, we can't list all of them without doubling the size of the book. It's big enough already, don't you think?

As with other kinds of Palm software, games are easy to try before you buy. Most have a trial period, usually from two weeks to a month, after which the game becomes disabled unless you register it (that is, pay for a code to unlock it permanently). Games usually cost $10–20, though a few will set you back $30. There's also a treasure trove of great freebies like these (all of them available at www.freewarepalm.com):

- **Cribbage 3.0**   Sure, you could pay 12 bucks or so for one of the commercial Cribbage games, but why? Well, the Palm tends to cheat a bit—but otherwise this is a freeware gem.

- **Mulg II**   Use your stylus to guide a marble through a maze within a fixed amount of time. Devilishly addictive.

13

■ **Napalm Racing**   Not the greatest racing game we've ever played, but surprisingly robust for a freebie.

■ **Patience Revisited**   An amazing collection of Solitaire games—21 in all, all in color, all free, free, free!

■ **PilOth**   A clone of the classic game of Othello.

■ **Pocket Video Poker**   Why take a trip to Vegas when you can gamble all you want for free? There's also Pocket Video Blackjack if that's more your speed.

■ **Sea War**   A nice implementation of the beloved game Battleship. There's even a high-resolution version.

■ **Solitaire Poker**   One of many variations on Solitaire, this one involving poker hands.

■ **Vexed 2.1**   One of the most addictive puzzle games ever, and a Palm OS freeware classic. The 2.1 version includes multiple puzzle packs with over 600 levels.

These freebies are a great place to start for anyone interested in a little fun on the run. In fact, there are enough freeware games to keep you entertained almost indefinitely. On the other hand, if you're willing to shell out a few bucks, you'll find some of the best mobile entertainment money can buy. In the following sections, we've listed some of our favorites, all divided into a few major categories.

Action and Arcade Games

Did you pump an untold number of quarters into arcade machines in the '80s? We sure did. These action games will make you long for the classics of yesteryear—and, in some cases, revisit them.

- **Galax**   An excellent retread of the inimitable (but often imitated) Galaxian.

- **Midway Arcade Classics**   Five flawless re-creations of arcade greats: Defender II, Joust, Root Beer Tapper, Sinistar, and Spy Hunter.

- **Sonic the Hedgehog**   Sega's console classic is now available for Palm OS 5 handhelds such as the Zire 71 and Tungsten T. Your kids will be in hog heaven.

- **Zap!2016**   A scrolling space-shooter with gorgeous graphics and terrific sound effects.

Card Games

Card games transition well to handheld PCs because they don't require fancy graphics or complicated controls. They're games you can relax with, maybe play in the bathtub. (On second thought, the bathtub is probably not the best place for

13

your PDA. Try the shower.) Poker, Hearts, Blackjack—there are versions of just about every classic card game you can think of.

- **AcidFreecell** Freecell is one of our favorite Solitaire games, and this version includes sound effects, photographic backgrounds, and other nifty perks.

- **KidzTalk GoFish** A memory game not unlike Concentration, the goal is to match pairs of cards from a spread-out deck of 20. As you make matches, a picture is revealed underneath. This OS 5–only game also talks to you in a real human voice. Great for little kids.

- **Texas Holdem Poker 1.2** Rick isn't much of a card player, but he is a big fan of the movie *Rounders,* hence his interest in this great little poker game.

- **Vegas Blackjack** Without a doubt the best-looking Blackjack game for the Palm OS, Vegas Blackjack plunks you down at a casino-style table for some serious hands of 21. Double down!

Board Games

There's a reason games like chess, Risk, and Monopoly have been around forever: they're fun, no matter where—or even how—you play them. Lots of the big-name board games are available for the Palm OS. These are the ones we like best:

- **Aggression** Remember Risk? Aggression is a visually striking re-creation of the beloved board game. It looks best on high-resolution color screens, but you can play it even on older grayscale Palms.

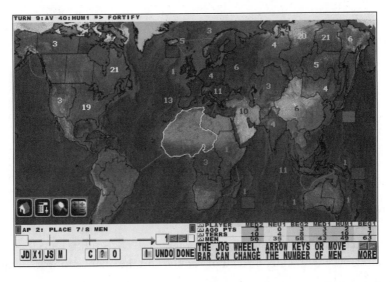

■ **Monopoly**   This needs no explanation, other than to say that 1 to 4 players can partake, human or computer, on the same handheld or several of them (the game supports play via infrared).

■ **Rook's Revenge**   Almost too fast-paced to qualify as a board game, Rook's Revenge is like chess with a jolt of caffeine. Move your pieces as fast as you can (they still have to be legal moves), without waiting for your opponent to make his moves. A great change of pace from boring old chess.

■ **Scrabble**   Like Monopoly, no explanation needed here. But how cool to play this old favorite anytime, anywhere, without having to worry about tiles spilling all over the place.

Puzzle Games

Some of the very best Palm OS games, bar none, are puzzle games. They're generally easy to learn, seriously addictive, and endlessly entertaining.

■ **Bejeweled**   Like TNT's "New Movie Classics," this game has been around for just a few years, but it's already achieved Tetris-like classic status. It requires zero time to learn to play—and all your free time once

13

you do. If by chance you've never heard of it, trust us and give it a try. It might just be the perfect game for PDAs.

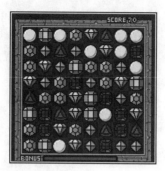

- **Bounce Out**   If you get tired of Bejeweled, try Bounce Out. It's the same game, only with balls instead of jewels, and the chance to work diagonally.

- **NetWalk II**   An oldie but goodie, NetWalk challenges you to make successful connections between your servers and your computers. Sounds like a tech-support nightmare, but it's actually a ton of fun.

- **Triclops**   How best to describe this game? There's a big triangle, see, and lots of little triangles fall into it, and you have to try to remove three or more like-colored triangles with each tap of the stylus. Okay, it sounds a little kooky, but it's a blast.

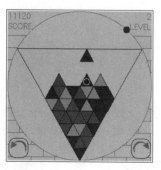

Word Games

Dave's not much for word games—too much stress on the brain—but Rick loves 'em. Nothing like keeping the old noodle active while you're passing the time.

■ **Bookworm**   Make as many words as you can from Bookworm's wall of letters. The trick is, the letters must be adjoining. We're not sure it'll actually increase your word power as the developer claims, but it's definitely an enjoyable challenge.

■ **Crossword Puzzles for Palm OS**   Whether you're a crossword-puzzle fanatic or you haven't looked at one in years, this excellent collection—derived from *Washington Post* puzzles—is an ideal way to pass the time. Sure beats carrying a big book of puzzles or getting newspaper ink on your fingers!

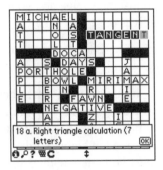

■ **Text Twist**   The first game Rick reaches for when he has five minutes to spare, Text Twist is a bit like Boggle. You're given six scrambled letters and a time limit; try to make as many words as you can from the letters *and* unscramble the six-letter word.

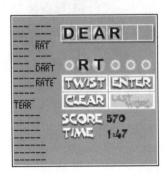

13

Strategy and Role-Playing Games

You might think a PDA isn't the best place to play a strategy or role-playing game. You might also think Dave is witty and urbane. In both cases, you'd be wrong. Although some strategy and RPG games do benefit from the big screens afforded by desktop computers, those clever Palm OS developers have created some mighty compelling stuff for handhelds. Witness:

- **Dragon Bane**   Remember Bard's Tale? It was a role-playing classic for desktop PCs. Dragon Bane brings the same medieval adventuring to your PDA, complete with monsters, spells, and your choice of character classes. Dungeons & Dragons lives on.

- **Galactic Realms**   Space-based action and strategy that's reminiscent of the great StarCraft.

- **Lemmings 4.1**   Show of hands: who remembers the Amiga? Lemmings was one of the all-time great games to emerge from that system. In this perfect re-creation, you must guide the dumb little guys to safety. It supports high-resolution screens, sound, memory cards, and so on—and it's a freebie! (The level packs will cost you a few bucks, though.)

Sports Games

Anyone for tennis? How about racing? Maybe even a little Quidditch? Sports games (even fictional ones based on an amazing book) aren't always ideal for a screen as small as the Palm's, but that hasn't stopped developers from making some admirable efforts. Golf, basketball, football, and even bowling are among the other sports represented as Palm games. Whatever your athletic passion—even if it's darts— you're sure to find a game to match.

Among the most impressive titles we've seen is TableTennis3D, a way-cool Ping Pong simulator. You can play against your PDA or another player via infrared.

Games for Which We Haven't Figured Out a Category

Okay, how would *you* classify a game involving a fish tank? Some games just don't fit a standard mold. Nevertheless, don't miss these amazing titles:

■ **Billiards 4.0** If you like pool, you'll love this dazzling interpretation. It's particularly great on HiRes+ screens, like the ones found in Garmin iQue and Sony CLIÉ NR/NX/NZ models.

13

- **Bump Attack Pinball** Pinball is really hard to do right on a PDA, what with the small screen, lack of flippers, and so on. Bump Attack Pinball gets it right, and with several beautiful-looking tables to boot.

- **Insaniquarium** Running a fish tank is hard work. You have to keep all the fish fed, gather up the coins they drop, fend off alien attackers—the usual stuff. Insaniquarium is like no other game we've seen, but it's definitely lots of fun. Your "tweens" and teens will love it, too.

Two-Player Infrared Games

As we already mentioned, two-player games are a cool way to pass the time when you're traveling with another handheld-equipped person. IS/Complete offers perhaps the largest collection of infrared-enabled games, including Palm OS versions of Battleship, checkers, chess, and even Hangman. They all work more or less the same way: you make a move, then tap a button. Your move is then beamed to your opponent's handheld, where the board is updated to reflect the new data. Then you perform the same process in the other direction.

The games and graphics are nothing spectacular, but they're still kind of cool. And you don't need to prearrange a gaming session with another player. That is, if you've got one of the IR games and your buddy doesn't, no problem—just beam it to him. Of course, there may be a few limitations, depending on whether the game in question is commercial or freeware. If it's commercial, the beamed copy will often work only with the one from which it was beamed. Or, it might stop working after a short period of time, like two weeks (this is to encourage "player 2" to buy his own copy).

If you're interested in more sophisticated IR games, check out Handmark's excellent versions of Monopoly and Scrabble. Both can be played either on a single device (with multiple players) or via IR.

Playing Text Adventures

Remember Zork? How about Douglas Adams' Hitchhiker's Guide to the Galaxy text adventure? What about Trinity? These games were popular decades ago, at the dawn of the modern computer age. Text adventures put you in a text-based world, with flowing narratives and extensive descriptions of your surroundings. When it was time to make your hero do something, you typed instructions into your PC. The computer then moved you along through the story based on your decisions. These games were often fiendishly clever, composed largely of logic puzzles and intellectual challenges.

So, why are we telling you all this? Text adventures are long-lost icons for the museum, right?

Not quite. Text adventures have made something of a comeback in the last few years, largely because handheld PCs like the Palm are an ideal platform for playing them. And although their identity has changed with the times—they're now usually called *interactive fiction* instead of text adventures—they're still a lot of fun to play. No serious gamer would consider his Palm complete without one or two interactive-fiction games installed for a rainy day at the airport (see Figure 13-1).

Unlocking Interactive Fiction Files

You can find hundreds of interactive fiction titles on the Internet. But these files aren't playable all by themselves. They usually come encoded in a format called *Z-Code*. Like a spreadsheet or document file, a Z-Code file is useless without the appropriate reader app. In this case, you need a program called Pilot-Frotz (or Frotz, for short). Install Frotz, and you can play any interactive fiction games you find and transfer to your Palm.

Frotz essentially gives you the same experience as when you played these text adventures years ago. It displays the game's text on the screen and provides you with a text prompt in which to enter your next move. When you start the game, you see the Frotz list view, along with any games you have currently installed. To play a game, tap its name, and then tap the Play button.

From there, you're taken to the game view, where you actually play the game. Unlike those early text adventures, Frotz gives you a few graphical tools that make these games easier to play. Here's how to use Frotz:

- If the game displays a long text description, you might see the word "MORE" to indicate more text occurs after this pause. Tap the screen to continue.

- To enter your text command, write it in the Graffiti area.

- You can display a list of common verbs and nouns (shown on the right in Figure 13-2) by tapping the right half of the Palm screen in any spot where no text exists. Instead of writing **Look**, for instance, tap the menu and tap the word "Look."

- You can tap any word in the story to make that word appear on the text prompt line. Thus, you can assemble your command from the menu and words already onscreen, instead of writing it all from scratch with Graffiti.

- If you want your character to move, tap any blank space on the left half of the Palm screen. You'll see a map window, like the one on the left side of Figure 13-2. Tap the desired compass direction. Other icons help you Enter, Exit, and go up or down stairs.

```
┌─────────────────────────────────┐
│▐North of House                  │
│of a white house, with a boarded front│
│door.                            │
│There is a small mailbox here.   │
│                                 │
│>n                               │
│North of House                   │
│You are facing the north side of a white│
│house. There is no door here, and all│
│the windows are boarded up. To the│
│north a narrow path winds through the│
│trees.                           │
│                                 │
│>▌                               │
└─────────────────────────────────┘
```

FIGURE 13-1   Interactive fiction combines good old-fashioned storytelling with a bit of brain-teasing puzzle solving.

TIP   *You can add custom words and phrases to the word list. Enter the desired word or phrase at the text prompt and select it with your stylus. Then choose List | Add from the menu. To see custom words, open the list menu and then tap on the first entry, USER LIST.*

Your position is automatically saved when you leave the game to do something else with your Palm. If you want to switch to another title, choose File | Force Quit to go back to the List view to choose another game. If you do that, though, your position in the current game is lost.

13

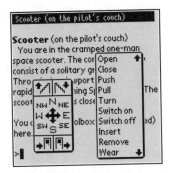

FIGURE 13-2   Frotz helps you play interactive fiction titles by displaying common commands and mapping tools.

Finding Interactive Fiction Titles

Interactive fiction is scattered around the Web. Try both of these sites:

- www.refalo.com/palm/interactive.htm

- www.csd.uwo.ca/~pete/Infocom/

If you're really diligent, you may be able to find some of the classic Infocom adventures (such as Zork and Planetfall). Check eBay to see if anyone is selling

Getting Started with Text Adventures

So, you want to try your hand at interactive fiction, but that text prompt is a little too intimidating? Fear not, because entering commands in a text adventure isn't too hard. You can enter just a verb—such as **Look**—or a complete sentence, such as **Pick up the compass**. Each game has something called a *parser* that's designed to decrypt your input. Here's a primer to get you started:

Directions

Compass points are frequently used: north, south, east, west, or any combination, such as northeast or southwest. You can also use one- and two-letter abbreviations, such as *n* and *se*. Also: up, down, in, out, enter, and exit.

Looking Around

The old-reliable command is simply Look. You can combine Look with anything that makes sense: "look up," "look down," or "look inside."

Action Verbs

Anything: push, pull, open, close, take, pick up, pump, give, swim, turn, screw, burn. When you deal with more than one object, you can use the word All, as in "Take All the coins."

Making Sentences

You have to combine nouns and verbs into complete sentences to accomplish much in these games. Manipulating objects is the name of the game and the way to solve the puzzles, as in "Take the money," "Pick up the compass," "Read the book," or "Close the gate with the red key."

them used, or do a Google search for Infocom. There may even be a site or two where you can pay for the adventures and download them directly, without having to purchase an actual CD. Look for bundles such as Lost Treasures of Infocom and Masterpieces of Infocom, which include multiple games.

Using the Palm as a Pair of Dice

If you like to play board games in the real world, you might be interested in using your Palm as a virtual pair of dice. After all, the Palm is harder to lose (we always misplace the dice that go with our board games). Several apps are available, but many of them have the disadvantage of requiring run-time modules of programming languages such as Forth or C. We don't care for that approach, because it's just extra stuff you have to install.

Some dice simulators you might want to try include Gamer's Die Roller, DicePro, and Roll Em.

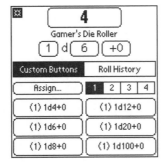

Where to Find It

Web Site	Address	What's There
Aladdin Systems	www.aladdinsys.com	Stuffit Expander file compression tool for the Mac
Astraware	www.astraware.com	Bejeweled, Bookworm, Bounce Out, Text Twist, Zap!2016, and many of our other favorites
FreewarePalm	www.freewarepalm.com	Freeware games (and other software)
Handmark	www.handmark.com	Midway Arcade Classics, Monopoly, Scrabble

13

Web Site	Address	What's There
IS/Complete	www.iscomplete.com	Several two-player-via-IR games
PalmGear	www.palmgear.com	Most of the games mentioned in this chapter
PalmGamingWorld	www.palmgamingworld.com	One-stop surfing for all sorts of Palm OS games
WinZip	www.winzip.com	WinZip file compression tool for Windows

Chapter 14

The Handheld Multimedia Machine

How to...

- Find e-books
- Choose a Doc viewer
- Read e-books on your Palm
- Convert text files to the Doc format
- Use your Palm camera
- Transfer images from the PDA to the PC
- View photos on your Palm
- Watch movies on your Palm
- Paint on the Palm
- Capture screenshots
- Play MP3s on your Palm
- Use the Palm to make music

You know the future has arrived when a device the size of a Pop Tart can hold an entire Stephen King novel, the full contents of a photo album, and a few of your favorite songs, and it takes pictures, too. Now that you've seen some of the minor miracles Palm devices can perform, it should come as little surprise to learn they're great for all sorts of multimedia tricks as well. In this chapter, you learn everything you need to know about using your Palm as a multimedia powerhouse.

Building a Library of E-Books

Before Palm devices came along, a slowly-growing collection of electronic books— mostly public-domain classic literature, such as Voltaire's *Candide* and Sir Arthur Conan Doyle's *Sherlock Holmes* stories—existed on the Internet. Because these works had already been converted to computer-readable text, why not copy them to Palm devices for reading anywhere, anytime?

In theory, you can simply paste the text into a memo. But there's a snag: documents are limited to about 500 words, so even short stories are out of the question. Hence the emergence of document and e-book viewers—these programs have no length limitation (other than the amount of memory in the Palm itself). One of the most common e-book formats is called Doc, named after the first document reader for the Palm.

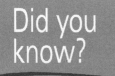

In this chapter, we mostly discuss reading documents, not editing them. If you want to learn more about creating and editing documents in a Palm word processor, see Chapter 11.

Choose a Doc Viewer

Many people make this mistake: they download a bunch of nifty e-books from a Web site such as MemoWare, load them onto their Palms, then scratch their heads, wondering why they can't see icons for their e-books in the Palm's Home screen. The reason, of course, is they don't have a Doc viewer installed. Without one, there's no way to view Doc files, which don't have their own icons.

Fortunately, there are plenty of Doc viewers out there—all free or inexpensive. The best place to start is with Palm's own program, Palm Reader (there are two versions—one that's free, and a $15 Palm Reader Pro with additional features).

Here are some other popular choices:

- **CSpotRun**   Not a bad viewer, but its best feature, perhaps, is that it's free.

- **TealDoc**   TealDoc's coolest feature is the screen rotation mode, which lets you view wide documents on a 320×240-pixel CLIÉ more accurately.

- **Isilo**   This supports HTML and plain .txt files as well as Doc files—also uses the Sony CLIÉ's 320×480-pixel resolution.

14

Did you know?

Doc Is an Equal-Opportunity Format

The Doc format works with both Palm OS devices and the Pocket PC. So sharing Doc files (such as e-books) with Pocket PC users is often as simple as giving them a copy of the file. If they have a Doc reader on their handheld, they can read the text without any sort of conversion process.

You can also use any of the word processors discussed in Chapter 11 (such as WordSmith, Quickword, Documents to Go, or FastWriter) to read Doc files. All of these programs are available from PalmGear.com.

Here's what some common e-book readers look like, side by side:

He looked apologetically at me. "There's no eavesdropping of course, but we don't want to upset our very excellent service with any rumours of ghosts in the place. There's too much shadow and oak panelling to trifle with that. And this, you know, wasn't a regular ghost. I don't think it will come again--ever."

"You mean to say you didn't keep it?"

"What sort of physique?" said Sanderson.

"Lean. You know that sort of young man's neck that has two great flutings down the back, here and here--so! And a little, meanish head with scrubby hair--And rather bad ears. Shoulders bad, narrower than the hips; turn-down collar, ready-made short jacket, trousers baggy and a little frayed at

▼ BM

say it," he said, "in all kindliness, but that is the plain truth of the case. Even at the first glance he struck me as weak."

He punctuated with the help of his cigar.

"I came upon him, you know, in the long passage. His back was towards me and I saw him first. Right off I knew him for a ghost. He was transparent and whitish; clean through his chest I could see the

NOTE *Not all readers can read all documents. Most of these programs handle the Doc format just fine, but some documents are stored in proprietary formats that only some of these readers can access. Isilo, for instance, has a special format that supports hypertext and fancy formatting. Palm Reader and TealDoc can't read Isilo documents. And commercial books made for Palm Reader can't be read in any other application.*

Make Room for the Books

Be forewarned: e-books can be large documents—another reason to consider buying a Palm device with lots of memory. Jules Verne's *The Mysterious Island,* for instance, takes a whopping 622K, and the infamous biography *Monica's Story* nabs 500K. You could wind up sacrificing a major chunk of your PDA's memory for only one e-book.

Fortunately, not all titles are quite so gargantuan. Most short stories are under 50K, and even Stephen King's novel, *The Girl Who Loved Tom Gordon,* is a reasonable 226K. If you're particularly strapped for space, you can always try deleting some infrequently used games and other applications, remove unwanted AvantGo channels, and clear out other e-books you've already read. On the other hand, as you learned in Chapter 4, you can store lots of extra programs and data—e-books included—on removable memory cards. Just make sure you get an e-book reader that supports such cards. Palm Reader, thankfully, does.

Free E-Books and E-Books for Sale

There are dozens of online sources for e-books, both free and commercial. The former are works considered public domain: either their copyrights have expired (as in the case of classic literature), or they've been written and released by authors not seeking compensation. There are literally thousands of titles available in the public domain, many of them already converted to the Doc format.

Commercial titles aren't unlike what you'd buy in a bookstore: they've simply been converted to some electronic format and authorized for sale online. Most commercial e-books are created using a proprietary format, meaning a special viewer is required. This is primarily to prevent unauthorized distribution—unlike actual books, commercial e-books aren't meant to be loaned out or given to others. When you buy one, you're effectively buying a license to read it on your Palm device and only your Palm device.

Our Favorite E-Books

Rick: I have turned into an e-book zealot in recent months, recommending MemoWare and Palm Digital Media.com to friends, family, and any strangers who will sit still for five seconds. Among the great titles I've read on my Palm are *Angela's Ashes, Battlefield Earth, Kick the Can,* and *The Corrections.* I also enjoyed rereading *The Most Dangerous Game,* a story I remembered fondly from high school. I got that one free from MemoWare.

Dave: I have to commend Rick on the progress he's made. When I met him a scant five years ago, he hadn't yet learned to master the written word. Since then, I've seen him get his equivalency diploma, start on "chapter books," and even sign his name in ink instead of crayon. Bravo, Rick! Well done! As for me, I find the best for the buck is the magazine *Fantasy & Science Fiction*—Palm Digital Media has a good assortment of them going back to 1997. I'm rarely disappointed by any of those tales, and there's a month's worth of bedtime reading in each collection.

Find Free Stuff

If one site is synonymous with Palm Doc files, it's MemoWare (www.memoware.com). Here you can find thousands of texts divided into categories such as business, history, travel, biography, sci-fi, and Shakespeare. Whether you're looking for a collection of Mexican recipes, a Zane Grey western, a sappy love poem, or a classic work by Dickens, this is the place to start.

MemoWare offers a convenient search engine, so you can type in a title or keyword to quickly find what you're looking for. It also has links to other e-book sites, although none are as comprehensive. Finally, MemoWare provides numerous links to software programs (most for Windows, a few for Mac) that turn computer documents into Doc files.

Find Commercial Stuff

The thing about public domain e-books is that most of them are, well, old. Somerset Maugham and Jack London are all well and good for catching up on the classics you promised yourself you'd read one day, but sometimes you just want a little Stephen King. Or Mary Higgins Clark. Or Captain Kirk. Fortunately, you can have them all on your Palm, provided you're willing to pay for them.

The top place to go for contemporary, mainstream fiction and nonfiction is, without a doubt, Palm's own online bookstore, Palm Digital Media. The site offers hundreds of books from many well-known authors.

 *When installing subsequent books, you need to install only the books themselves—you already have the Palm Reader.*

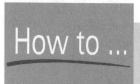 **View Palm Digital Media Books**

When you purchase a book from Palm Digital Media, you supply your name and credit card number, then receive a Zip file to download. This file contains the e-book itself (in an encrypted .pdb format), along with the Palm Reader program. If you don't already have the Palm Reader installed on your PDA, be sure to install it before trying to read your new book.

You also receive, via e-mail, a code number that's used to "unlock" the e-book. You need to enter this number on your Palm device the first time you open your e-book.

Other Sources for Contemporary E-Books

Palm Digital Media may be a large source for commercial e-books, but other Web sites also offer contemporary works. You may also want to check out the following:

eBookMall	www.ebookmall.com
PerfectBound	www.perfectbound.com
Fictionwise	www.fictionwise.com
MobiPocket	www.mobipocket.com

Making Your Own E-Books

Become a published author! Well, not published in the "Stephen King" sense. More in the "kooky old uncle who staples his warnings about how mailboxes are alien mind control devices to telephone poles" sense. Nonetheless, if you have your own documents, short stories, novellas, or doctoral thesis that you'd like to covert to a format that's readable on the Palm, you have a lot of options, including these most common ones:

- Word and text (.txt) format documents are fine if your audience is using a Palm word processor such as WordSmith, FastWriter, Documents to Go, and so on. But you can't read a Word file in an e-book app such as Palm Reader, so this is not the most common solution.

- Palm eBook Studio is a $30 program available from the Palm Digital Media Web site that lets you easily convert text and images to a format that's compatible with both Palms and Pocket PCs.

- MakeDoc (for Windows users) and MakeDocDD (an equivalent program for Mac users) are free, no-frills, doc converters.

14

Read in Bed Without Disturbing Your Spouse

Since the dawn of time, one seemingly insurmountable problem has plagued the human race: how to read in bed without disturbing one's spouse. Torches didn't work: they crackled too loudly and tended to set the bed on fire. Battery-operated book lights didn't work: they made books too heavy, leading to carpal reader syndrome. But finally there's an answer: the Palm handheld. Just load up a novel and turn on the backlight. You'll have no trouble seeing the screen in the dark, and your spouse won't even know it's on. PDA or marriage saver? You be the judge.

Taking Pictures with Your Palm

Digital cameras have been around for less than 10 years, but they have already dramatically changed the way we think about photography. Almost everyone we know, for instance, owns a digital camera and uses it to take snapshots at family outings. The pictures can be immediately e-mailed to friends and relatives, posted at an online photo site, or mailed out on CD-ROM. Even people who would never haul around a 35mm camera embrace the simplicity and convenience of a digital camera.

What does all that have to do with your PDA? Plenty. A few models come with a built-in digital camera; most others can accept add-on cameras. Want to see what all the excitement is about? At the time this book is being written, here are your options:

- **Zire 71** This PDA has a built-in camera capable of shooting VGA quality (640×480-pixel) images.

- **CLIÉ NR, NX, and NZ** Various Sony PDAs have integrated digital cameras. The NZ90, for instance, has a massive two-megapixel camera and flash, which makes it powerful enough to take pictures you can print at 8×10 inches. Some of these models can also record video as well.

■ **Veo Photo Traveler**   This camera-on-an-SD card is an accessory that works with any Palm device with an SDIO slot—such as any m-series or Tungsten model. There isn't even any Palm OS software to install; just slip the camera into the SD slot, and you can immediately take pictures that are transferred to the PC when you HotSync.

Using the Zire 71

Your Zire 71's camera is a snap to use. Slide the front of the case up and you'll find a shutter release button at the bottom of the PDA (you can see the front and back of the Zire 71 in Figure 14-1). Just aim and shoot.

That said, be aware that the Zire 71 has a long "lag" between the time that you press the shutter button and when the picture is actually taken. It takes about a full second for the picture to get captured, so you need to get in the habit of holding the Zire very still until you see the finished image appear on the screen. If you don't, you'll get nothing but a terrible blur, as shown in the following illustration:

FIGURE 14-1   The back of the Zire 71 hides the camera lens.

Like any digital camera, the Zire 71 has some options. You can configure the camera by tapping the Options button in the bottom-left corner of the screen when the camera is running. Here is what the Options screen looks like:

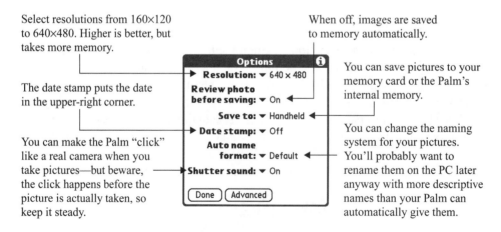

Select resolutions from 160×120 to 640×480. Higher is better, but takes more memory.

The date stamp puts the date in the upper-right corner.

You can make the Palm "click" like a real camera when you take pictures—but beware, the click happens before the picture is actually taken, so keep it steady.

When off, images are saved to memory automatically.

You can save pictures to your memory card or the Palm's internal memory.

You can change the naming system for your pictures. You'll probably want to rename them on the PC later anyway with more descriptive names than your Palm can automatically give them.

Adjusting White Balance

Your Zire 71 has a four-position control called "white balance" hidden in the Advanced button on the Options screen. Your old 35mm film camera didn't have anything like it. So what the heck is white balance? In a nutshell, different light sources have different color temperatures, meaning that a scene will appear to have a different color tone depending upon how it is illuminated.

You can get a sense of this yourself. Candlelight appears more yellowish than sunlight, for instance. And other sources—such as tungsten lights— can cast strange, greenish glows around a room. But in general, our brains automatically adjust for different color sources and make the color correction for us. We usually don't even notice.

Your Zire's white balance control works like the human brain. It adjusts the exposure so your pictures have the same color cast no matter what light source you use. When properly balanced, your camera won't apply strange color casts to your pictures even if you shoot indoors, outdoors, in fluorescent lighting, and in candlelight.

Most of the time, your PDA is fine if you leave it set on auto (as in the following image). If you notice that your camera is taking pictures with a weird color cast—everything is coming out greenish or bluish, for instance—try one of the preset white balance settings and see if that improves your shots.

14

Using Your Pictures on the PC

When you HotSync your Zire 71, the pictures are automatically HotSynced and stored on your computer's hard drive. How you interact with those pictures, though, depends upon whether you set your Zire 71 to save the images on the handheld or the SD memory card (which you can set using the Options button when the camera mode is engaged).

Pictures Saved on the Handheld

If the Zire is configured to Save To Handheld, images will appear in the Palm Desktop—even if you use another PIM, such as Outlook, for your primary synchronization. To find them, just start the Palm Desktop and click on the Palm Photos button on the left side of the screen. You'll see something like Figure 14-2.

As you can see in Figure 14-2, the Palm Desktop gives you some tools for working with your images. Select one or more images and use the icons in the toolbar to rotate, e-mail, or delete them. You can also double-click an image to open the Editor, which is a very simple image editing program. Here, you can crop, remove red eye, and perform other simple tasks.

The pictures are also stored directly to a folder on your hard drive, and you can look for them there if you want to. You can specify which folder the Palm Desktop uses to save your pictures by choosing Tools | Preferences from the menu; by default, it'll store them in a folder called Palm Photos within your My Pictures folder. Since they're standard JPG images, you can do anything you like with them—such as crop, rename, e-mail, post to the Web, or use as a wallpaper image in Windows.

> **TIP** *You can't use the Palm Desktop to print images. If you want to print, you'll need to do that in your favorite image editor; drag the image you want to print to the Windows desktop, then print it from there in a program such as Paint Shop Pro or Adobe Photoshop Elements. Heck, you can even print using the Paint program (found in the Accessories folder of the Start menu) that comes with Windows!*

Pictures Saved on the SD Card

If the images are saved to your SD card, they don't appear in the Palm Photos module of the Palm Desktop. Instead, your only way to interact with them is by opening the folder into which the HotSync Manager saved them. Just like images stored on the handheld, these SD images end up in whatever folder is specified in the Tools | Preferences menu of the Palm Desktop.

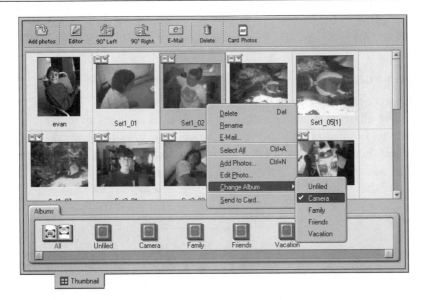

FIGURE 14-2 Your Zire 71's images are stored in the Palm Desktop, and a right-click on any image gives you a whole bunch of options for managing or sharing them.

To see and work with these pictures, you can use Windows to open the folder or let Palm Desktop find them for you. Open Palm Desktop, click the Palm Photos icon on the left side of the screen, and click Card Photos in the toolbar at the top of the screen. You'll see a dialog box with a button that says Open Windows Explorer.

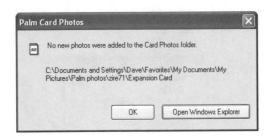

Click it, and you'll immediately see your images stored in their folder. Working with these images is a snap; since they're already standard JPG images, you can load them into an image editor, e-mail them, or perform any other option you like.

 *Looking for your pics? The Palm stores them in two folders—Expansion Card and Handheld—in a folder named after whatever your device name happens to be, which in turn is in the Palm Photos folder in My Pictures.*

Showing Your Pictures on the Palm

Half the fun of taking pictures is getting to show off your results. The Zire 71 comes with a photo album that lets you store any number of images (up to the limit of your memory) and show them off to anyone you can stop long enough to point the Zire in their face. By default, all the pictures you take with your camera appear in the album, and you can add more images from your PC.

To open the Album, find the icon in the Home screen. It looks like this:

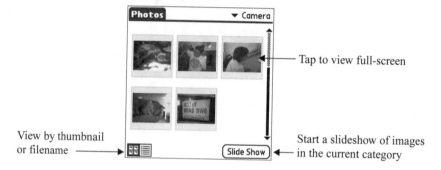

The Photo menu gives you additional options. You can delete, rotate, and copy images to the SD memory card or handheld, depending upon where the image is to begin with. You can also beam images to another PDA, as long as that device has an application that can view JPG images.

To rename or categorize your image, choose Photo | Details from the menu. The Details dialog box looks like this:

Since the memory card is a category as far as the Palm OS is concerned, you can't categorize any images stored on a card.

Synchronizing Images Between PDA and PC

We saved the best for last. Any images in the Palm Photos section of the Palm Desktop are automatically synchronized with the Photos application on your Zire. That means you can use the Palm Desktop to rename, edit, and arrange your images, and they're automatically updated on your Palm as well. When using the Palm Desktop and the Photos app as a digital substitute for your wallet photos, consider these issues:

- Any changes you make to images in the Handheld storage on the PDA or in the Palm Photos view of the Palm Desktop are automatically updated in both locations. You can use the Enhance tool in the Editor to improve a photo, for instance, and the updated picture will appear on the Palm after a HotSync.

- If you make changes to the actual image, stored in the My Pictures folder of your hard disk, those modifications aren't reflected on your PDA.

- You can drag and drop images to the Palm Desktop (or use the Add Photos button in the toolbar) to add pictures from elsewhere on your hard disk to your Palm. If you do, the images aren't resized or modified at all; they are copied to the Palm at their full resolution. You might want to reduce their size first, since a multi-megapixel image from a digital camera can consume storage space on your Palm very rapidly.

- By default, all of the images displayed in the Palm Desktop are stored in the handheld's main memory. To transfer it to your Palm's SD card, right-click on an image and choose Send to Card.

Building an Electronic Photo Album

The Photos app in the Zire 71 is great, but what if you don't have a Zire? Is it still possible to keep a digital photo album in your pocket? You bet. With the right photo viewer software, you'll never be without a picture of your spouse, kids, cats, or other loved ones. The process is quite simple: electronic images on your desktop PC are converted to the right format, then installed when you HotSync. Then you load up your viewer and, well, view 'em.

14

Choosing Photo-Viewing Software

Many programs enable you to view images on your PDA, some of them quite similar in their form and function. Here are some of the most popular programs:

- **AcidImage**   An excellent photo viewer that reads plain-old JPG images off your PDA's expansion card, so you don't have to use a cumbersome desktop conversion program first. Just drag and drop JPG images from the PC onto your Palm.

- **HandStory Suite**   This multifaceted program displays e-book doc files, Web clips, memos, and digital images. The desktop transfer process is very elegant; just right-click on an image on the desktop and choose Save to Palm from the menu.

- **SplashPhoto**   A more "traditional" photo album, it relies on a desktop converter to crop and edit images down to size for the Palm's screen. It also reads pure JPG images as well.

- **Photogather**   Similar to SplashPhoto, Photogather has a desktop converter as well. Beware, though: Photogather sends full-resolution images to the Palm instead of shrinking them to fit on the screen—and that can eat up a lot of memory very quickly.

Watching Movies on Your CLIÉ

Dave: Personally, I love the idea of watching a TV show I saved off of my VCR on plane trips. But you, Mr. Blows-in-the-Wind, what's your opinion of PDA movies now? For years you told me that it was silly to watch movies on a small handheld screen, and even when I suggested that faster processors, better screens, and improved sound would someday make watching a movie on your PDA commonplace, you poo-poo'd the idea as insane. But I know you're using Kinoma to watch SpongeBob episodes on your CLIÉ, so what's your excuse? What made you decide that video on a PDA was a good idea? I expect to hear a lot of groveling, with the words, "You were right, Dave."

Rick: The day those words escape my lips is the day I've been drugged, beaten, and threatened with having to see Kristin Hersh in concert. Years ago, when you were going ga-ga over postage stamp-sized slideshows playing on your

Palm without sound, I did indeed poo-poo the notion of handheld video. And on most Palm-based handhelds, the experience is still extremely lame. But on a Sony CLIÉ —especially one with a high-resolution color screen and enhanced sound—mobile movies are pretty cool. There are still plenty of obstacles, such as making space for the video files (a mere half-hour show can eat up over 64MB). But we're getting there, and I can't wait for the day when I can walk into an airport and download *Moulin Rouge* to my PDA from a kiosk.

Watching Movies on Your PDA

It wasn't all that long ago that watching an entire feature-length movie on a PDA would have been considered insanity. These days, though, there's no reason not to use your Palm to fire up *The Matrix* or an episode of *The Simpsons* on a long flight.

Of course, you'll want to have a lot of memory. A 128MB card is the bare minimum for watching a short TV show, and you'll probably want to have a 256MB or 512MB for serious watching—otherwise, you'll have to break things up in multiple sections and put them on several cards.

Getting Video into Your Palm

Though there are several video players to choose from, we recommend using either TealMovie or Kinoma—or, if you have a Sony CLIÉ, the Movie Player application that accompanies many of the newer models. All of these applications come with desktop converters that you can use to import movies in a variety of formats. TealMovie, for instance, accepts video in AVI and the QuickTime MOV formats. Kinoma has broader support for video formats, working with QuickTime, MPEG-1, MPEG-4, AVI, and even Macromedia Flash.

Having a video player on your PDA is all well and good, but it's a lot like being all dressed up with nowhere to go: where do you get the movies for your PDA to begin with? The reality is that you have an embarrassment of riches when it comes to sources for video. People who watch movies on their PDAs can draw on television and videotape, DVD, their digital camcorders, and even the Internet. Here's the skinny:

14

- **Television programs**   Whether live off the air or stored on videotape— TV is a common source. You might want to copy this week's episode of *Friends* or *24*, for instance, so you can watch it when you travel. You'll need some mechanism on your computer, such as a composite-video-in or S-Video input, to capture analog video and store it on your PC. Some multimedia computers ship with video capture capabilities. If your computer doesn't already have this, you can add an ATI All-in-Wonder card to your PC, which has video inputs and the necessary software to store video on a hard disk. Another alternative: Dazzle's Digital Video Creator is a USB hub that sits outside your PC and lets you capture video onto your PC via composite video or S-Video ports.

■ **Digital Video**   This is getting very popular as well. Digital video, from a DV or Digital8 camcorder, requires a FireWire port (also known as IEEE-1394 or i.Link). Many computers come with at least one FireWire connection, but if yours doesn't, you can add one for under $100. Just fire up your video editing software (which often comes with the camcorder or FireWire card) and capture your movie on the computer's hard drive. When you're done, you may need to save or export the video in a different file format— but we'll talk about that in the next section.

■ **DVD**   DVD is the way most of us watch our movies these days, so it stands to reason that we'd want to be able to copy DVD to PDA. PDQ. Suppose you just rented *Terminator III* but you're going out of town before you have a chance to watch it. The problem, of course, is getting the movie off of the silver platter and onto your computer's hard disk. Since DVDs are copy-protected, this might initially seem like a hopeless task. Fret not—there are several programs around that make this possible. Programs such as DVD-to-AVI (www.dvd-to-avi.com) and MovieJack (www.moviejack.org) can "rip" the content from DVD and store the movie as an AVI or MPEG file on your computer's hard drive. From there it's a matter of synchronizing the movie with your PDA.

■ **The Internet**   The Internet is teeming with movies and television shows if you know where to look. Peer-to-peer services such as Kazaa and LimeWire have many videos you can download from other people's computers, though some of the material may be copyrighted—be careful that you don't break any laws!

Converting Your Video

So, you have a movie or two and a video player on your PDA. Think you're done? Think again. In some cases, you might really be ready to kick back and watch *Logan's Run* on your Tungsten T. But much of the time, you still need to convert, compress, and synchronize. Not all video players recognize the same file formats, and that's where some video utilities can come in handy.

Consider this: you download a vintage Throwing Muses music video from Beestung.net with plans to play it on your Tungsten T via the Kinoma Player. When you inspect the video, though, you find that it's in a format called DIVX—and Kinoma's desktop Producer software doesn't recognize DIVX files. Game over? Nope. You just need to convert the file from DIVX to a format that Kinoma understands, such as MPEG.

To do that, you'll need an intermediate utility that lets you save a video file in a different format. There are two excellent utilities that we recommend without reservation: EO-Video and TMPGEnc. EO-Video is a polished, easy-to-use video tool that lets you load files in a broad range of formats and save them as almost anything else. You can load a QuickTime file, for instance, and save it as an MPEG-1 video. More to the point, you can load WMV files—created expressly for Microsoft's Windows Media Player—and save them as general purpose AVI or MPEG videos that Palm OS players can understand.

If you have a DIVX video—and that's an increasingly popular format on the Web—then EO-Video won't be of much help, since the program doesn't have a DIVX decoder. Instead, turn to TMPGEnc, which can take DIVX and other file formats and transform them into common MPEG movies.

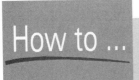 **Watch a Movie on Your Palm**

So, you're ready to copy an episode of *Friends* to your Zire 71? The exact method will vary depending upon which movie player software you use and what format the original movie is in. But here's a general step-by-step guide to making it happen:

1. Find the movie you want online at a site such as Kazaa and download it to your PC. You find it's in MPEG format, which means that TealMovie Encoder can't work with this file.

2. Start EO-Video and click on the Converter tab. Drag the movie to the file list on the right side of the screen.

14

3. Configure EO-Video to make an AVI movie. Choose AVI from the drop-down list atop the screen.

4. Set the movie to a size appropriate to your Zire 71. Click on Output Size and make sure it's set to 320×240 (or something similar). Remember that if you create a video that's bigger than your PDA's screen size, you're wasting memory and slowing down the video unnecessarily.

5. Click the Convert button.

6. After the movie is finished, load it into TealMovie Encoder and create the PRC file.

7. Add the finished PRC file to your HotSync session using the Install tool. Be sure to change the file's destination—copy it to the memory card, not your PDA's system memory.

8. HotSync, then watch the movie!

Painting on the Palm

You're probably wondering why you might want to paint on a handheld computer so small that it fits in your pocket. Well, in the world of computers, the answer is often "because you can." Programmers have never let something as silly as a technical limitation get in the way of doing something, so when PDAs first came out, programmers seemed to scramble to become the first to create a paint program for their favorite handheld PC.

But, aside from that admittedly flippant answer, the capability to sketch things out on your Palm is a handy feature. You can draw a map to sketch the way to lunch, outline a process, or design a flowchart. You can also just doodle—use the PDA as a high-tech Etch-a-Sketch for those boring times when you're waiting for the train or pretending to take notes in a meeting. Perhaps most importantly, you can draw on top of pictures you've stored on your Palm, giving you the ability to annotate images and add captions.

Painting on your Palm is fun and productive, but you need to remember these limitations:

- Palm models vary in resolution from 160×160 all the way up to 480×320. The more pixels you have, the better, but even the highest-resolution devices don't give you a lot of room in which to draw. After your images are transferred to a PC, you'll find that they're still quite small. So, drawing something on the PDA you later plan to export to, say, a PowerPoint presentation, generally isn't a practical plan.

■ Few paint programs support printing directly from the Palm, and not all even let you transfer completed art back to the PC. That means, in some cases, what you draw on the screen pretty much stays on the screen. If you *can* print your work of art, it'll print just as rough and jagged on paper as it looked onscreen.

Choosing a Painting Program

There are a ton of painting and drawing applications available for the Palm. Indeed, if you're an adventurous sort of person, search the archives at PalmGear.com for painting programs, and you'll be amazed by what you find. Nonetheless, here are a couple of the best options you may want to try:

■ **TealPaint**   Perhaps the most full-featured paint program for the Palm, TealPaint seems to do it all. The program has a complete set of painting tools, including lines, shapes, fill tools, an eraser, and a variety of brushes. The program starts you in this screen, which displays thumbnail images of your pictures and lets you view, edit, or animate them. Using TealPaint, you can copy and paste selections of your image, not just within the same picture, but in any picture in your database. TealPaint is also an animation tool. We discuss animation programs later in this chapter, but it's worth pointing out that you can use TealPaint to create animations by playing all the images in a particular database in sequence. To make a simple bouncing ball, for instance, make a series of images in which the ball moves a bit in each successive image. Then tap on the Anim button and tap the first picture in your series.

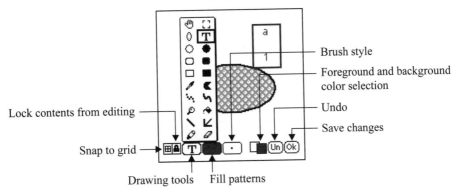

14

Lock contents from editing

Snap to grid

Drawing tools   Fill patterns

Brush style

Foreground and background color selection

Undo

Save changes

■ **Diddle**   Diddle is a free, neat little drawing program that enables you to
sketch with a minimum of clutter to get in the way of your drawing. The
interface is composed of a set of graphical menus at the top of the screen—
you can choose from among various drawing styles, line thickness, and
text. For the most part, the program is easy to explore on your own—just
start drawing.

Collaborating on a Sketch

Drawing on a Palm is usually a solo affair, but what if you're in a meeting trying
to lay out office furniture with your business partner? What then, huh? Okay, there
may be some better examples, but just work with us for a moment.

Okay, we have a better example! Suppose you're in a long, boring meeting.
If you have the right drawing software, you can doodle on your Palm and have it
immediately show up on a partner's PDA, who can then add to your drawing and
beam it back to you. All the while, your boss is none the wiser.

Anyway, if your buddy, business partner, or intern owns a Palm, the two of you
can sketch your ideas on your PDAs. The results can appear simultaneously in both
devices more or less in real time. That's totally cool, if you ask us.

Most collaborative sketch programs do their magic via the CLIÉ's IR port.
Here are some popular apps you can try:

■ **Beamer**   This simple program has just a few buttons, but it's free. You
can write short notes in a screen that resembles the Note Pad or draw
free-form images in a blank sketchpad. When you're ready, tap the beam
button (it looks like a tilde sign) to beam it to another nearby Palm
Powered PDA. The recipient can add to your drawing and beam it back.

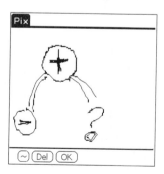

■ **Zapster**   Very similar to Beamer, this program has a slightly more elegant interface. On the downside, it's shareware and costs $10. Like Beamer, you use it to draw, then beam your work to another CLIÉ, where it can be edited and returned.

If you have a Tungsten T or a Palm with a Bluetooth card, you can use Palm's BlueBoard application to doodle with up to four people at once.

Capturing Screenshots of the Palm Display

Perhaps you've thumbed through this book, some Palm Web sites, or magazines such as *Handheld Computing* and *Mobility* and wondered what it would be like to have lunch with Dave and Rick. (Answer: like keeping a pair of 6-year-olds entertained at McDonald's.) You might also have wondered how everyone seems to be able to capture screenshots of the Palm display and publish them in ordinary desktop software. As it turns out, capturing PDA screens isn't that hard to do because several tools are available to automate the process for you.

The easiest way to capture a screen from your Palm—and our favorite, by far—is by using ScreenShot, from LinkeSoft. There are two versions of ScreenShot available: one that works with X-Master or HackMaster for older Palm devices (see Chapter 12), and a version designed just for Palm OS 5. ScreenShot is a great general-purpose tool because you needn't do anything special to activate it. There are no countdowns until the screen is captured (unless you specifically set a capture delay) and no funky menu selections. Just display the screen you want to capture and draw the screen capture gesture in the Graffiti area.

```
┌────────────────────────────────┐
│ ScreenShot                      │
│   Active       │  Inactive      │
│ Activation:  ▼ Silkscreen       │
│   ▼ From Find    ▼ To Fav       │
│ Delayed: 3  sec                 │
│   ▼ From Fav     ▼ To Find      │
│ ☑ Beep                          │
│ Licensed to                     │
│ t                               │
│ Screenshots: 3 (600 KB)         │
│ (View) (Remove Last) (Remove All)│
└────────────────────────────────┘
```

14

Listening to MP3s on Your Palm

It hasn't been very long that Palm PDAs could play digital music—before models such as the Tungsten T, Zire 71, and Sony CLIÉ NX70, Palms just weren't fast or spacious enough to accommodate hours of CD-like music. But that was then, and this is now. Many new Palms come with digital music players. Palm bundles the RealOne player with many of its models, and Sony includes its own player in CLIÉ models.

 *If you have a Palm device running OS 5, and you don't already have a copy of RealOne, you can download it from www.realone.com.*

Installing Music

Assuming that you're using the RealOne player, it's quite easy to install some tunes. In fact, you can choose either of two methods:

■ Use Palm's Install Tool to install music. Just remember that you must deposit the songs in the memory card, since the Palm can't play music that's installed in main memory. That shouldn't be a problem, since the Install Tool should automatically install MP3 files in expansion memory without even being told.

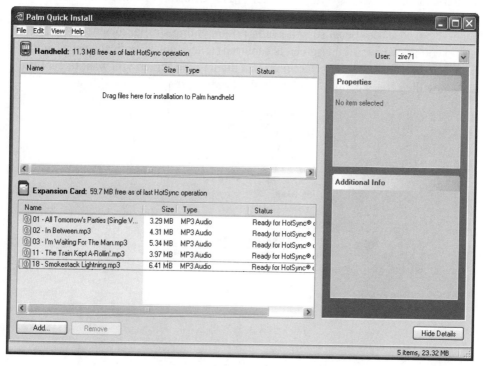

AudioPlayer Alternatives

Want to experiment with digital audio? You're not stuck with RealOne or the Sony audio player—several options are available. Here are some MP3 players you might want to check out if you're in the mood to explore:

- **AeroPlayer**   A gorgeous-looking MP3 player with extensive skin support.

- **eNeRgy**   A small, functional, freeware MP3 player. Download it from PalmGear.com.

- **AJVMP3**   A pretty-looking MP3 player intended for CLIÉ owners. Find it at http://ajvmp3.paradise.net.nz.

- Insert your Palm's expansion card in a desktop card reader and simply drag and drop the MP3 files to the card, being sure to install the files in the proper folder. RealOne looks for digital music files in a folder called AUDIO.

Making Music on the Palm

When you tire of simply listening to music and instead want to be in the band, it's time for some music software. And believe it or not, you can indeed use the Palm for a large number of music applications. The Palm has a built-in speaker, and the display is perfectly suited for music notation in a small space. If you're a musician, be sure to check out some of these applications.

Metronome and Drumming Software

It doesn't take a rocket scientist to figure out the Palm's sound capabilities aren't exactly symphonic in nature. So, one obvious application for your Palm is to keep time. In fact, this would have come in handy a long time ago—Dave used to carry a guitar around wherever he went, and having a metronome or mini-drum machine in a box as small as the Palm would have been really cool.

- **Meep**   This is your standard metronome. Meep has a slider for choosing any tempo from 40 to 280 beats per minute, and you can select up to 8 beats per measure, as well. You can work from onscreen counts or add an audible beep to each beat.

14

■ **Pocket Beat**   This app simulates a drum kit right on your Palm. It can remember two distinct tempos, and you can switch between them easily by using onscreen controls or the Scroll button. Pocket Beat can also play straight or shuffle beats, and it can vary between 40 and 196 beats per minute. The best part, though, is you can tap out your own meter on the screen—Pocket Beat memorizes the tempo and plays it accordingly.

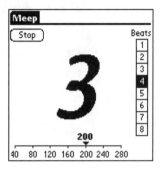

Portable Music Lessons

Budding musicians can carry around the following applications to bone up on notes, keyboard positions, and fingering:

■ **MusicTeacher**   This program can be used as an aid to learning to sing *prima vista*—that is, by reading sheet music by sight. Several tunes are stored in the MusicTeacher database, and you can also enter your own using the onscreen keyboard.

   This program is interesting because it's written in Java and uses a Java interpreter on the Palm to run. Because it's only a Java app, the MusicTeacher program can also be found on the Web and runs from within a Web browser window. You can find it at www.wabasoft.com.

■ **McChords**   If you're learning piano, McChords is an essential portable tool for working through chord fingerings. It shows you which keys to press to form the majority of chords you need to master basic piano playing.

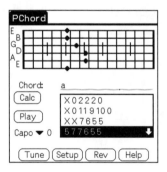

- **PChord**   This program, shown in the following illustration, is indispensable for anyone trying to get the hang of the guitar. In fact, PChord also supports mandolin, banjo, violin, and other stringed instruments. Choose a chord and PChord displays a variety of ways to finger it. PChord includes every chord we could think of, including obscure (minor 9th and stacked fourths) chords you might play only once in a great while. As such, it's a good memory jogger even for experienced players. Similar programs to try include Guitar Power, FretTrainer, and CDB FretBoard Trainer.

Tools for Musicians

Tuning—bleh. We hate tuning guitars. If only there were some automated way to. . .

Well, of course there is. Every guitarist on Earth probably owns a $30 electronic tuner, but did you know you can use your Palm for tuning as well? We've found a bunch of tuners—one good example is a program called Guitar Tuner Lt. Dave has used it himself on several occasions. It comes with standard and alternative tunings. Tap on the appropriate onscreen string, and the tone plays for several seconds. Or, tap the Auto button to hear each string's tone in turn.

14

Music Annotation and Recording

You may have experimented with (or frequently use) applications on the Mac or PC that enable you to compose and play music. Those programs generally let you drag notes onto musical staffs or play an onscreen keyboard to construct musical compositions. Well, you can do the same thing on the Palm—the screen is just a bit smaller, and you don't have multiple voices to hear your multitimbral creations. Here are a few applications you can try:

■ **miniPiano** This program enables you to play an onscreen keyboard while the notes you strike get added on a staff. You can then play back your creation. miniPiano has a Free Play mode in which the keys are duration sensitive—the longer you hold the stylus on the key, the longer it plays.

■ **PocketSynth** This program enables you to create music by tapping on an onscreen keyboard. PocketSynth enables you to select note lengths and rests, for some compositional flexibility.

 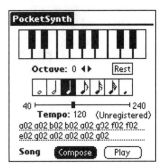

Where to Find It

Web Site	Address	What's There
EO Video	www.eo-video.com	EO Video video conversion utility
PalmGear	www.palmgear.com	Virtually all the applications found in this chapter
SplashData	www.splashdata.com	SplashPhoto
TealPoint Software	www.tealpoint.com	Home of TealPaint and other Teal products
TMPGenc Net	www.tmpgenc.net	TMPGenc video conversion utility
TriVista	www.trivista.com	A Smaller Image
Palm Digital Media	www.palmdigitalmedia	Palm Reader

Chapter 15

Accessories and Upgrades

How to...

- Choose a case
- Choose a stylus
- Choose a keyboard
- Protect your screen from dust and scratches
- Navigate the world with a GPS receiver
- Turn your PDA into a digital camera
- Recharge your handheld's battery while on the road
- Magnify your handheld's screen
- Mount your PDA in your car (or golf cart)
- Help a lost PDA find its way home

There's more to Palm devices than just software. We're talking gadgets, gear, accessories—the stuff that makes your handheld your own and extends its capabilities beyond what mere software can accomplish. Take the Targus USB Charge and Sync Cable, an invaluable travel companion that lets you synchronize—and recharge—your handheld by plugging it into any USB port. Or the Stowaway XT keyboard, which puts a full set of keys beneath your fingers for desktop-like data entry. In this chapter, we look at these and other accessories and upgrades. For starters, let's tackle cases—a subjective category if ever there was one.

NOTE   *Most of the items we spotlight in this chapter are for Palm-branded handhelds, but some are compatible with other models. If you own, say, a Handspring or Sony device, check the manufacturers' Web sites for leads to product-specific accessories and upgrades.*

Pick a Case, Any Case

As a new Palm owner, one of the first things you need to determine is how you plan to convey the device. In your pocket? Briefcase? Purse? Clipped to your belt? Backpack? Dashboard? Your answer will help determine the kind of case you should buy.

There are cases for every Palm model and every occasion, and picking one can be a tough call indeed. Do you opt for practical or stylish? (The two are often mutually exclusive.) Do you look for lots of extras such as card slots and pen holders, or try to keep it as slim as possible? Do you shell out big bucks for a titanium shell that can withstand being run over by a car? (This happens quite a bit, believe it or not.)

> **NOTE** *Some Palm OS handhelds have "built-in" screen covers that negate the need for a protective case (though you may still want one to hold a pen, paper, business cards, and so forth).*

Because there are so many varieties out there, and because everyone's case needs are different, we're going to start by steering you to the case manufacturers themselves, then offer a few general tips and suggestions.

Company	URL	Our Favorite
Arkon Resources	www.arkon.com	Car mounts
Dooney & Bourke	www.dooney.com	Various
E&B Company	www.ebcases.com	Various
InnoPocket	www.innopocket.com	Metal Deluxe Case
MarWare	www.marware.com	SportSuit IV
Palm, Inc.	www.palm.com	Slim Leather Case
Proporta	www.proporta.com	Aluminum Case
Saunders RhinoSkin	www.saunders-usa.com/rhinoskin	Aluminum HardCase

Here are some things to keep in mind as you shop for a case:

- **Style**   If you're an executive-minded person, you may have purchased a Palm Tungsten T and want a case to match. That means leather. If you're planning to tote the Palm in a suit pocket, look for something that doesn't add much bulk, like E&B's Slipper or Palm's Slim Leather Case (see Figure 15-1).

- **Portability**   In the summer, when the tight clothes come out and the jackets get stowed, pockets are hard to come by. That's when something like a belt-clip case can come in mighty handy.

15

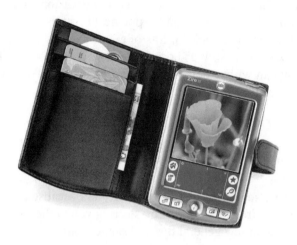

FIGURE 15-1 The Palm Slim Leather Case is available for most models.

- **Screen protection** When your Palm is bouncing around in a pocket, purse, or briefcase, the last thing you want is for some piece of flotsam to gouge or scratch the screen. That's one of the main reasons behind getting a case in the first place.

- **Drop protection** Gravity—it strikes without warning (especially if you're a klutz like Rick), and it can fatally wound a Palm device in a matter of milliseconds. A case made of neoprene or metal, like MarWare's SportSuit or InnoPocket's Metal Deluxe, can save the day if your Palm gets knocked or dropped to the floor.

- **Moron protection** We've heard more than a few stories of people driving over their Palm devices. Why they're being left in the driveway in the first place is beyond us, but there are aluminum and metal cases that can handle such punishment. Okay, maybe they won't survive being run over, but they can help you weather everyday hazards (such as shark attacks and mortar fire).

- **Velcro** Some cases rely on Velcro to keep your Palm device secured. Although we look upon this as a necessary evil (who wants a big square of the stuff stuck to the back of their Palm?), we do try to avoid such cases when possible.

The Stylus Decision

Many Palm users are perfectly happy with the stylus that came with their Palm device—until they get a look at some of the alternatives. Indeed, even though those bundled plastic pens do get the job done, they're not as comfortable or versatile as they could be. For instance, wouldn't a thicker or heavier writing implement feel better in your hand? And wouldn't it be nice if it doubled as an ink pen? These are just some of the options available to the discriminating Palm user.

As with cases, we wouldn't presume to pick a stylus for you. That's a matter of personal preference. So, here's a look at some of the stylus makers and their offerings.

Product	URL	Comments
Cross DigitalWriter	www.cross.com	Various executive-minded sizes and styles, many with multifunction designs
LandWare Floating Point	www.landware.com	Unique flexible tip lends the feel of writing on paper
PDA Panache	www.pdapanache.com	Wide assortment of sizes and styles
Pentopia Chameleon	www.pentopia.com	Multifunction replacement styluses

There are basically two kinds of styluses: those that are too large to fit in a Palm's stylus holder, and those that aren't. The former we'd classify as "executive" styluses: they seem right at home in a suit pocket or briefcase. The Cross DigitalWriter falls into this category—it's big, comfy, and has that classy business look.

Replacement styluses, on the other hand, supplant the stock Palm pen. These include the LandWare Floating Point and Pentopia Chameleon. Both fit snugly in your Palm's stylus silo, and the latter doubles as a ballpoint pen.

 TIP

If your Palm should happen to crash, the last thing you want is to have to hunt down a toothpick or paper clip in order to press your Palm's Reset button. Thus, look for a stylus that hides a reset pin. Most of them do; it's usually accessible simply by unscrewing one end of the barrel.

15

Keyboards

If you typically enter a lot of data into your Palm device—memos, e-mail messages, business documents, novels—you've probably longed to replace your stylus with a keyboard. After all, most of us can type a lot faster than we can write by hand.

Fortunately, there are a multitude of keyboards available for Palm devices, all of them priced under $100.

Okay, but what kind? Handheld keyboards fall into two basic categories: full-sized models that allow for touch typing and palm-sized models that give your thumbs a workout (not unlike the keyboards built into PDAs such as the Handspring Treo and Palm Tungsten C). In the sections that come, we give you the skinny on a few of our favorite keyboards. You're sure to find one—or maybe more than one—that meets your needs.

 *There's an easy argument to be made in favor of owning two or three keyboards for your handheld PC. You could keep a full-sized model on hand for boardroom note-taking and carry a thumb 'board for when you're out and about. That's what we do—and we're professionals!*

Full-Sized Keyboards

We don't blame you if the notion of carrying around a standard computer keyboard for use with your tiny little handheld PC is making you chuckle. That would be pretty silly, wouldn't it? Still, what better way to do some serious writing than a full-sized set of keys? Of the handful of options now available, there's no solution we like better than the Stowaway.

As you can see in Figure 15-2, this amazing keyboard folds up to the size of a small diary, and unfolds to produce a set of keys comparable to a notebook PC's. It's a bit pricey (we've found better prices on eBay, especially for the versions that

FIGURE 15-2   The Palm Portable Keyboard (a.k.a. Stowaway) puts a comfy set of keys beneath your fingers, then folds up and fits in a pocket.

are compatible with older Palm models), but you won't regret the investment. Check out the Stowaway XT, too—it's even more compact than the original.

For Palm-branded handhelds, the Stowaway and Stowaway XT are sold under the names Palm Portable Keyboard and Palm Ultra-Thin Keyboard, respectively.

The Stowaway does have one disadvantage: limited compatibility. That is, you have to buy the version that's designed to work with your particular handheld model, and if you decide to upgrade someday, the keyboard probably won't be compatible with your new handheld. This is a problem that plagues just about all portable keyboards—but there's a solution.

It's called the Pocketop Portable Keyboard, and instead of requiring a direct connection to your handheld, it works wirelessly via infrared ports. That means it's compatible with virtually any model (including handhelds that use Microsoft's Pocket PC operating system), so it should be able to "stay with you" for the duration.

15

The Pocketop's keys are smaller and less comfortable than those of the Stowaway, but it also becomes even more compact when folded. It's a truly ingenious product, one that's well worth investigating.

 *If you're intrigued by this idea of a "wireless" keyboard, Belkin and Targus now offer similar products—the Wireless PDA Keyboard and Universal Wireless Keyboard, respectively.*

Thumb-Style Keyboards

If you've ever seen one of those BlackBerry pagers or taken a gander at one of Handspring's Treo handhelds, you may have noticed that in place of a Graffiti area, they have tiny built-in keyboards.

For anyone who's now thinking, "Say, I wish *my* handheld had one of them thar keyboards!", we'd like to remind you that "them thar" is not proper grammar, no matter how many times you hear Dave use it. Fortunately, you can buy a clip-on "thumb board" for just about any handheld, usually for less than $50.

The one we like best is Seiko's aptly named ThumBoard, which is available for the Palm V, m500, and Visor series. The ThumBoard connects to the bottom of the device, enveloping roughly the bottom third of it (including the buttons and Graffiti area). It includes power, application, and function buttons, plus separate number and arrow keys. Most Palm OS operations are available as secondary-key functions. The only downside? You can't beam anything when the keyboard is attached.

Protecting Your Screen

Keeping your screen pristine is the first rule of Palm ownership. Why? One word: scratches. A scratch in the Graffiti area can result in inaccurate handwriting recognition. A scratch on the main screen can impair its visibility. Fortunately, it's relatively simple to forestall such disasters.

What causes scratches? If your Palm device is flopping around unprotected in a purse or briefcase, any loose item—keys, paper clips, a pen, or pencil—can create a scratch. That's why we highly recommend a case (see the first section of this chapter). More commonly, however, little specks of grit and other airborne flotsam accumulate on your screen, and when you run your stylus over one of them—scratch city.

CAUTION *Dave is a big fan of tapping on his screen with his big grubby fingers. They leave behind oil and smudges, which are more likely to trap dust and grit. Rick, who is much daintier, says that if you must use a finger, at least use your fingernail.*

We recommend you buy a lens-cleaning cloth, the kind used to wipe dust from eyeglasses and camera lenses. Every day, just give your screen a little buff and polish to keep it free of dust and grit. Or, consider one of the following products.

15

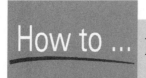 **Protect with Scotch Tape**

The Graffiti area is where most stylus contact occurs, and therefore it's where scratches are most likely to result. If you want simple, inexpensive protection, buy yourself a roll of 3M's Scotch Magic Tape 811. It's exactly the right height for most Graffiti areas, and one roll will last you a lifetime. Plus, its slightly rough surface makes for less-slippery handwriting—always a plus. Just cut a piece to cover the input area and replace it every month or so. You'll never see a single scratch.

ClearTouch

Our new favorite screen protector is the BoxWave ClearTouch. This plastic overlay covers your screen from top to bottom, thus ensuring your stylus causes no damage. It also cuts down on glare and helps keep dust away. Better still, unlike other screen protectors we've tried, which are disposable and must be replaced every month or so, ClearTouch is designed to be removed, cleaned, and reapplied. It leaves behind no gummy residue (do we sound like a floor-wax commercial or what?), and it seems to have endless lasting power. We've had one on a Sony CLIÉ for nearly six months, and it shows no signs of wear.

PDA Screen Protectors

We're not sure this deal will still be around by the time you read this, but it's worth checking out. At a Web site called FreeScreenProtectors.com, you can order an entire box of CompanionLink PDA Screen Protectors and pay only for shipping. That's right—just enter the coupon code "FREESP" when placing your order, and the sheets are free. Sounds too good to be true, but we placed an order and received our box within about three days. Shipping cost about six bucks. Woo-hoo—free stuff!

Navigating the World with a GPS Receiver

Dave is a huge fan of the Global Positioning System, the network of orbiting satellites used to pinpoint one's exact position on the planet. That's because he tends to get lost in his own driveway. Still, GPS is undeniably valuable if you're driving on unfamiliar roads or trying to find your way to, say, a new client's office. If you're interested in turning your PDA into a GPS, check out the following products and companies:

Company	URL	Product
Delorme	www.delorme.com	Earthmate GPS
Magellan	www.magellangps.com	GPS Companion for Palm m500 series
Mapopolis	www.mapopolis.com	GPS hardware/software bundles for many Palm OS devices

If you're really a fan of GPS, check out the Garmin iQue 3600, the first Palm OS handheld with a built-in GPS receiver. And may we also humbly recommend *How to Do Everything with GPS,* a book (due for publication in November, 2003) that covers all manner of GPS technology, including everything you need to know about turning PDAs into sophisticated, practical GPS systems.

See Chapter 9 for more information on using your PDA and GPS.

Turning Your PDA into a Camera

If you're jealous of the picture-taking capabilities found in PDAs such as the Palm Zire 71 and Sony CLIÉ NX70V, despair no more. The Veo Photo Traveler is a $99 digital camera that plugs into your handheld's SD expansion slot and captures 640×480-pixel color photos—the same resolution afforded Zire 71 owners. Its lens even swivels, so you can easily take shots of your own lovely mug. On the downside, it occupies your SD slot, so you can't store images directly to a memory card— they have to reside (at least temporarily) in main memory. Still, it's a nifty little accessory, and having a camera always at the ready is handier than you might think.

Magnifying Your PDA Screen

Having a hard time reading the tiny text on your handheld's screen? You can, of course, switch to a larger font in the core Palm OS apps (Address Book, Date Book, Memo Pad, and To Do List)—just tap Menu | Options | Font. But that doesn't help you in other applications. Magnifico is a clip-on lens that promises 2X magnification and compatibility with any PDA. There's also a Combo version that includes a stand—ideal if you're using a portable keyboard.

Recharging Your Batteries While Traveling

A Palm handheld with a rechargeable battery is a mixed blessing. Sure, you don't have to keep a pocketful of fresh Duracells on hand, but what happens if you're on the road and the PDA runs out of juice? Fortunately, there are plenty of portable-power solutions that can save the day.

If you own a Palm-brand handheld that has a Universal Connector (that's anything in the m500 series, the Tungsten series, the m130, the i705, or the Zire 71), consider Palm's Power To Go. It's a clip-on battery pack that connects to the bottom and back of the handheld and provides instant power and eventual recharging. And it has its own Universal Connector, so it gets its own charge right from your HotSync cradle. The $99.95 Power To Go is a good solution if you fly a lot or don't have easy access to an AC outlet.

On the other hand, if you spend most of your time in offices or other places where AC power is readily available, Palm's $29.95 Universal Travel Charger Kit can keep your battery powered up even when there's no cradle around. It also includes adapters for charging in the U.K., Europe, and Australia, so it's a must-have for global travelers.

In Chapter 9, you learned a bit about USB chargers—cables that draw power from a computer's USB port to gradually recharge your handheld. We're partial to the BoxWave MiniSync, which is available for a wide variety of handheld models and couldn't be more compact. Normally it measures just a few inches from end to end, but when you pull the plugs, they extend on thin cords to nearly three feet. When you're done charging, the spring-reloaded spindle retracts the cords. Pretty cool, and it doubles as a HotSync cable.

Finally, don't forget car chargers. You can top off your handheld while tooling around town, or supply extra power if you're using your PDA for GPS navigation or some other in-car application. The Expansys Car Charger for Palm M Series and Tungsten is one option; the company offers chargers for many other models as well.

A Disposable Power Source for Your PDA (and Other Devices)

One very unique travel-charging option is Instant Power. Instead of charging your batteries from a wall outlet, Instant Power tops off your PDA with a disposable

15

power source. The charger is actually a sort of fuel cell that combines a safe embedded fuel with oxygen drawn from the air. Stored in its aluminum pouch, the charger has a shelf life of about two years. Once you open the pouch, it's good for about three months. That means you can put one in your travel bag and have the peace of mind that you'll have power anytime you need it.

To get started with Instant Power, you need to buy an Instant Power Charger kit that includes a single disposable power cartridge and a connection cable for whatever model handheld you own. There are versions for just about every Palm OS–powered PDA, as well as wireless modems, digital cameras, Pocket PCs, and even camcorders. Since the power cartridges are interchangeable, you can charge up your entire mobile arsenal without worrying about carrying three different kinds of batteries or chargers.

You should be able to charge your PDA about three times with a single Instant Power cartridge. After you deplete it, just toss it in the trash, but keep the cable— you need to replace only the interchangeable cartridges.

One Portable Charger Does It All

One of the coolest travel-charging solutions we've seen yet is the Triple Power Source Emergency Charger from Proporta. Compatible with the m500 series, Tungsten series, and Zire 71, it includes three parts: a USB HotSync/charge cable, a cigarette-lighter charge cable, and an adapter for charging from an ordinary 9-volt battery. We especially like the latter, because you can pick up a 9-volt cell just about anywhere in the world.

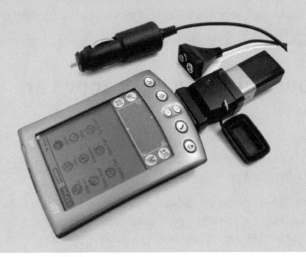

Our Favorite Accessories

Rick: Three items I never travel without: my ClearTouch screen protector (it's earned a permanent home on my CLIÉ), my MiniSync USB charge/HotSync cable, and my 128MB Memory Stick. The latter I use to store everything from games and e-books to MP3 files and movies. Oh, and I should also mention Boostaroo (www.boostaroo.com), which wasn't specifically designed for PDAs but comes in very handy on noisy airplanes. It amplifies the audio from any standard headphone jack, meaning I can actually *hear* my MP3s when there's a lot of ambient noise. A great little accessory.

15

> **Dave:** I used to be an accessory nut like Rick. I'd carry all sorts of silly PDA gadgets and accessories. But they just bogged me down. More recently, Bluetooth has changed my life. These days I carry three things, and only three things: my Tungsten T, a Sony Ericsson T68i mobile phone, and a Bluetooth earpiece. Working in concert with each other, I can place phone calls from my Tungsten and talk without ever touching my phone, check e-mail, and even surf the Web. Oh, I also have a 256MB SD card in my Tungsten, carry a travel charger, use Bose Quiet Comfort headphones to listen to my Tungsten's MP3s on noisy airplanes, and sometimes bring a Bluetooth GPS receiver for my Tungsten. But that's all.

Mounting Your Palm Device in Your Car (or Golf Cart)

Is your car your castle? Your office? Your home away from home? If so, your Palm device deserves a place of honor—and a place where you can access it while keeping at least one hand on the wheel.

 *In all seriousness, you should never, ever try to use your Palm while driving. If you must look something up or write something down, wait until you're stopped at a light. Or, ask a passenger to do it for you.*

Arkon Resources' CM620 Universal PDA Windshield Mount Solution (see Figure 15-3) puts your Palm device at arm's reach. The CM620 can hold virtually any model, and comes with hardware for attaching to your car's windshield (other mounting solutions are also available). You may also want to check out the Powered Multimedia PDA Mount, which not only supplies power to your handheld, but also includes an amplified speaker—great for listening to MP3 tunes, audiobooks, GPS-navigation directions, and so on.

Fore!

There are several nifty golf scorecard programs available for the Palm—any serious golfer would do well to consider one. (We're partial to IntelliGolf, which you can find at www.intelligolf.com.) Of course, you'll need a place to store your Palm while you're on the links. Revolve Design offers pull-cart and electric-cart adapters for the UniMount, so you can have easy access to your electronic scorecard.

| FIGURE 15-3 | The Arkon CM620 Universal Car Mount uses suction cups to attach to your windshield. |

Recovering Lost Handhelds

No one ever means to lose anything, but it happens. The only thing worse than losing your PDA would be realizing that whoever found it probably wouldn't know how to go about returning it to you. Sure, an address label pasted to the back might do the trick, but we have a better solution: StuffBak.com.

For as little as $1.95, you can buy a specially coded StuffBak label to paste on the back of your handheld. The finder need only call a toll-free number or visit the StuffBak Web site to arrange for its return, which requires little effort and includes a reward. You pay a $14.95 transaction fee, plus shipping charges and any cash reward you care to offer. (StuffBak's own reward is a pack of its labels, valued at $20.) If you believe people are generally honest, this is an inexpensive and potentially painless way to help a lost handheld find its way home.

15

 *Some Palm-brand handhelds come with a similar product already in the box. It's called Boomerangit, and it works just like StuffBak. Check to see if there's a Boomerangit label mixed in with the materials that came with your PDA.*

Where to Find It

Web Site	Address	What's There
Arkon Resources	www.arkon.com	CM620 Universal Car Mount
Belkin	www.belkin.com	Wireless PDA Keyboard
BoxWave	www.boxwave.com	ClearTouch, MiniSync
Expansys	www.expansys.com	Expansys Car Charger
Instant Power	www.instant-power.com	Instant Power Charger
Officeonthegogo.com	www.officeonthegogo.com	Magnifico
Palm	www.palm.com	Palm Portable Keyboard, Power To Go, Seiko ThumBoard, Universal Travel Charger Kit
Pocketop	www.pocketop.net	Pocketop Portable Keyboard
Proporta	www.proporta.com	Triple Power Source Emergency Charger
StuffBak.com	www.stuffbak.com	StuffBak labels
Targus	www.targus.com	Universal Wireless Keyboard
Think Outside	www.thinkoutside.com	Stowaway keyboards
Veo	www.veo.com	Veo Photo Traveler

Chapter 16

Problems and Solutions

How to…

- Reset your Palm device
- Avoid battery-related problems
- Prevent and fix scratched screens
- Fix a screen that no longer responds properly
- Resolve Hack conflicts
- Fix alarms that don't "wake up" your Palm
- Deal with a handheld that suddenly won't HotSync
- Solve common HotSync problems
- Manage two Palms on one PC
- HotSync one Palm on two PCs
- Upgrade from an old Palm device to a new one
- Obtain warranty repairs
- Obtain nonwarranty or accident-related repairs
- Find answers to problems on the Web

No computer is perfect. Windows is about as far from the mark as you can get, Macs have problems of their own, and even Palm devices suffer the occasional meltdown. Usually it's minor: an alarm that fails to "wake up" the unit or a wayward Hack that causes the occasional crash. But sometimes something downright scary happens, like a sudden and inexplicable lockup that wipes the Palm's entire memory. In this chapter, we help you troubleshoot some of the most common Palm maladies and, hopefully, prevent the worst of them.

NOTE   *Many common problems are addressed on Palm's Web site (and the sites of other Palm device manufacturers). We're not going to rehash them here, but we are going to suggest you check out those sites if you have a problem we haven't addressed. Chances are good you'll find a solution.*

We also look at some upgrade options, including moving from an old Palm device to a new one—a very common practice these days.

Curing Most Problems with a Reset

Just as rebooting a computer will often resolve a glitch or lockup, resetting your handheld is the solution to many a problem. And it's usually the first thing you need to do if your device crashes—or just acts a little strangely.

Just What Is a "Crash," Anyway?

When a computer crashes, that generally means it has plowed into a brick wall and can no longer function. Fortunately, whereas a car in the same situation would need weeks of bump-and-paint work, a computer can usually return to normal by being rebooted. In the case of Palm devices, a "reset" is the same as a "reboot."

When a Palm device crashes, one common error message is "Fatal Exception." Don't be alarmed; this isn't nearly as morbid as it sounds. It simply means that the Palm has encountered a glitch that proved fatal to its operation. Very often an onscreen Reset button will appear with this error, a tap of which performs a "soft reset" (as we describe in the next section). Sometimes, however, the crash is so severe that even this button doesn't work. (You know because you tap it and nothing happens.) In a case like that, you have to perform a manual reset.

Different Ways to Reset a Palm Device

On the back of every Palm device, there's a little hole labeled RESET. (On some models, such as the Kyocera 6035 and Zire 71, the hole may be tucked inside the battery compartment or beneath the camera lens cover.)

Hidden inside this hole is a button that effectively reboots the unit. When that happens, you see the Palm OS startup screen, followed a few seconds later by the Prefs screen. That's how a successful reset goes. About 98 percent of the time, everything will be as you left it—your data, your applications, everything.

Technically speaking, there are three kinds of resets: soft, warm, and hard. (Mind out of the gutter, please.) The details:

- **Soft**   Only in rare instances do you need to perform anything other than a soft reset, which is akin to pressing CTRL-ALT-DELETE to reboot your computer. You simply press the Reset button, then wait a few seconds while your Palm resets itself. No data is lost.

- **Warm**   This action, performed by holding the Scroll Up button while pressing the Reset button, goes an extra step by bypassing any system patches or Hacks you may have installed. Use this only if your Palm fails to respond to a soft reset, meaning it's still locked up, crashing, or stuck in a "boot loop" (the

16

Palm logo is flashing or the screen is displaying garbage). No data is lost, but you have to manually re-enable any system patches or Hacks.

- **Hard** With any luck, you'll never have to do this. A hard reset wipes everything out of your Palm's memory, essentially returning it to factory condition. In the exceedingly rare case that your Palm is seriously hosed (meaning it won't reset or even turn off), this should at least get you back to square one. If it doesn't, your handheld is toast and will need to be replaced (more on repair/replacement options later in this chapter). The good news is this: even after a hard reset, all it takes is a HotSync to restore all your data. Some third-party applications may have to be re-installed manually, but most will just reappear on your handheld. It's like magic!

The Toothpick Story

A couple years ago, Rick was having lunch with a couple of his buddies when he pulled out his PalmPilot Personal to jot a few notes. To his horror, it wouldn't turn on (a problem he later attributed to the extremely cold weather, which can indeed numb a pair of batteries). A press of the Reset button was in order, but Rick didn't have the right tool—namely, a paper clip. So he asked the waitress to bring him a toothpick—the other common item that's small enough to fit in the reset hole. Presto: the Palm sprang back to life.

The moral of the story is, be prepared. If your Palm crashes and you need to reset it, the last thing you want is a desperate hunt for a paper clip or toothpick. Fortunately, many styluses have "reset tips" hidden inside them. And now, a tip about tips.

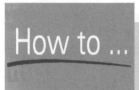 **Perform Warm and Hard Resets**

There's a bit of a trick to doing a warm or hard reset successfully. With your Palm device on or off (it doesn't matter), hold down the Scroll Up button (for a warm reset) or the power button (for a hard reset), then press and release the Reset button on the back of the unit. Now, here's the trick: *wait until the Palm logo appears onscreen* before releasing the scroll or power button. If you release both buttons simultaneously, before the logo appears, all you get is a soft reset.

TIP

If your handheld has a metal stylus, it may surprise you to learn that it's stowing a reset tip. Where's it hiding? Unscrew the top (or, in some cases, the bottom) from the barrel to find out. If your handheld came with a plastic stylus and uses AAA batteries, you can break a toothpick in half and stow it in the battery compartment, resting between the two cells. Now you'll always have a reset tip handy.

Nine Great Tips & Tricks

These handy little secrets will help you on your way from novice user to Palm pro.

1. **Find the latest freeware**   At PalmGear.com, click the Software link at the left-hand side of the main page, then find Latest Freeware Software near the top of the Software Categories page that appears. Presto: nothin' but freebies.

2. **…And download it quick**   To save yourself the hassles of downloading, unzipping, and queuing Palm software (freeware and commercial apps alike) for installation, grab PalmGear's StreamLync utility. It's free, and it allows you to download and install software from PalmGear with just a few easy clicks.

3. **Hotwired HotSync**   Can't HotSync all of a sudden? Try a soft reset of your handheld. More times than not, this solves the problem.

4. **HotSync with the Web**   Did you know you can synchronize your handheld with Yahoo! Address Book, then access your calendar, contacts, and memos from any Web-enabled computer? Just visit Yahoo! Mobile (mobile.yahoo.com), click the PDA Downloads link, then look for Intellisync for Yahoo! It's free, as is the account you'll need to set up with Yahoo! Follow the instructions carefully, however, because you could accidentally wind up unable to HotSync with your PC.

5. **Multiple-personality buttons**   Your handheld's four application buttons needn't be limited to launching four applications. Utilities such as QLaunch and SmartLauncher let you program the buttons to launch multiple programs with multiple presses.

6. **Sync with your spouse**   It's one thing to sync two handhelds to the same PC. It's another to have access to each other's schedule. DualDate, a Palm freebie, puts your calendar side by side with a spouse, friend, co-worker, and so on for at-a-glance comparison.

16

7. **Happy holidays** Want to add all the holidays to your Date Book? Just download 2004 USA Holidays 1.1 (www.freewarepalm.com). It contains 36 U.S. and religious holidays. While you're at it, get the 2005 through 2010 calendars as well. Just import the file(s) into Palm Desktop, then HotSync.

8. **Louder alarms** If you've set the alarm volume to "High" in Prefs, but your alarms still aren't loud enough, try switching to a different alarm sound. In Date Book, tap Menu | Options | Preferences. Tap the arrow next to Alarm Sound, then choose a tune. You'll hear it played immediately. Find the one that's loudest, then tap OK.

9. **Graffiti at a glance** Swipe the stylus from the bottom of the screen to the top and a handy Graffiti reference chart will appear.

Avoiding Battery Problems

Batteries are the lifeblood of any Palm device. When they die, they take your data with them, effectively returning your handheld to factory condition. That's why it's vital to keep a close eye on the battery gauge shown at the top of the Applications screen (see Figure 16-1), and to take heed when the device notifies you that your batteries are low.

The battery gauge tells you how much juice your PDA has left

FIGURE 16-1 All Palm OS devices equipped with Palm OS 3.0 and later have this handy—and fairly accurate—battery gauge at the top of the screen.

Of course, if you HotSync regularly, a wiped handheld isn't the end of the world. Once you've replaced (or recharged) the batteries, a HotSync is all it takes to restore virtually everything. Still, there's no reason to let things reach that point. Following are some tips to help you avoid most battery-related incidents.

Keeping 'Em Fresh

Suppose you head off to Bermuda for a two-week getaway (you lucky vacationer, you), leaving your work—and your Palm—behind. When you return, don't be surprised to find the Palm dead as a doornail. That's because it draws a trace amount of power from the batteries, even when off, to keep the memory alive. If the batteries were fairly low to begin with, the long period of inactivity might just polish them off.

The obvious solution is to keep your Palm with you as much as possible. (It's great for games, e-books, and other leisure activities, remember?) Alternatively, if you know you're going to be away from it for a while, just leave it in the cradle (or put in a pair of new batteries before you leave if it's not a rechargeable model).

> TIP
>
> *In nonrechargeable models, you can use rechargeable batteries in place of alkalines, but be aware that the battery meter won't accurately display their charge status—and you may have a shorter window of opportunity to change the batteries once you receive a low-battery notification. NiMH rechargeables work best—we recommend avoiding rechargeable NiCad and alkaline cells.*

Swapping 'Em Quick

The documentation for nonrechargeable Palm devices says that when replacing batteries, you shouldn't leave them out for more than 60 seconds (lest data loss occur). This is true, to a point. Near-dead batteries aren't supplying much power to the memory, so when you remove them, the memory can indeed fade fast. On the other hand, if you're replacing batteries that are still reasonably healthy, it can be half an hour or more before the memory gets wiped.

Of course, it can be difficult to gauge the batteries' precise remaining strength, so follow this rule of thumb: swap them fast. Pop the old ones out, pop the fresh ones in, and you're done. It's exceedingly rare to lose data when you adhere to this method—but you should always do a HotSync first anyway, just to be safe.

16

Emergency Rescue for Rechargeable Palms

You've been on the road for weeks, your handheld has warned you repeatedly that the battery is low, and there's not a charging cradle in sight. That's the Catch-22 of the rechargeable battery: no Duracells to buy, but no easy way to recharge on the road. That is, unless you have one of the many portable charging accessories now available. See Chapter 15 for more details.

Fixing Scratched Screens

Scratches happen. They happen most often when your stylus hits a piece of dust or grit. That's why it's important to keep your screen as clean as possible (we recommend a daily wipe with a lint-free, antistatic cloth). Better still, take a few preventative steps:

- **Tape** A piece of Scotch Magic Tape 811 placed over the Graffiti input area (where most scratches occur) not only makes existing scratches less tangible while you're writing, but also prevents future scratches and provides a tackier writing surface.

- **Screen protectors** As discussed in Chapter 15, products such as the BoxWave ClearTouch are plastic overlays that protect the entire screen. They won't remove scratches, but they will prevent them and, like the tape, make them less pronounced.

- **PDA ScreenClean** Fellowes wash-and-dry system may remind you of those wet-nap packets you get in those greasy-spoon restaurants Dave likes to eat in. One packet contains a wet cloth you use to wash and wipe the screen, the other a dry cloth used for drying and buffing. These won't repair scratches, but they will remove all the dust and grit that can lead to them, and leave your screen looking pristine.

Fixing a Screen That No Longer Responds Properly

As noted in Chapter 2's discussion of the Digitizer option, it's not uncommon to experience some "drift" in the screen's response to your stylus taps. An example: you have to tap just a bit to the left or right of your desired target for the tap to be recognized. This occurs over time, when the accuracy of the digitizer (the hardware that makes the screen respond to your input) degrades.

Unless the digitizer has gotten so off-kilter that you can no longer operate your Palm device, the solution is to hit the Prefs icon, then choose Digitizer from the list of choices. Here you can reset the digitizer, effectively making your handheld good as new. If you can't even manage to tap Prefs, you can do a soft reset (as described earlier in this chapter). That gets you to the Prefs screen, where you should at least be able to select the Digitizer option.

Solving Memory-Related HotSync Failure

If you try to install a new program or database, and your Palm device doesn't have enough memory, the HotSync will fail—and fail again every time thereafter. Assuming you can't free up enough space on your handheld to accommodate the new item(s), you have to venture onto your hard drive. Specifically, locate the C:\palm*yourusername*\ install or C:\program files\palm*yourusername*\install folder (the "holding tank" for software waiting to be installed during HotSync), and delete everything that's in there. Now you should be able to HotSync successfully.

> NOTE *Deleting programs and data from the Install folder doesn't permanently delete them from your hard drive. When you choose items to be installed on your Palm device, copies are placed in the Install folder. The original files remain.*

How to ... Cure "Mad Digitizer Syndrome"

What happens when the digitizer gets so out of whack that your Palm device essentially becomes inoperable? This problem, which some have dubbed "Mad Digitizer Syndrome," tends to plague older models, though it can strike even if your handheld is only a year or two old. One very effective way to cure MDS is with a utility called AutoDigi, which automatically recalibrates the digitizer after a reset. You can buy the $15 program at PalmGear (www.palmgear.com). If your screen is really giving you trouble, check out OnDigi, a Hack that automatically recalibrates the digitizer each time you turn on your handheld.

16

Resolving Hack Conflicts

It bears repeating (see Chapter 12 for the first time we said it) that as marvelous as Hacks are, they can wreak havoc on Palm devices. This is especially true if you run more than two or three simultaneously, as these little bits of code can conflict with one another. If you find that your Palm is crashing on a regular basis, you may have to investigate your Hacks. Here's what you should do:

1. Start X-Master, then uncheck the box next to each Hack to disable it.

2. Go back to using your Palm device. If you find that the crashes no longer occur, a Hack is the likely culprit. To help pin down which one, go on to step 3.

3. Launch X-Master again, then enable just one Hack. Use your Palm device normally, and see if the crashes return. If not, enable a second Hack. Through this process of elimination, you should be able to figure out which one is causing the problem. When you do, stop using it.

Fixing a Palm That Won't "Wake Up" for Alarms

It's easy to fall out of love with your Palm device when an alarm you set fails to go off (meaning the Palm doesn't "wake up" and beep). There are several reasons this can happen, from low batteries to a corrupted alarm database to a conflict with third-party software. The first is easy to resolve by making sure your Palm has fresh batteries (or is adequately charged). For the other two problems, try a soft reset, which very often does the trick.

If you use a third-party program that has anything to do with alarms (such as ToDo Plus, DiddleBug, and so forth), it's very possible this is causing the snafu. To troubleshoot it, try doing a warm reset (hold the scroll-up button while pressing the Reset button). This will disable any Hacks or third-party applications that tie into the operating system. Set an alarm in Date Book and see if it works. If so, then another program is very likely to blame. A process of elimination should help you determine which one. In any case, you may have to discontinue using that program if it keeps fouling up your alarms.

If none of these options work, it's possible your Palm device is damaged. Contact the manufacturer for service.

Curing Beaming Problems

Having trouble beaming? Chances are good the problem is caused by one of three factors. First, make sure the two handhelds aren't too close together. People often make the mistake of holding their Palm devices right next to each other, which can give the infrared transceivers trouble. Keep the units at least a foot or two apart (their range is about five feet).

Second, make sure the Beam Receive option is checked in the Prefs | General (or Power) screen. Although you may not have unchecked it yourself, sometimes it just seems to happen.

If neither of these suggestions solves the problem, try moving to a darker area. Beaming doesn't always work if you're in a brightly lit room or outdoors on a sunny day.

If all else fails, you might want to perform a soft reset on both Palms; that should clear up whatever problem was keeping your devices from chatting with each other.

The Date Won't Advance

This is a known issue that afflicts mostly the Palm IIIx and Palm V. According to Palm, it's caused by low batteries, meaning the problem should abate if you replace or recharge yours. At the same time, try a soft reset.

If this doesn't do the trick, third-party software or a hardware defect may be to blame. The only real effective way to find out for sure is to do a hard reset, which will wipe all third-party software and restore the Palm to its factory settings, then set the clock to 11:59 P.M. and note the date. Wait a minute, then turn the unit on and see if the date has advanced. If so, it's probably a software glitch. If not, a repair may be in order.

It's no mean feat to pin down a software conflict. It could be a Hack or an application that has some link to the calendar. If you're able to figure out which program is the culprit, contact the developer to see if there's a fix (or at least some acknowledgement of the problem).

16

The Last Chapter

Dave: Well, this is the last chapter… and it's almost complete. It was a blast to write this book, but I have to admit that I'm kind of burnt out on all this tech writing stuff. I think I'll take my half of the advance (a cool half-million or so) and move to Bermuda. There, I'll build a cottage on the beach and let my army of trained monkey butlers bring me cool drinks all day long. I'll pass the time staring at the waves as they gently break onto the sandy, white beach, and occasionally dabble at writing a best-selling novel on my Palm with a Stowaway keyboard. My MP3 player will be loaded up with Kristin Hersh music and my cats will be napping in my lap. Yep, that's what I'm going to do…

Rick: Always with the monkey butlers. As for me, now that the yoke of another book has been lifted, I'll be returning to the soup kitchen where I volunteer three times a week, though not before I finish the urban-beautification program I spearheaded and the fundraiser for Greenpeace. Just have to decide which charities will be getting my royalty checks this year—always a tough choice. Honestly, there's no better reward for months of hard work than good old philanthropy. Oh, but, uh, your plan sounds really good, too…

Dealing with a Handheld That Will No Longer HotSync

It worked fine yesterday, but today your handheld just refuses to HotSync. We hear your pain—this drives us up the wall, too. We wish we could blame Windows, because it's just the kind of nonsense we've come to expect from it, but this is usually due to a Palm software, hardware, or cradle problem.

Best bet? Start with a soft reset. Use the end of a paper clip (or unscrew the barrel of your metal stylus to find a hidden tip) to press the Reset button on the back of your handheld. In many cases, this will solve the problem outright, and you can get back to playing Bejeweled. If it doesn't, consider re-installing Palm Desktop. This action won't affect your data, but it will provide a "fresh" version of HotSync Manager—which often solves HotSync problems. If you're not comfortable with that step or it doesn't work, consult your manufacturer's Web site for other remedies.

The Mysterious m500/m505 Cradle Crisis

Has your Palm m500 or m505 suddenly stopped synchronizing? The culprit may be electrostatic discharge (ESD), which has fried more handhelds over the years than Palm would like to admit. In this case, it's fried cradle. Palm *has* admitted that some m500 and m505 cradles are more susceptible to ESD than others, and will replace yours if it has the problem. Visit Palm's Web site (www.palm.com/support) for information on the exchange program.

Resolving COM Port Issues

Ah, the wonders of the PC's COM ports. COM ports are communication ports usually associated with the serial ports on your PC. If you are connecting your Palm to a Windows-based PC, and your HotSync cradle uses an old-fashioned serial port, you'll need to know just a teeny-tiny bit about COM ports—unless something goes awry, in which case you'll need to know more. If you have a Mac or a USB HotSync cradle, you can sit this one out.

Knowing Your COM Ports

For starters, your Palm's HotSync cradle needs to be plugged into a serial port, and the COM port associated with that port can't be shared with anything else.

Ninety-nine percent of the time, the Palm Desktop installation software figures out what COM port to use all by itself. If you later move things around, though, you may need to do some detective work. Use this table to figure out what COM port you're using:

If...	Then...
There's only one serial port on my PC	It's COM1.
The cradle is plugged into a small 9-pin port	It's COM1.
The cradle is plugged into the big 25-pin port	It's COM2.
The cradle is plugged into a serial port that is part of an expansion card	It's a little hard to say from here. Experiment!

16

NOTE   *These port descriptions apply to older PCs and may not match yours. Consult your system documentation for specific COM port identifications.*

Troublesome USB Ports

Most HotSync cradles and cables now have a USB connector that lets you connect without fiddling with all the bizarre serial port issues that can crop up. But if you have USB, you're not out of the woods yet. Keep these things in mind:

- On a Windows system, USB is guaranteed to work only with Windows 98 or higher. If you still have Windows 95, get with the program—and upgrade if you expect to reliably use USB devices such as the Palm's HotSync cradle.

- If your HotSync cradle sometimes fails to work, you might have too many USB devices connected to a single USB port. Move the cradle to another USB port, or try disconnecting one or two other devices.

- You might need a powered USB hub—there may not be enough juice in the port to supply power to all the devices you have connected, and that may cause the HotSync cradle to cut out.

Check your handheld manufacturer's Web site for more USB troubleshooting information, and try Microsoft support as well (support.microsoft.com).

 If you have only one of those big, 25-pin ports available on the back of your PC, it's probably COM1, and you can use the 9-pin-to-25-pin adapter that came with your Palm to make the connection.

Troubleshooting HotSync Glitches

If you can't get your Palm to talk to your PC, there are a number of likely causes. Consider the following list a checklist for resolving the issue.

- Start by making sure the HotSync cradle is plugged securely into its serial or USB port.

- Verify that the correct COM/USB port is configured in the HotSync Manager (see Chapter 3 for details on this). If you're in doubt, try the other COM port choices available in the HotSync Manager to double-check.

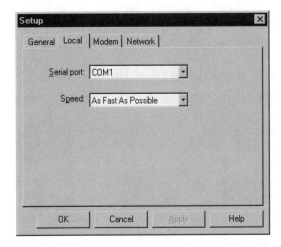

■ Shut off any applications that might be trying to take control of the COM port, such as fax programs or remote-control applications.

■ Try a lower HotSync speed. This is especially important on older laptops or early Pentium/486-based PCs.

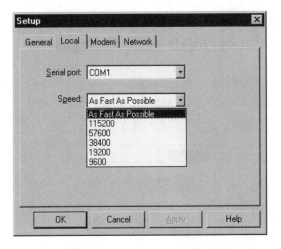

■ Close the HotSync Manager and restart it. Also, as noted earlier, try a soft reset on the Palm itself.

■ Upgrade to the newest Palm Desktop software, which you can download from Palm's Web site. It may include a slightly updated version of HotSync Manager that addresses common problems.

16

If none of those things works, your Palm or the HotSync cradle may be defective. If possible, test the system on another PC.

The Palm Reports a COM Port Conflict

A device or application is probably just hogging the port. Communication software such as fax programs and remote-control software are designed to grab and hold a COM port, so they might interfere with the HotSync Manager. Disable those programs before HotSyncing.

> **NOTE**   *The HotSync Manager hogs the COM port as well. If you disconnect the HotSync cradle and plug something else in—such as a modem—the new device won't work unless you shut off the HotSync Manager.*

The Palm Aborts a HotSync Immediately

If you press the HotSync button on the cradle, and the Palm immediately insists that the COM port is in use—so fast that it doesn't seem possible for the Palm to have even checked—the solution is to perform a soft reset on your Palm. After it resets, the HotSync should work fine.

When HotSyncing, the Palm Displays the HotSync Screen but Absolutely Nothing Else Happens

Frequently, this problem is just a result of the HotSync Manager not running on the PC or one of the HotSync dialog boxes is open. If you open the Custom dialog box to change conduit settings, for instance, the HotSync will not run, and you won't get an error message—so look on the desktop for an open dialog box.

The Battery Conspiracy

That may sound ominous, but we just wanted to get your attention. If you have a Palm that uses alkaline batteries, don't leave it lying in the HotSync cradle for an extended period of time. That's because the HotSync cradle drains the batteries. At least, that was the case with older models such as the Palm III. If you have a Palm device that has rechargeable batteries, you needn't worry about that, because the cradle actually recharges the batteries.

When HotSyncing, This Message Appears: "An application failed to respond to a HotSync"

This one is easy to fix. When you started the HotSync, an Address Book or Date Book entry was probably left open in Palm Desktop. Your Palm can't successfully HotSync with one of those entries open for editing, so you should close the entry and try again.

Outlook HotSync Problems

As you learned in Chapter 3, most Palm devices come with a special conduit for synchronizing with Microsoft Outlook. It's called PocketMirror, and we could fill a separate book with information on using and troubleshooting it. Fortunately, you can get lots of helpful assistance from Chapura, the company that makes it (www.chapura.com).

Working with Windows 2000

If you're a Windows 2000 user, you'll be glad to know the OS gets along with Palm Desktop just fine. However, at press time there were a few known issues you should consider:

- Windows 2000's "hot undock" feature, usually found on notebook systems, may not work with HotSync Manager running. Solution: shut down HotSync Manager before performing the undock.

- Infrared HotSyncs won't work. Solution: download the HotSync 3.1.1 updater from Palm.

16

Working with Windows NT 4.0

Just one item to be aware of here: Windows NT 4.0 doesn't support USB, so you can't use a handheld that has a USB cradle. It may be possible to purchase a serial cradle for any given model—check with the manufacturer.

Working with Windows XP

As with every new version of Windows, XP brought with it a raft of synchronization and other problems. Many Palm, Handspring, and Sony users reported they couldn't HotSync with the new OS, and others encountered problems with XP's multiple user profiles. You may need a patch, a new version of Palm Desktop, or some other solution entirely. Visit your handheld maker's Web site for more details. In the meantime, consider this: If you upgrade your PC to Windows XP or buy a new one that has it already installed, you need to make sure you use Palm Desktop 4.0.1 or later. If you have an earlier version, you can download the latest one from Palm's Web site.

 *Palm Desktop doesn't support Windows XP's "switch user" option, which allows multiple users to log onto their PCs at the same time. If you have multiple user profiles set up, each person needs to log out at the end of their session, while the next person logs in.*

Managing Multiple Palms or PCs

The Palm OS allows you to HotSync the same Palm to more than one PC, or to HotSync several Palms to the same PC. Surprisingly, most Palm owners are reluctant to try this out ("I was always kind of afraid to HotSync two Palms to my PC," Rick once told Dave in a particularly confessional moment). But it's easier, and less fraught with complications, than you might think.

Two Palms on a Single PC

If you have two Palms and only one computer, you're not alone. In fact, it's a pretty common scenario: many married couples have their own Palms and want to HotSync to the household computer.

TIP

Once you're successfully syncing both handhelds, install DualDate on them. This free program replaces the stock Date Book application with one that lets you view two calendars side by side. Now you can see your spouse's schedule, and vice versa. DualDate can be downloaded from PalmGear.com.

Here's what you need to do:

1. Be absolutely sure that both Palms have different usernames. Check this by tapping on the HotSync icon on each Palm and looking at the name in the upper-right corner. Identically named Palms, HotSynced to the same PC, will irretrievably thrash the data on the PC and both Palms.

2. Put the Palm in the HotSync cradle and go. The first time the second Palm is inserted, your PC will ask if you want to create a new account for the other Palm. Click Yes.

CAUTION

If both Palms have the same username for some reason, do not attempt to HotSync them to the same PC! In fact, change their names before you HotSync at all, to prevent accidentally HotSyncing the Palms in the wrong PC.

TIP

As long as you're using two Palms in the same family—such as a pair of m500s—you can use one HotSync cradle for both handhelds. However, you can't always mix and match. A Palm V, for instance, won't work with an i705 cradle, and vice versa. However, it is possible to have multiple cradles connected to the same PC. You could have one plugged into a serial port and another into a USB port, for instance, or plug two cradles into two USB ports.

Two PCs with a Single Palm

Your PDA can keep two different PCs straight just as easily as one PC can keep a pair of PDAs straight. When you HotSync, the handheld updates the second PC with whatever data it previously got from the first PC, and vice versa. This is a great way to keep your office PC and home computer in sync, or a PC and a Mac— the Palm can serve as a nonpartisan conduit for keeping all the data in agreement.

16

> TIP
>
> *Although this is not essential, we recommend making sure that you have the same version of the Palm Desktop on both PCs. If you're using a PC and a Mac, you can't do that, but you should keep up with the latest release of the Mac Palm Desktop.*

Of course, the most efficient way to use a dual-PC system is to acquire a second HotSync cradle. You can buy an additional one for about $30, or you can get a HotSync cable instead, which is a little more streamlined for traveling. See Chapter 15 for information on USB HotSync cables that also charge your battery.

Upgrades

If you're like Dave, you're probably a little obsessed with having the latest and greatest of everything. Gotta have the latest Palm, the latest version of the OS, and the fanciest wetsuit. This section helps you manage two key maneuvers—upgrading to a new Palm device, and upgrading to OS 3.5.

Upgrading from an Old Handheld to a New One

To those of you still living with a Pilot 5000, we salute you. But when you finally decide you're ready for a nicer screen, more memory, and a bunch of cool accessories that won't work with your old model, we'll be here for you. Specifically, we're here to help you make the move from an older handheld to a new one—an increasingly common task these days, now that the devices have been around for so many years.

Unlike upgrading to a new PC (which requires an obnoxious amount of effort), upgrading to a new Palm device is shockingly easy. Here's the process in a nutshell:

> TIP
>
> *Before you perform step 1, take the time to "clean out" the old handheld by deleting applications and data you're no longer using. At the same time, disable any Hacks that may be running—especially if you're upgrading to a model with Palm OS 5. In fact, as you learned in Chapter 12, Hacks are incompatible with OS 5, so you should not only disable the Hacks from your old model, you should delete them—and your Hack manager as well—before your "final HotSync." Finally, search your computer's hard drive for a file called Saved_prefs.prc, and delete it. The end goal here is to avoid transporting old, unnecessary, and potentially incompatible stuff from the old device to the new one.*

1. Do one last HotSync of your old Palm device.

2. Turn off your PC, unplug the old HotSync cradle, and plug in the new one. (Chances are good the new handheld won't be able to use the old cradle. C'est la vie.) If your new cradle has a USB connector, install the new version of Palm Desktop *before* plugging in the new cradle.

3. Turn on your PC and install the Palm Desktop software that came with your new handheld. Go ahead and place it in the same C:\Palm directory (or whatever's appropriate) where the previous version was installed. Don't worry—all your data will be preserved!

4. HotSync your new handheld. When you do, a box appears listing your username from your old model. Click it, then choose OK. This will restore all your data.

NOTE *Most of your third-party applications will be re-installed along with your data, but a few may not. Thus, you may have to manually re-install some programs. At the same time, you may have to re-enter registration codes for any software you've paid to unlock.*

Upgrading the OS

Sorry, Charlie. (You're not Charlie? What are you doing with Charlie's book!) It's impossible to upgrade the OS in most Palm OS handhelds. (There are some exceptions—m500 and m5150 users can upgrade from Palm OS 4.0 to 4.1 at www.palm.com/us/support/upgrade/—but there are no upgrades available for most modern models.) However, your device manufacturer may issue "patches" (software updates) designed to fix problems or add features, so check their Web sites periodically.

Obtaining Service and Repairs

Palm problems, although relatively infrequent, come in all shapes and sizes. Yours may be as simple as an alarm that won't go off or as dire as a device that won't turn on. Fortunately, technical support and repair services are available from the

16

respective manufacturers. Here we've compiled a table of their phone numbers and Web addresses:

Company	Tech Support	Web Site
Palm	(847) 262-7256	www.palm.com
Handspring	(716) 871-6448	www.handspring.com
Sony	(877) 760-7669	www.sony.com

Obtaining Nonwarranty or Accident-Related Repairs

Right up there with the awful sound of your car crunching into another is the sound of your Palm device hitting the pavement. A cracked case, a broken screen, a dead unit—these are among the painful results. And unfortunately, if you drop, step on, sit on, or get caught in a rainstorm with your Palm device, your warranty is pretty much out the window.

All is not lost, however. If your Palm is damaged, or develops a problem after the warranty has expired, you may still have options. For a fee (usually $100–125), Palm and Handspring, for instance, will usually replace a broken or out-of-warranty unit with a refurbished one. It's not cheap, but it's probably cheaper than buying a brand-new Palm. Other manufacturers may handle such situations differently. The bottom line is, if something terrible happens to your device, it's worth a phone call to the company to see what options are available. You may be able to pay for repairs or buy a refurbished one for less than the cost of a new unit.

Extended Warranty Plans

If you have at least 90 days remaining on your original one-year warranty, you may be able to purchase an extended warranty directly from Palm (for Palm-branded products only, and available only to U.S. residents). Alternatively, you can purchase a one-time screen-replacement plan within the first 30 days of your purchase date. (The screen is the most likely casualty in a Palm mishap, and the standard warranty doesn't cover it.)

Plan prices vary a bit depending on your model. See Palm's Web site for details.

Other Sources for Help

As we've noted many times already, you can find oodles of help on handheld manufacturers' Web sites. In addition, there are several independent sites that offer tips, tricks, hints, and technical solutions. If you're looking for answers that aren't in this book or on the Palm/Handspring/Sony Web site, try some of these:

Site	Description
www.palmgear.com	Look for the Tips & Tricks section.
www.pdabuzz.com	This site has a message board area in which you can post questions and read answers to common questions. It also contains Palm-related product news and reviews.
alt.comp.sys.palmtops.pilot comp.sys.palmtops.pilot	These newsgroups are available to anyone with a newsreader such as Outlook Express. They are threaded message boards that contain questions and answers about Palm issues. You can post your own questions, respond to what's already there, or just read the existing posts.

Where to Find It

Web Site	Address	What's There
Fellowes	www.fellowes.com	PDA ScreenClean and other accessories
PalmGear	www.palmgear.com	DualDate and a zillion other Palm OS programs
Palm, Inc.	www.palm.com	Extended warranty programs

16

Index

INTERNATIONAL CONTACT INFORMATION

AUSTRALIA
McGraw-Hill Book Company Australia Pty. Ltd.
TEL +61-2-9900-1800
FAX +61-2-9878-8881
http://www.mcgraw-hill.com.au
books-it_sydney@mcgraw-hill.com

CANADA
McGraw-Hill Ryerson Ltd.
TEL +905-430-5000
FAX +905-430-5020
http://www.mcgraw-hill.ca

**GREECE, MIDDLE EAST, & AFRICA
(Excluding South Africa)**
McGraw-Hill Hellas
TEL +30-210-6560-990
TEL +30-210-6560-993
TEL +30-210-6560-994
FAX +30-210-6545-525

MEXICO (Also serving Latin America)
McGraw-Hill Interamericana Editores S.A. de C.V.
TEL +525-117-1583
FAX +525-117-1589
http://www.mcgraw-hill.com.mx
fernando_castellanos@mcgraw-hill.com

SINGAPORE (Serving Asia)
McGraw-Hill Book Company
TEL +65-6863-1580
FAX +65-6862-3354
http://www.mcgraw-hill.com.sg
mghasia@mcgraw-hill.com

SOUTH AFRICA
McGraw-Hill South Africa
TEL +27-11-622-7512
FAX +27-11-622-9045
robyn_swanepoel@mcgraw-hill.com

SPAIN
McGraw-Hill/Interamericana de España, S.A.U.
TEL +34-91-180-3000
FAX +34-91-372-8513
http://www.mcgraw-hill.es
professional@mcgraw-hill.es

**UNITED KINGDOM, NORTHERN,
EASTERN, & CENTRAL EUROPE**
McGraw-Hill Education Europe
TEL +44-1-628-502500
FAX +44-1-628-770224
http://www.mcgraw-hill.co.uk
computing_europe@mcgraw-hill.com

ALL OTHER INQUIRIES Contact:
McGraw-Hill/Osborne
TEL +1-510-420-7700
FAX +1-510-420-7703
http://www.osborne.com
omg_international@mcgraw-hill.com

Subscribe Today!